BYRON, SHELLEY
AND THEIR PISAN CIRCLE

VILLA LANFRANCHI, PISA

From a drawing by O. F. M. Ward

Byron, Shelley and their Pisan Circle

By

C. L. CLINE

THE UNIVERSITY OF TEXAS

"Our roots never struck so deeply as at Pisa, and the transplanted tree flourishes not."

SHELLEY

LONDON

JOHN MURRAY, ALBEMARLE STREET, W

First Edition, 1952

Made and printed in Great Britain by
William Clowes and Sons, Limited, London and Beccles
and published by John Murray (Publishers) Limited

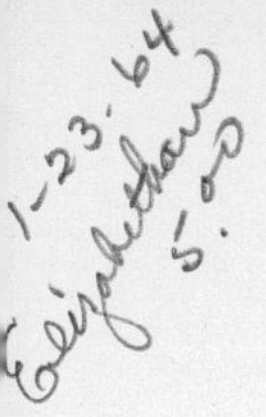
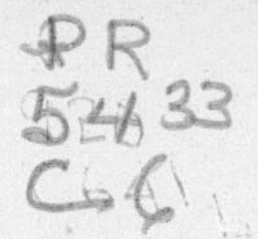

Contents

Page

Preface ix

1 The Shelleys at Pisa 1

2 The Irish Expatriate: John Taaffe, Jr. 16

3 Beginnings of the Pisan Circle . 26

4 Lord Byron Comes to Pisa . . 38

5 The Winter of 1821–22 . . 60

6 The Affair with the Dragoon: the Afternoon of March 24, 1822 . 91

7 Reverberations of the Dragoon Affair 107

8 The Summer Colonies . . . 155

9 The End of the Pisan Circle . 185

10 After Pisa 193

Appendix A 203

Appendix B 208

Appendix C 213

Notes 223

Index 251

List of Illustrations

Villa Lanfranchi, Pisa *Frontispiece*

From a drawing by O. F. M. Ward

Lord Byron, as he appeared after his daily ride at Pisa and Genoa *facing page* 56

From a silhouette cut in paper by Mrs. Leigh Hunt

Tita *facing page* 90

From a drawing by Daniel Maclise, R.A.; at Hughenden

Deposition to the Police at Pisa, signed by Byron, Trelawny, Shelley and Hay *facing page* 108

In the possession of Sir John Murray

Preface

AFTER a century and a quarter of Byron-Shelley scholarship, it might seem at first glance unlikely that much of value could be added to the biographies. Yet, although the fine life of Shelley (1940) by Professor Newman I. White may serve adequately the needs of Shelley students for many years to come, a full-scale biography of Byron is badly needed. This book is an attempt to write a segment of that biography.

My excuse for retelling the main events in the lives of Byron and Shelley during the Pisan period must be the availability of important new material. The main part of it consists of the following: the unpublished Byron-Dawkins and Taaffe-Dawkins correspondence, with certain other letters from Byron to Taaffe and Captain Roberts and from Count Guiccioli to his lawyer, Vincenzo Taglioni, in The University of Texas Library; an unpublished autobiography of Taaffe and a considerable collection of letters and other documents, in the possession of his great granddaughter; and numerous letters from Byron to Kinnaird and to Byron from Taaffe, Medwin, Trelawny, Hay, Dawkins, Kinnaird, and others, as well as a series of letters from Taaffe to John Murray, in the possession of Sir John Murray. In addition, I have been able to supplement these materials with letters of Byron, Trelawny, and Taaffe in the Keats-Shelley Memorial in Rome; letters of Trelawny and Taaffe in the library of Mr. Carl Pforzheimer; letters of Byron in the Morgan Library and the Berg Collection; unpublished portions of the *Journal of Edward Ellerker Williams* from the manuscript in the British Museum, and a great mass of court records from the State Archives at Pisa, Florence, and Lucca.

In recording my indebtedness to others, I must begin with those who have placed at my disposal materials without which the book could not have been written. To Mrs. Cesira More O'Ferrall I am grateful not only for making available to me the mass of materials relating to her great grandfather, John Taaffe, Jr., but also for her warm hospitality, which will always remain a most pleasant memory. Nor shall I soon forget a visit to Smarmore Castle, where I was cordially received by Mr. Randal Taaffe, present head of the family, and permitted to examine and use freely all of the Smarmore papers relating to John Taaffe, Jr. To Sir John Murray, who gave me access to his great Byron collection and allowed me to use many letters and documents from it, and to Mr. John Grey Murray, from whom I have received many courtesies, I wish to record my grateful thanks. Mr. Carl Pforzheimer, the trustees of the Pierpont Morgan Library, the trustees of the Berg Collection of the New York Public Library, the trustees of the Keats-Shelley Memorial in Rome, and the Keeper of the Manuscripts of the British Museum have also generously supplied me with various materials which are duly acknowledged at the appropriate places in the text. My thanks are also due to Mr. Duncan Gray, Librarian of the City of Nottingham, who greatly facilitated my examination of the Byron materials at Newstead Abbey, and to the Reverend Dermot MacIvor, of Ardee, who was of invaluable assistance in helping me to trace materials relating to Taaffe.

One of the pleasures of scholarship is always the unfailing helpfulness and kindness of other workers in the field. Of these I wish to mention particularly Professor Leslie A. Marchand, of Rutgers University, who allowed me to draw freely on his extensive knowledge of Byron during the composition of this book and who saved me from numerous errors by reading it in manuscript; Miss

R. Glynn Grylls (Lady Mander), who has furnished me with some of the details of Trelawny's life which I have used; the Marchesa Iris Origo, who has been helpful in answering many questions relating to Teresa Guiccioli and her family and who was kind enough to make several excerpts for me from Teresa's unpublished *Vie de Lord Byron en Italie*; and Professor Frederick L. Jones, the late Professor Newman I. White, and Mr. Edmund Blunden, all of whom have furnished me with information about Shelley. Professor Robert Metcalf Smith likewise helped me to obtain some information about John Taaffe, Jr.

Not the least of my obligation is to my own colleagues at The University of Texas: Professors Harry H. Ransom and Guy Steffan, who have read the book in manuscript and offered many valuable suggestions; Miss Fannie Ratchford, Curator of Rare Books, who has been from the beginning most sympathetic and helpful in a hundred practical ways; Professors D. L. Clark and Willis Pratt, who have allowed me to draw upon their broad knowledge of Shelley and Byron; Professor Robert Adger Law, who has read the book in page proof; and Professor Powell Stewart, who assumed many of my academic duties during the writing of the book and to whom I therefore owe a special debt of gratitude.

I wish to record my thanks to the American Council of Learned Societies for a travel grant which enabled me to go to Ireland and England and to Dean A. P. Brogan and the Research Council of The University of Texas for numerous grants-in-aid. And, lastly, I would record my thanks to my wife for her able assistance in proof-reading and for her encouragement when it was needed most.

C. L. CLINE

Austin, Texas
July 1951

CHAPTER I

The Shelleys at Pisa

THE winter of 1819–20 was the severest winter that the city of Florence had experienced in sixty years.[1] To Percy and Mary Shelley, who had come to Florence in October expecting to remain six months, the weather was unexpectedly disagreeable. Shelley, whose health was never robust and who was suffering from an almost constant pain in his side that was aggravated by the cold and damp, in a wry poetic moment called it "an epic of rain with an episode of frost & a few similes concerning fine weather."[2]

The Shelleys had come to Florence from Leghorn in order that Mary might have, during her approaching confinement, the services of Dr. John Bell, a Scottish physician who had attended her in Rome during the preceding spring and then had moved on to Florence. Looking backward in December, Mary Shelley felt that coming to Florence had been a mistake. Having meanwhile learned of the reputation of Dr. Vaccà [3] in Pisa, she decided that she might have had equally good medical attendance at lower cost there. In Florence they were virtually friendless; but at Leghorn, only a short distance from Pisa, lived Mr. and Mrs. Gisborne,[4] the latter an old friend of Godwin's who had already shown her desire to help the Shelleys. Florence, it is true, had famous art galleries and fine classical architecture, but of what value were they to Mary if she was confined to her own rooms? And now that the winter had turned out to be wet and cold, they thought of Pisa, situated in a depression that sheltered it from the penetrating "tramontanes" of Florence, and famous for its pure water.

"Tuscany is delightful eight months of the year," Shelley wrote to his cousin Tom Medwin, then at Geneva, "but nothing reconciles me to the slightest indication of winter: much less such infernal cold as my nerves have been racked upon for the last ten days." [5] Since the baby, born on November 12, was flourishing, only the severity of the weather, which discouraged travelling, and a reluctance to interrupt the musical progress of Claire Clairmont—the daughter of Godwin's second wife and an often unwelcome member of the Shelley ménage—kept them at Florence. A sudden break in the weather, bringing almost spring-like days, was too tempting to resist: it was suddenly decided that they should go to Pisa—and by boat. "We *embark*," Shelley wrote to Mr. Gisborne; "and I promise myself delight from the sky, and the water, and the mountains. I must suffer at any rate, but I expect to suffer less in a boat than in a carriage." [6]

Early on the morning of January 26 they began their journey. The weather, with its promise of spring, turned out to be deceptive: a sharp wind swept across the river, cutting through them and reminding them that winter had not yet spent its force. After some five uncomfortable hours they landed at Empoli, where they took a carriage for Pisa. A jolting drive brought them to their destination about six o'clock, and they found lodgings at the Albergo delle Tre Donzelle in the Lung' Arno Regio. So came to Pisa the first of the little group that Trelawny was to designate "the Pisa Circle." It was to be Shelley's home, in the words of Mrs. Angeli, "for a longer period than he ever sojourned in any other place since the doors of his paternal home had been closed against him." [7]

Circumstances had made Shelley an exile. Deprived by a Chancery decision of his children by Harriet, threatened with arrest by creditors, looked at askance by neighbours at Marlow, some of whom suspected that the baby Allegra

(Byron's daughter by Claire Clairmont) was Shelley's child by Claire, and worried into almost chronic ill-health, Shelley, Mary, and their two children, with Claire Clairmont, Allegra, and two servants, left England on March 12, 1818. After a leisurely journey through France, they crossed the Alps into Italy on March 30. The interval between their arrival in Italy and their coming to Pisa included a summer (1818) at the Bagni di Lucca, about sixty miles north of Leghorn, a winter (1818–19) at Naples, three months (March–June, 1819) at Rome, almost four months at Leghorn, and the period at Florence already referred to.

The almost two years that the Shelleys had spent in Italy had been marked more by grief and suffering than by happiness. In September, 1818, while they were staying in the vicinity of Venice so that Claire might see Allegra, who had been given over to Byron upon their arrival in Italy, their younger child, Clara Everina, died. Then, in the following June, their son William died. The losses were almost more than Mary could bear: with the death of Clara she gave way to a mood of despondency that deepened with the death of William and was only stopped short of despair by the birth of Percy Florence on November 12. Shelley, too, suffered deeply. The benefits of the southern climate were all overbalanced by the physical and mental agonies that he endured. Mary's outcry, "We went from England comparatively prosperous & happy—I should return broken hearted & miserable—I never know one moments ease from the wretchedness and despair that possesses me——"[8] is matched by Shelley's lament, "O that I could return to England! How heavy a weight when misfortune is added to exile, and solitude, as if the measure were not full, heaped high on both. O that I could return to England!"[9]

But they could not return to England; instead, bruised and lonely, they took up life anew at Pisa. This was not their first acquaintance with the town. They had spent several days in it, lodging at the Tre Donzelle, shortly after their arrival in Italy. And on their way from Leghorn to Florence in August, 1819, they had broken their journey there and had formed an acquaintance that was later to be of considerable value to them, especially to Claire Clairmont—that of the Masons, as Lady Mountcashell and her common-law husband, George William Tighe, were known in Pisa.[10] When Lady Mountcashell was a child in Ireland, Mary Wollstonecraft, Mary Shelley's mother, had been governess in the household of Lord Kingston, father of the future Lady Mountcashell. The story of the elopement of Shelley and Mary had been related by Mrs. Godwin in a letter to Lady Mountcashell, who thus received the pair with unusual interest. When the Shelleys met her in Pisa, she had separated from the Earl Mountcashell and had been living for eight years with Mr. Tighe, by whom she had two daughters.

Pisa had not impressed the Shelleys very favourably at first sight. To Shelley it seemed "a large disagreeable city, almost without inhabitants"[11]; and indeed its population, once said to be 120,000, had by 1820 shrunk to some 18,000. Mary, in writing to Leigh and Marianne Hunt, gave a more detailed explanation of their dislike:

> Pisa is a dull town situated on the banks of the Arno—it has a fine cathedral but not to be compared to that of Milan—and a tower which has been so shaken by an earthquake that it leans many feet on one side—Its gallery of pictures or whatever it contains we did not see putting that off untill our return to the town—One thing however which disgusted me so much that I could never walk in the streets except in misery was that criminals condemned to labour work publickly in the streets heavily ironed in pairs with a man with a gun to each pair to guard against their escape—These poor wretches look sallow and dreadfully wretched and you could get into no street but you heard the clanking of their chains.[12]

It is probable that Hunt's impression of the town was juster than the Shelleys', for with time Pisa was to improve in the Shelleys' estimation. To Hunt it was "a small white city, with a tower leaning at one end of it, trees on either side, and blue mountains for the background. . . . You cross a bridge, and cast your eye up the whole extent of the city one way, the river Arno (the river of Dante, Petrarch, and Boccaccio) winding through the middle of it under two more bridges; and fair elegant houses of good size bordering the white pavement on either side. This is the Lung'arno, or street 'Along the Arno.'"[13] Far from disagreeable, it was "a tranquil, an imposing, and even now a beautiful and stately city. It looks like what it is, the residence of an university: many parts of it seem made up of colleges; and we feel as if we ought to 'walk gowned.'"[14]

Three days after their arrival in Pisa, the Shelleys and Claire found lodgings at the Casa Frasi, on the Lung' Arno. "We have two bed rooms 2 sitting rooms kitchen servants rooms nicely furnished—& very clean & *new* (a great thing in this country) for 4 guineas & a ½ a month," Mary wrote to Marianne Hunt.[15] But Shelley, who had no study, felt cooped up and was unable to resume his literary work for the time being.[16] When on March 14 they moved from the mezzanine to roomier quarters on the third floor of the Casa Frasi, he was much more content.

In the beginning they knew only Mr. and Mrs. Mason in Pisa, and Mary's and Claire's journals are full of references to associations with the Masons during the following months. "Almost every day for six months the Shelleys and Claire went there for tea, dinner, or an afternoon or morning call," observes White.[17] Shelley, who read Greek with Mrs. Mason, took to her from the first; later he was to modify his opinion somewhat.[18]

> She is everything that is amiable and wise, and he is very agreeable [he wrote to Leigh Hunt]. You will think it my fate either to find or to imagine some lady of 45, very unprejudiced and philosophical, who has entered deeply into the best and selectest spirit of

the age, with enchanting manners, and a disposition rather to like me, in every town that I inhabit. But certainly such this lady is.[19]

There was apparently never any real affection between her and Mary, but to Claire, who was much more intimate with her, she proved to be a sincere friend and counsellor.

With better working conditions Shelley was engaged in study and composition; from his never prolific pen came the *Ode to Liberty*, *The Sensitive Plant*, which owes something to Mrs. Mason and her garden, and *A Vision of the Sea*. That he wrote in the hope of finding readers is quite clear, and equally clear is the disheartening effect of finding none. "I am devising literary plans of some magnitude," he wrote to his friend Peacock later. "But nothing is so difficult and unwelcome as to write without a confidence of finding readers. . . ."[20] Any hopes that he would find an audience with *The Cenci*, which was published in March, were soon blasted; the reviews were for the most part savage, and Shelley could draw little consolation from the frequent concession of his genius, so severe was the condemnation of his views.[21]

Claire Clairmont continued to be a source of friction in the household. Mary's attitude toward her was much what it had been three years earlier when, in writing to Shelley her requirements in a house, she had specified one with a lawn, a river or lake, noble trees, and divine mountains, and then had written abruptly: "But never mind this—give me a garden & *absentia Clariae* and I will thank my love for many favours."[22] Now she wrote in her journal (June 8): "A better day than most days and good reason for it, though Shelley is not well. Clare away at Pugnano." Claire's journal offers similar evidence of friction (July 4):

> Heigho the Clare and the Ma
> Find something to fight about every day.

It could hardly have been otherwise. Aside from very real

differences in temperament, the constant presence of another woman in the household would have irritated a better-natured woman than Mary. But Claire was alone in the world and had no one else but the Shelleys to turn to; this in itself was enough to secure for her Shelley's affection and protection and in turn Mary's jealousy. Freer of duties than Mary, Claire went about more, particularly with the Mason children, and occupied herself with her music and dancing lessons. She likewise read a great deal, translated a French work, and wrote "Letters from Italy," a literary composition now lost.[23]

Warm weather, the Pisan water, and the medical advice of Vaccà all combined to improve Shelley's health. ". . . I feel myself most materially better at the return of spring," he wrote to Peacock. "I am on the whole greatly benefited by my residence in Italy, and, but for certain moral causes, should probably have been enabled to reinstate my system completely."[24] Vaccà, though he was unable to effect a cure, sensibly advised using no medicines and trusting to Nature. An even warmer climate than Pisa's was desirable but impractical because of danger to the baby, Percy Florence.[25] At first the Shelleys planned to spend the summer of 1820 at the Baths of Lucca; but they suddenly decided, instead, to go to Leghorn in the middle of June and occupy the house of the Gisbornes, who were in England arranging business affairs. The change in plans was made in order to enlist the aid of a lawyer, Federico del Rosso, in circumventing the blackmailing attempts of a rascally former servant, Paolo Foggi, who had been discharged earlier by the Shelleys. Shelley's own words are that Paolo was attempting "to extort money by threatening to charge me with the most horrible crimes,"[26] while Mary wrote to Mrs. Gisborne that Paolo had entered "into an infamous conspiracy against us."[27]

It is clear enough that all of this had to do with a mysterious episode in Shelley's life dating back to the winter of 1818 in Naples. On December 27, 1818, Shelley had sworn before a magistrate that a child, who was given the name of Elena Adelaide Shelley, was born to him and Mary. It is certain that such a child existed, and also certain that it could not have been Mary's child. Since Paolo was later responsible for the story told Mrs. Hoppner by Elise Foggi, his wife, that the child was the offspring of Shelley and Claire Clairmont, it does not require much imagination to guess that he was threatening to spread such a story now unless bought off by Shelley.* "We have had a most infernal business with Paolo whom, however, we have succeeded in crushing," Shelley wrote to the Gisbornes.[28] In this belief, unfortunately, he was mistaken.

That in the midst of such vexation Shelley could compose his immortal lyric, *To a Skylark*, is surely more marvellous than most of its readers can ever have realized. "It was on a beautiful summer evening," Mary Shelley later recalled, "while wandering among the lanes, whose myrtle hedges were the bowers of the fire-flies, that we heard the carolling of the sky-lark, which inspired one of the most beautiful of his poems."[29] Not only is it one of Shelley's most beautiful poems: it is much more. It is the poignant outcry of a great poet who recognizes his own powers but has met with neglect or rejection by a heedless world.

Their business apparently accomplished, the Shelleys and Claire moved on to the Baths of Pisa in August to escape the heat, but Claire stayed only a short time before returning to Leghorn; then in October, on the advice of Mrs. Mason, she went to live in the home of Professor

* For all this, see White, II, chapters XX and XXVII. Because the discreet journals of all concerned are silent on this affair, the facts are not likely ever to be fully known. But White's hypothesis, that Elena Adelaide Shelley was an adopted child whom Shelley hoped to introduce into his own household and have accepted by Mary but was prevented by circumstances, is so reasonable as to compel belief. The fact that adoption had no legal status in England until the following year might account for the subterfuge. The child died on June 9, 1820.

Bojti at Florence, a move made doubly expedient by the machinations of Paolo.[30] Shelley accompanied her to Florence and on his return to the Baths of Pisa brought with him his cousin and former schoolmate, Thomas Medwin, whom he found in Pisa.

Medwin, though four years older than Shelley, had been at Sion House, Brentford, with him, and the two had spent most of their vacations together at Horsham. Entering the army about 1813, Medwin went with his regiment to India. During his years in the East, according to Medwin, he and Shelley corresponded, but he failed to preserve Shelley's letters. One day just before his departure from Bombay, Medwin found in a bookstall a copy of *The Revolt of Islam*, which renewed his interest in Shelley. On landing at Liverpool in the spring of 1819, he learned that Shelley was in Italy and wrote to him there. Whenever Shelley had an establishment, he always sent out invitations to the few friends he possessed to come and visit him—whether there was room or not. The correspondence now resumed brought repeated invitations from Shelley to Medwin to visit him and Mary in Italy, "the Paradise of exiles, the retreat of Pariahs," [31] though in order that there might be no misunderstanding he warned, "I ought to tell you that we do not enter into society." [32] When at last Medwin arrived at Pisa, he found that the Shelleys were away. He was referred to Mrs. Mason for information about them, and on the following day Shelley, having returned from Florence, called on him at the Tre Donzelle. Thus it was that Medwin accompanied Shelley to the Baths of Pisa.

At the end of October, heavy rains caused the Serchio to break its banks, flooding the Shelleys' house with four feet of water and driving them and their guest into Pisa, where they took an apartment at the Palazzo Galetti.

> We are now removed to a lodging on the Lung Arno, which is sufficiently commodious, and for which we pay thirteen sequins a month [Shelley wrote to Claire]. It is next door to that marble

palace, and is called Palazzo Galetti, consisting of an excellent mezzanino, and of two rooms on the fourth story, all to the south, and with two fireplaces. The rooms above, one of which is Medwin's room and the other my study (congratulate me on my seclusion) are delightfully pleasant, and to-day I shall be employed in arranging my books and gathering my papers about me. Mary has a very good room below, and there is plenty of space for the babe.[33]

Medwin was already an author of sorts at the time of his arrival in Pisa, having published *Oswald and Edwin: an Oriental Sketch* at Geneva in the preceding February.[34] Shelley read sympathetically the manuscript of Medwin's *Sketches in Hindoostan*, which Ollier, probably on Shelley's recommendation, published in 1821. Shelley regarded it as "highly fit for popularity" and admired "equally the richness and variety of the imagery with the ease and profusion of language in which it is expressed." A severe critic, he confessed, might find "some single lines and expressions" that might be changed for the better, but they were very few, indeed, he added, and he was unqualified "to do more than point them out." [35]

In the beginning the Shelleys found Medwin a pleasant addition to their household. Shelley speaks of his "cheerful conversation," calls him "very agreeable," and says that "he plays at chess, and falls into our habits of reading in the evening, and Mary likes him well enough." [36] But Medwin's conversation ran too much to India and lion hunts—one is reminded of Jos Sedley—and his own literary projects for this state of affairs to continue for long. Possibly his illness of some weeks' duration in November and December, during which Shelley nursed him with the tenderest care and consequently could not escape him, marked the beginning of a changed attitude toward him. Not long thereafter Mary wrote to Claire:

You have no idea how earnestly we desire the transfer of Mxxxxn to Florence—in plain Italian he is a *Seccatura*—He sits with us & be one reading or writing he insists upon interrupting one every moment to read all the fine things he either writes or reads. . . . S[helley] does nothing but conjugate the verb seccare

& twist & turn Seccatura in all possible ways. He is Common Place personified—[37]

It was Mary's desire to become acquainted with some of the Italian people, but at Pisa, as she wrote to Marianne Hunt, she found the prospect discouraging:

. . . Its inhabitants w[oul]d exercise all Hogg's * vocabulary of scamps, raffs &c &c to fully describe their ragged-haired, shirtless condition. Many of them are students of the university & they are none of the genteelest of the crew. Then there are *Bargees*, beggars without number; galley slaves in their yellow & red dress with chains—the women in dirty cotton gowns trailing in the dirt—pink silk hats starting up in the air to run away from their ugly faces in this manner: [*a sketch here illustrates*] for they always tie the bows at the points [of] their chins—& white satin shoes—& fellows with bushy hair—large whiskers, canes in their hands, & a bit of dirty party coloured riband (a symbol of nobility) sticking in their button holes that mean to look like the lords of the rabble but who only look like their drivers. The Pisans I dislike more than any of the Italians & none of them are *as yet* favourites with me.[38]

Months later, when she had had more opportunity to observe them, she recorded in her journal that life in Pisa would be pleasant enough if she but had a carriage in which to escape from her house to the country without coming in contact with the inhabitants: "but the Pisans and the Scholari, in short, the whole population, are such, that it would sound strange to an English person if I attempted to express what I feel concerning them. . . ." [39] Yet it turned out that there were people in Pisa who were, after all, unobjectionable to Mary. Within two weeks of her damning characterization of the Pisans, her journal begins to be sprinkled with the names of new acquaintances, among them several native Italians—first Pacchiani; then Sgricci, Prince Mavrocordato, his cousin Princess Argiropoli, Mr. Taaffe, Emilia Viviani, Madame Tantini, Signora Bernardini, Contessa dei Conti, and others.

* Thomas Jefferson Hogg, who was expelled from Oxford with Shelley.

Most of these new acquaintances were introduced by Professor Pacchiani, known as the Devil of Pisa, who, until the Shelleys learned that the sobriquet was deserved, was a favourite of theirs. A churchman who had remained in orders but had deserted the church for the university, Pacchiani became a professor of logic and metaphysics at the University of Pisa in 1801. In the following year he occupied the chair of physical chemistry and might have had a distinguished career had not indolence prevented his carrying out his studies to their ultimate conclusion. Medwin speaks of his office as that of *Belles Lettres* at the time the Shelleys knew him.[40] When Madame de Staël was in Pisa in 1816, she joked with Pacchiani about his imaginary tragedies because of his frequent quotations from literary compositions that never appeared and were probably never written.

Suspected of being the author of scurrilous anonymous publications, and known to subsist in part by robbing his own servant and by collecting commissions from language teachers, artists, landlords, and merchants for whom he obtained customers, he had fallen into discredit locally by the time the Shelleys knew him; but they were slow, naturally, in learning of these unsavoury details. A brilliant conversationalist, he exercised a charm upon Shelley, who, Medwin tells us, "listened with rapt attention to his eloquence, which he compared to that of Coleridge."[41] Mary was equally taken in by him. "He is really the only Italian who has a heart and soul," she wrote to Hunt. "He is very high spirited, has a profound mind and an eloquence which enraptures. . . . Every evening he comes to our house and always delights us with his original ideas."[42] But within a month their enthusiasm cooled when they found him to be of an inquisitive and indelicate nature.[43]

With Pacchiani came Sgricci, an *improvvisatore* then in popular favour, whose performances, especially in tragic scenes, showed remarkable ability. On December 20 the

Shelleys went to hear him improvise on the subject of Iphigenia in Tauris, a performance which Mary pronounced a "most wonderful and delightful exhibition."[44] She went three weeks later to hear him again at Lucca, this time on the subject of Inez di Castro, and thought he "acquitted himself to admiration in the conduct and passion & poetry of his piece." [45] She and Shelley heard him again in Pisa on January 22 in the Death of Hector, but he did not long remain in favour with Shelley, whom he disgusted with his talk against the Neapolitan insurgents.

Prince Mavrocordato, an exile from Turkish rule in Greece who was to return and play an important part in the struggle for Greek independence, was Mary's favourite among their new acquaintances. Presently she wrote to Mrs. Gisborne: "Do you not envy my luck, that, having begun Greek, an amiable, young, agreeable, and learned Greek Prince comes every morning to give me a lesson of an hour and a-half ? This is the result of an acquaintance with Pacchiani. So you see, even the Devil has his use." [46]

Shelley, who tolerated Mavrocordato for Mary's sake, might well have used the same expression, for it was Pacchiani who formed the link with Emilia Viviani. The pretty daughter of the governor of Pisa, Emilia had been placed in the Convent of St. Anna by her mother because of jealousy of Emilia's talents and beauty.[47] When the Shelleys—and Claire, back in Pisa on a visit—met her in November, she had been a "prisoner" in the convent for three years, and Shelley's hatred of tyranny was instantly roused on her behalf. Throughout Claire's stay in Pisa, her journal records almost daily visits to Emilia. Presently Shelley was drawing up a petition for her liberation, which he requested Claire, then back in Florence, to find means of presenting to the Grand Duchess. Inspired by friendship with Emilia, Shelley wrote his *Epipsychidion*, which he called "an idealised history of my life and feelings," and sent it off to Ollier in February for limited publication.[48] Until shortly before her marriage the following September, the Shelleys saw Emilia and corresponded with her frequently. Mary, who found her too demonstrative and who was charged by Emilia with *freddezza* or coldness, later referred to the episode as "Shelley's Italian platonics."[49] She was no doubt grateful for the family interdiction which forbade Emilia to see the Shelleys for a period preceding her marriage on September 8. But with the completion of *Epipsychidion* she had ended her usefulness to literature and might pass on into the obscurity of an unhappy marriage, assured of a gratuitous immortality.

The first circle of acquaintance formed by the Shelleys in Pisa was, as we have seen, comprised of Italians and exiles from their native countries. The principal figures were Pacchiani, Sgricci, Mavrocordato, Emilia Viviani, and one who has not yet been identified—John Taaffe, Jr., an Irish expatriate—who likewise was probably introduced by Pacchiani and whose first recorded appearance in the Shelley household is mentioned in Claire's journal on November 28, 1820: "Pacchiani calls his priests cap a Tartuffeometro—or measure for hypocrisy. Mr. Taaffe calls." A few days later (December 3), Mary's journal contains the first of many entries bearing his name: "Mr. Taaffe in the evening." An aspiring poet, Taaffe had already published *Padilla, A Tale of Palestine* in 1816. Shortly after coming to Italy in 1815, he had begun the study of Dante as a means of perfecting his Italian; later he was to engage the assistance of both Shelley and Byron in getting the fruits of his labours, his *Comment on Dante*, published. A minor figure certainly, he appears in all the biographies of Byron and Shelley, frequently misnamed "Count" Taaffe, often misspelled "Taafe." Garnett, in the introduction to the *Journal of Edward Ellerker Williams*, says of him: ". . . Even Taaffe had had romantic adventures in his youth, which this is not the place to record." Since Taaffe was, with the exception of the in-and-out Medwin, the earliest recruit to the real Pisan circle that was to supersede the short-lived one composed of Italians and expatriates, and since he was a prominent figure in two episodes involving Byron and Shelley, this is the logical place to record those "romantic adventures."

CHAPTER 2

The Irish Expatriate: John Taaffe, Jr.

"If I had to choose a genealogy," John Taaffe writes complacently in his unpublished autobiography, "it would be my own." The eldest son of John Taaffe of Smarmore by his second wife and cousin, Catherine Taaffe, John Taaffe, Jr. (1787 or 1788–1862) was descended on both paternal and maternal sides from a prominent Catholic family that had come to Ireland with Richard Strongbow in 1170 and settled first in County Louth.[1] His paternal grandfather and his father, for a time, kept a distillery and had other commercial interests in Ardee, County Louth, but this was before the time of John Taaffe, Jr., whose earliest memories, he recalls, were of living at Smarmore, a castle with a tower said to date back to Danish times. Here the family lived bountifully, after the openhanded, hospitable fashion of the gentry of the time, on what Taaffe estimates was an income of £8,000 per annum.[2]

Taaffe professed not to know his birth date; he was born "about 1788," he says. His first instruction was at the hands of an older half-sister, Eliza, to whom he expresses his gratitude in his poem *Padilla*. After an unfortunate period at a school in Inch (halfway between Drogheda and Dublin), he was enrolled at Stonyhurst, a Jesuit school, where he acquired "a tolerable knowledge of Latin, Greek, and even mathematics." A sensitive, self-conscious youth, he blushed so easily that his schoolmates nicknamed him Betty Black. Being short-sighted, he was not proficient at most sports and cultivated a compensatory love of solitude. His future was in good part determined by the praise of one of his teachers, who told Taaffe that he was the only real poet in the school. "I used to hug myself with transport when alone and where nobody could see me repeating the Professor's words and determining to do my best to verify them," he reports.

For his last year he transferred to Ulverstone (near Preston); there he translated Horace, wrote "a heap of idle rhymes," and acquired dandified manners. Returning to Ireland in the autumn of 1807, he spent the three happiest years of his life at Smarmore—the Eden which, like Adam, he was to forfeit by his own folly. Here he lived the life of a well-to-do Irish gentleman, hunting, breeding horses and hounds, and continuing his studies of Latin, Greek, and French under the guidance of a priest. But the love of literature and the desire to become a poet were so strong within him that he could not continue to enjoy such a life, however pleasant. He regarded his life at Smarmore as misspent and yearned to go to college. His father consenting, Edinburgh was at last settled upon as least likely to damage his religious principles.

"In an evil hour," he writes, "I set out for Edinburgh"—hoping that his talents would one day enable him to do honour to his name and grace his beloved Smarmore the better upon his return. The event turned out otherwise. Except for an acquaintance with Scott, who received him hospitably, the winter of 1810–11 which he spent at the university profited him little. On the contrary he became involved in a love affair, of which he writes obscurely in his autobiography and which was to cost him his inheritance and drive him into exile for the rest of his life. From family papers at Smarmore it is clear that he contracted what Scottish law calls a marriage by "cohabitation and repute" with a Mrs. Belinda Colebrooke, whom he describes as beautiful, brilliant, and rich.[3] His family tried to break off the affair, arranging a career for him first in the diplomatic corps and then in the army. On both occasions Taaffe made promises to them which he failed to keep. Instead he "attempted to marry" Mrs. Colebrooke.*

The affair was of short duration. By his own account it ended after a few months in her attempt to murder him, an act which he could only ascribe to madness.† He returned, humiliated, like the Prodigal Son, to his parents. To escape the legal consequences of his folly, it was decided that he should travel for the next few years.

Before setting out sadly from his home for what was to be a life of exile, Taaffe chanced upon a fragment of a poem he had earlier composed. "I promised," he says solemnly, "that if I lived I should try to compose something less unworthy of the dear parents who were even at that time my audience." Though his father forgave him, the legal jeopardy in which he lived henceforth caused his father to make a new will in favour of his younger brother, George. Thereafter he was to live on the modest allowance of a cadet, with none of the expectations of an eldest son. It was in 1812 when he set out upon his travels, which, like Childe Harold's pilgrimage, began in Portugal, where he travelled extensively, and included Gibraltar, North Africa, and Spain. During the course of his travels he wrote *Padilla*, *A Tale of Palestine*,

* The nature of this attempt is not clear. Taaffe's words are: "I attempted to marry her—who (I now see) was only deceiving me. She could not marry me nor anyone else—at least not without divorce; for married she was already, and her husband alive. Yet let me not do her injustice; she is dead many years. It was not so much deceit in her as mutability of mind. . . . She seemed to doat on me and no doubt did doat on me very ardently—and on her husband no longer, and desired he would forget her as well—and never spoke to me of him but as a discarded and never favoured lover—without even the shadow or pretence of a legitimate claim or connection."

† According to Taaffe, Mrs. Colebrooke crept stealthily upon him, with an open razor in her hand, as he lay sleeping on a couch. He awoke in the nick of time, and she slunk back into her room. Of the episode, Taaffe writes: "The Physicians declared her mad. But the lawyers declared otherwise. . . . Madness is the excuse for an attempt at murder. It was necessary to cure her; which the courts prevented."

which he sent home for publication and which appeared in print in 1816. By a curious coincidence he first entitled it *Lara*, though he declares that he knew nothing of Byron's *Lara* until sometime later. The poem attracted little attention, but the hopeful author was reluctant to accept the public verdict as merited.

In June, 1815, he first touched foot upon the soil of Italy, which henceforth was to be his home, though he did not know it then. At Genoa he formed one of the warmest friendships of his life, that with Madame Regny.[4] The tie between them was cemented when her twelve-year-old daughter Natalie died in Taaffe's arms. Physicians subsequently ordered Madame Regny to Pisa for her health, and Taaffe accompanied her and her baby, Ida. He expected to stay a few months; he was destined to stay for many years. To Madame Regny, who must have been a woman of unusual culture and personal charm, were opened the doors of the first society of Pisa, Lucca, and Florence, and, through her, to Taaffe. Since Madame Regny was a painter of ability, her circle of acquaintances included the painters and intellectuals of Tuscany. The Florentine Academy elected her an honorary member; and Taaffe, in his autobiography, reels off the names of counts, marquesses, dukes, princes, and archbishops whose salons were frequented by the two. When Madame de Staël came to Pisa in 1816, Taaffe became acquainted with her, addressed some complimentary verses to her, and after her departure from Pisa received several letters from her.[5]

Taaffe, who took great pleasure in riding, kept a horse in Madame Regny's stables, which by the desire of M. Regny, then at Rome, were under his direction. His habits were those of an unascetic scholar: he spent his mornings in study, rode out in the afternoons, dined with the family of Madame Regny, whose father and sister had joined her, and went into society in the evenings, often returning to write well into the early hours of the morning.

Now occurred the most curious episode of Taaffe's career. The brilliant society which received him was not enough to satisfy him. He married—but married under most extraordinary circumstances. This is the story. In 1816 or 1817 Taaffe met in Pisa Catherine Fitzgerald, the daughter of General Andrew Fitzgerald,[6] an elderly officer who had served in India, and married her. The ceremony, performed by an English Catholic priest, took place on an English vessel out of sight of land off Leghorn, with only Madame Regny as witness. Towards evening the vessel put in close to shore, and the bride, bridegroom, and witness went ashore in a small boat that had been in tow. Catherine Taaffe, who had been visiting in Leghorn, remained there, while Taaffe returned to Pisa without her. Since his wife came to him without a dowry, and since he himself had only a slender income dependent upon his father's generosity, Taaffe realized that his family would regard the alliance as unfortunate and therefore resolved to keep it from them and from public knowledge. More important, since Mrs. Colebrooke was still alive he undoubtedly feared legal difficulties if the marriage became known. When, therefore, in the course of the evening he encountered General Fitzgerald, no mention was made of the new relationship that, unknown to the general, existed between them. The secret was later revealed to Catherine Taaffe's young brother, just before he sailed for India, and the three, with Madame Regny again as witness, bound themselves by solemn promises to preserve it.

It must have been a difficult secret to keep, for Catherine Taaffe bore a daughter, Isias, in 1818, and a son, John, in 1819. She died in childbirth with the birth of her second child. In his autobiography, Taaffe passes swiftly over this portion of his history, not even recording the name of his wife. Vaccà, who attended her, knew the secret, and, in addition to Madame Regny, two ladies knew "part of it," according to Taaffe. Madame Regny was Catherine Taaffe's shield in those days when concealing an advanced state of pregnancy from the eyes of father and friends must have been a difficult task indeed. Upon the death of his wife, Taaffe took the puzzling position that only her brother had the right to make the marriage known, though after the death of Taaffe's father in 1825, he casually informed his brother and sister, who were visiting in Italy, that he had a son and a daughter by a now dead wife.

Each child was put out to nurse with an Italian family as soon as it was born, but this arrangement could not last indefinitely. Taaffe hoped that Madame Regny would offer to take Isias, but since she did not, he made an arrangement with Mr. and Mrs. Fortis, acquaintances of his at Milan, to take her.[7] Since they had recently lost their only child, they took Isias in the hope that she would help to fill the void in their lives.

This, then, is the history of John Taaffe, Jr., up to the time that the Shelleys arrived in Pisa. Unfortunately, the journals of Mary and Claire give no personal details of him. But the portrait painted by Madame Regny shortly after the break-up of the Pisan circle reveals him to have been a small, compact man with a broad face and short nose, dark brown hair receding from the forehead, and a firm mouth. Punctilious in manner and dress, he enjoyed society—particularly "good" society—but there is no evidence that he valued his titled friends more than his artist friends. The shyness that had marked his youth appeared in the man as a slightly exaggerated regard for his own dignity: he was looked upon by the members of the Pisan circle as inclined to vanity. In 1820, despite the failure of *Padilla*, he was as determined as ever to write poetry that would win him immortality, and the presence of Shelley and later of Byron naturally strengthened this resolution. Toward carrying it out, he devoted himself industriously to serious studies. The waste books that he left behind are full of criticisms of the great number of books—more history and philosophy than literature—

that he was reading in various languages. His study of Italian having led him to Dante, he laboured on his translation of the *Divine Comedy*, which Byron and Shelley jested about; but the translation led, in turn, to a more meritorious work, his *Comment on Dante*, which both recommended highly to their publishers. Except for some occasional verse—the lines to Madame de Staël, an elegy on the death of a Saxon prince in Pisa in 1822, and some birthday verses addressed to an unidentified young lady, possibly one of the Misses Beauclerk[8]— his study of Dante was his principal literary occupation during the years from 1816 to 1822.

After Taaffe's first visit to the Shelley household on November 28, 1820, he was a frequent visitor until the end of March, 1822, when his connection with the little circle became less intimate than formerly as a result of his conduct in an altercation with a dragoon. Until that time, it was not uncommon for him to visit the Shelleys three or four times a week. Mary's journal is full of such entries as "Mr. Taaffe in the evening," "Emilia Viviani and Mr. Taaffe," "In the evening the Williams', Prince Mavrocordato, and Mr. Taaffe," "Mr. Taaffe calls," and so on. Within a month the acquaintanceship had developed to the point that Shelley presented Taaffe with a copy of one of his dramatic compositions, probably *Prometheus Unbound*, published only a few months before, and received in return a letter of generous praise. There is no reason to think that Shelley, who longed for an audience, was less grateful than he appeared in his letter of acknowledgment to be: "You have gratified my literary vanity, & if I dared to trust myself I should say a purer feeling, in a manner, which never has before fallen to my lot; & you must bear the burthen of my thanks."[9]

A little later Taaffe submitted to Shelley for criticism or approval some verses written by a Mrs. Thomas,[10] an Englishwoman who, with her family, spent several years in Pisa, Genoa, and vicinity. Since Shelley's opinion was written to Taaffe instead of to the author, he could be entirely candid in judging them. "Your own conscience will tell you that the verses are insufferable trash," he wrote, in a note accompanying the return of the verses, "& it gives me great regret to state that mine agrees with yours in this particular."[11]

Although a bond of sympathy may have been created between Taaffe and Shelley by the failure of each to find an audience for his poetry, an obstacle to any real sympathy existed, on the other hand, in their differing attitudes toward religion. Taaffe remained to the end of his life, as he had begun, a staunch Catholic, whereas Shelley came to Pisa a confessed atheist who had been publicly branded and defamed as such. Shelley's kindly nature attracted Taaffe, who, serious student that he was, found in Shelley intellectual qualities that commanded his admiration. Looking further, Taaffe perceived that the label *atheist*, in terms of the man, was meaningless. A passage in his autobiography reveals not only Taaffe's affection for Shelley but also his ability to estimate Shelley's character at something like its real worth:

> Shelley was a sweeter poet and better man than he got credit for. The World treated him too harshly. I apprehend his father began the unjust persecution against him; unjust both when he was too young to be really wicked (only boyishly headstrong) and when he had grown wiser that extreme cruelty to his juvenile errors irritated and impelled him to some unwarrantable exposure during a few years of his advanced youth. He had become an exemplary moralist when I met him; and probably would have lived down calumny had his earthly career lasted a little longer.
>
> Some call him an Atheist, but it is not true; at least he was none when I knew him. He died none. He called himself an Atheist; still it is not true. He was at that moment pretty much like the deer who, when run down, turns on her hunters when her few butts only increase the barbarous outcry and display the cruelty clearer. Shelley once (ridiculously enough) called himself what he was not; and he had ceased calling himself so a long time before I made his acquaintance.

His fancy was so ardent that it perhaps saw resemblances where most people saw none. But his language was rich and musical: he knew English better than any person I ever met with. If he disdained to be understood it was more in his printed books than in his conversation, which was almost always eloquent, singularly mellifluous and full of heat and in a most wonderful and attractive degree uniting gentleness and vigour—his unquenchable courage contrasting strangely with his feeble frame and girlish voice.

I do not think I ever beheld such an instance of the mind's mastery over its body. No Anchorite dieted more parsimoniously. He told me he composed best when he was ill. He had the custom of lying on the carpet like a dog—particularly when in his study alone to read in winter on a rug near the stove, and in summer on the marbled floor. His pockets were usually crammed with books, papers, bread and raisins. Very seldom indeed he used to drink small wines; and hardly ever (if ever) taste strong ones or spirituous liquor. He could stick on a horse tolerably well; for I have seen a horse rear violently with him and not throw him; but he generally went on foot and had a peculiar bent in his elastic gait. Although then he was not tall and looked about thirty—having the Spirit of an heroical man in a boyish frame; not but there was something wizened in his freckled face—or if you will, withered—something of the faded flower indication of past sufferings or ominous of future ones, or both. So it frequently struck me; which grieved me, for I loved him.

Shelley, for his part, regarded Taaffe with mixed feelings. On the one hand he respected Taaffe's scholarship and valued his literary judgment sufficiently to submit *Adonais* to him for criticism, and upon Taaffe's advice omitted in the Preface a long passage relating to his own personal wrongs. On the other hand Shelley did not care for formal calls, for drawing-room small talk, or for pointless anecdotes, of which Taaffe seems to have had a supply. He was alive, too, to a certain ridiculousness about the man which sometimes manifested itself in his manner and sometimes in his verses. "Mr Taaffe rides, writes, indites,[12] complains, bows & apologizes: he would be a mortal bore if he came often,"[13] Shelley wrote to Claire Clairmont from the Baths of Pisa after he had had ample opportunity to become well acquainted with Taaffe, and his words suggest an over-mannered, slightly ridiculous person. Mary was accustomed to sneer at Taaffe: it was she who contemptuously called him "the poet laureate of Pisa" and "this wise little gentleman" and who, in a letter to Mrs. Gisborne, selected for ridicule some verses of his written on the occasion of a young lady's birthday:

> Eyes that shed a thousand flowers
> Why should flowers be sent to you
> Sweetest flowers of heavenly bowers,
> Love & friendship are what are due.

"Then," continued Mary, "he wrote an elegy on the death of a saxon Prince[14] beginning Woe! woe! but he put in another woe! lest woe should be read whoo! & that at the beginning of his poem was too great a kindness to bestow on his readers, it ought to have been geho!"[15]

Taaffe had his ridiculous side, which was the one that Mary viewed exclusively. Shelley, looking closer, saw that there was another side, which he was able to respect. Moreover, Shelley must have felt some gratitude to Taaffe for the value that he placed upon Shelley's own verses. How many other appreciative readers had Shelley in the world in 1820?

CHAPTER 3

Beginnings of the Pisan Circle

IN January, 1821, Edward and Jane Williams, friends of Medwin, arrived in Pisa. "It was under the idea that their enlightened society and sympathy would tend to chase Shelley's melancholy, that I allured them to Pisa from Chalons [*sic*]," writes Medwin. "Their arrival was a great event, and they formed a most agreeable addition to our little party." [1] It was the Williamses' intention to stay in Pisa for a month and then go on to Florence; at least that was Mary Shelley's understanding.[2] She hoped fervently that they would take some of the burden of Medwin off her shoulders and that he would either go to Florence with them or, better still, precede them there. Having landed at Leghorn on January 13, the Williamses were in Pisa a few days later, occupying the lodgings that Medwin had engaged for them. The Shelleys lost no time in calling on them, and the two couples were soon well acquainted. The Williamses, the Shelleys, Taaffe, and Medwin (so long as he remained) constitute the nucleus of the Pisan circle that was now forming in the little Tuscan town.

Williams, a year younger than Shelley, had been briefly at Eton, after leaving which he entered the navy; but about 1811 he obtained a commission in the Eighth Dragoons and went to India,[3] where he served with Medwin. About 1819 he returned to England as a lieutenant on half-pay, accompanied by Jane, his common-law wife, who bore him a child, Edwin Medwin, in February, 1820.

Edward Trelawny, who was later to join the Pisan

circle, relates the story of his meeting three young men recently returned from India at the house of Sir John St. Aubyn, near Geneva. They were George Jervoise, of the Madras Artillery, Williams, and Medwin. "Medwin was the chief medium that impressed us with a desire to know Shelley," writes Trelawny; "he had known him from childhood; he talked of nothing but the inspired boy, his virtues and his sufferings, so that, irrespective of his genius, we all longed to know him."[4] When in the autumn of 1820 Trelawny was called back to England, the Williamses decided to spend the winter in the south of France, and Trelawny drove them in his carriage to Chalon sur Saône, promising to rejoin them in the spring "and to go on to Italy together in pursuit of Shelley."[5]

As it turned out, the Williamses came to Pisa and found Shelley almost exactly a year sooner than Trelawny. Medwin was waiting for them, and it was he who introduced them to the Shelleys at the first opportunity. As though he had accomplished his mission at Pisa with that act, he did not remain long thereafter; he departed on February 27. It was a fine exchange for the Shelleys: they lost a bore and gained two friends that they soon learned to value. A second child was born to the Williamses on March 16. Mary brought the news to Williams, who had retired to the Shelleys' apartment "to avoid the confusion and feelings such scenes occasion."[6]

From the first Williams appealed to Shelley. "W[illiams] I like," Shelley informed Claire later, "& I have got reconciled to Jane."[7] In the beginning Shelley held Jane Williams's "lack of literary refinement" against her, but gradually her good nature, her grace of motion, and her love of music overcame his initial prejudice.[8] "We see the Williams's constantly—nice, good-natured people, very soft society after authors and pretenders to philosophy," Shelley wrote to Claire,[9] the barbed arrow being directed primarily at Medwin.

On March 5 the Shelleys moved to Casa Aulla, and not long afterwards the Williamses took "the beautiful villa of Marchese Poschi, at Pugnano, about seven miles and a half from Pisa." [10] Both Medwin and Taaffe testify to the remarkable effect that companionship with Shelley had upon Williams. Before his acquaintance with Shelley his most serious pursuit in life had been hunting and sports. Taaffe, who regarded Williams as "a gentlemanly amiable young man," says that Williams in India had taken great delight in hunting lions and tigers and had kept a journal full of drawings of his hunts. According to it he had killed or been at the killing of eighteen lions and twenty-six tigers.[11] While Italy could hardly have afforded anything as exciting as one of the tiger hunts which Taaffe narrates, in which Williams and his mahout narrowly escaped death, proximity to Shelley caused Williams to abandon all sports (except the one that he shared with Shelley, sailing) in order to give himself up entirely to study and writing.

During the first three months of his stay at Pugnano, Williams was engaged in the writing of a play, *The Promise, or a Year, a Month, and a Day*, based upon two stories by Boccaccio, and Shelley not only encouraged and aided him [12] but also wrote an epithalamium for the play. In the following July it was sent to a friend of Williams's in England to be offered for performance in the theatre, and Shelley thought that, if accepted, it stood an excellent chance of being successful. In the end, however, it was rejected.

The strongest tie between Shelley and Williams was the passion that each had for sailing. Shelley's "great rage is a boat," Byron remarked later to Medwin,[13] and it was true. Vaccà had suggested that Shelley should buy a saddle horse for the sake of his health, but Shelley felt that the same benefit could be derived much less expensively from a boat. Accordingly he requested Henry Reveley, Mrs. Gisborne's son, to purchase a small boat for him at Leghorn. For a few pauls Reveley acquired a boat about ten feet long and flat-bottomed so that she could operate on the shallow Arno, and fitted a mast, sails, and rudder to her. Shelley and Williams went to Leghorn on April 16 to take possession and insisted on sailing her home from Leghorn to Pisa through the canal by moonlight.

Fortunately Mrs. Gisborne urged that Henry should accompany them, for about half-way to Pisa Williams, contrary to his sailorly training, stood up in the boat and, in catching hold of the mast to steady himself, upset the boat. Able to swim a little, he made shore safely, while Reveley, instructing Shelley to remain calm, caught hold of him and started toward shore with him. "All right; never more comfortable in my life," replied Shelley; "do what you will with me." But for all his courage at the moment of danger, Shelley fainted when they got ashore. Reveley left Shelley in Williams's care and rescued the boat; then, with Shelley sufficiently recovered, all three walked to a nearby *casale* or large farmhouse, where fires were blown up, warm clothing obtained, and the shipwrecked mariners spent the rest of the night. Next morning Shelley and Williams walked to Pisa, and Reveley took the boat back to Leghorn for repairs.[14] If the accident was a warning from the gods, Shelley did not heed it. He awaited with much impatience the repairs on the boat, which included, at his direction, changing the position of the rowlocks and adding a false keel for safety.

On April 1 the Shelleys were electrified by the news that Greece had asserted her freedom and was in full revolt. Warned by Mavrocordato, they had been expecting the announcement, which Mary hastened to pass along to Claire at Florence:

Greece has declared its freedom! Prince Mavrocordato has made us expect this event for some weeks past. Yesterday, he came *rayonnant de joie*—he had been ill for some days, but he forgot all his pains. Ipselanti, a Greek general in the service of Russia, has collected together 10,000 Greeks and entered Wallachia, declaring the liberty of his country. The Morea—Epirus—Servia are in revolt. Greece will most certainly be free. The worst part of this news to us is that our amiable prince will leave us—he will of course join his countrymen as soon as possible—never did man appear so happy—yet he sacrifices family—fortune—everything to the hope of freeing his country.[15]

On May 8 the Shelleys moved to the Baths of Pisa, from which it was only four miles to Pugnano and the Williamses, an easy walk or an even more delightful sail by way of the canal that connected the Serchio with the Arno. Williams and Shelley were together oftener than ever now, spending many a happy hour in the little boat. Shelley's fragmentary poem, *The Boat on the Serchio*, gives some clue to the pleasures of Lionel and Melchior (Shelley and Williams), who "from the throng of men had stepped aside," given care to the winds—"they can bear it well" —stowed their boat with provisions, and then with full sails

the boat makes head
Against the Serchio's torrent fierce

and "sweeps into the affrighted sea." The beginning of the poem, which tells of the two friends coming upon their sleeping boat, contains some of Shelley's finest descriptive verses:

The stars burn out in the pale blue air,
And the thin white moon lay withering there;
To tower, and cavern, and rift, and tree,
The owl and the bat fled drowsily.
Day had kindled the dewy woods,
And the rocks above and the stream below,
And the vapours in their multitudes,
And the Apennines' shroud of summer snow,
Are clothed with light of aery gold
The mists in their eastern caves uprolled.

Day had awakened all things that be,
The lark and the thrush and the swallow free,
And the milkmaid's song and the mower's scythe,
And the matin-bell and the mountain bee:
Fireflies were quenched on the dewy corn,
Glow-worms went out on the river's brim,
Like lamps which a student forgets to trim:
The beetle forgot to wind his horn,
The crickets were still in the meadow and hill:
Like a flock of rooks at a farmer's gun
Night's dreams and terrors, every one,
Fled from the brains which are their prey
From the lamp's death to the morning ray.

Except for Williams, whom he always welcomed, and Emilia Viviani, whom he usually went to see twice a week, Shelley cared to see no one; he enjoyed the solitude at the Baths of Pisa as much as anything else. But in spite of his wishes they had visitors. Prince Mavrocordato came several times, and Shelley wrote to Claire: ". . . I reproach my own savage disposition that so agreable accomplished and ammiable [a] person is not more agreable to me."[16] With the rest of the Greek refugees, however, he was soon removed from the scene. On June 8 Shelley wrote to Claire: "A vessel has arrived to take the Greek Prince and his suite to join the army in Morea. He is a great loss to Mary and *therefore* to me . . . but not otherwise."[17] Nevertheless Shelley admired Mavrocordato's patriotism and courage and in 1822 dedicated to him *Hellas*, the last book published in his lifetime.

Except for the Williamses, now the Shelleys' closest friends, Taaffe was the most frequent visitor to the Shelleys at the Baths. In May he attempted to persuade the Shelleys to visit Como, where he planned to go, during the summer, but the distance, the inconvenience, and the lack of any real desire to go caused them to decline. Taaffe, possibly at Shelley's suggestion, had decided to have his *Comment* printed at Pisa and then try to find an English publisher who would engage to sell it, and he was busy at this time in seeing a portion of it through the press. Shelley, though occupied in finishing his own *Adonais*, obligingly read proof for him. On returning a batch of proof, he sent Taaffe the following note:

Bagni—Tuesday Noon [18] [June 5, 1821]

Dear Taaffe

I send you the proofs & after having carefully looked over them, I am not so fortunate as to have found any errors.—I am anxious to see the conclusion & to put it in train for publication in England. —We have expected to see you these several evenings, & I am sorry to hear that fatigue prevents you; yet we can offer you a bed if the ride home alarms you, or if you at any time like to share the gaieties of this place: Heaven knows what they are.

Faithfully yours,
S.[19]

[P.S., written crosswise at the top] Mrs. S sends her best comp^ts & desires me to remind you of her Guinea pigs—

The guinea pigs were a gift from Taaffe to Mary, who wrote a note about them to Taaffe later in the same day:

My dear Sir

I send my servant for the Guinea Pigs, and am extremely obliged to you for the book.

The Williams' are very well and desired regards if I should see you; but I am afraid that this *tempo matto* [20] does not accord with you or your little horse.

Shelley will be very glad to receive the next proof.

Your obedient Servant
Mary Shelley[21]

Teusday evening [June 5, 1821]
Baths of St. Giuliano

[P.S.] I send you some lists of articles that some friends of ours [22] going to England wish to sell. Perhaps you would have the kindness to shew them to any of your friends. Mad^me Regny [23] might like to buy some of the music for Ida. Those marked with a cross are already sold[.]

With the guinea pigs Taaffe sent an accompanying note, at the end of which he wrote, "O, that I were one of those guinea pigs, that I might see you this morning!" [24] Mary derived almost as much scornful amusement from the note as from Taaffe's absurd birthday verses.

Shelley tried to be of assistance to Taaffe in finding an English publisher for his *Comment.* As he had done for Medwin in the preceding November, he wrote a letter of recommendation to his own publisher, Ollier, accompanied by specimens of the *Comment* and the translation:

> . . . The more considerable portion of this work will consist of the comment. I have read with much attention this portion, as well as the verses, up to the eighth Canto; and I do not hesitate to assure you that the lights which the annotator's labours have thrown on the obscurer parts of the text are such as all foreigners and most Italians would derive an immense additional knowledge of Dante from. They elucidate a great number of the most interesting facts connected with Dante's history and the history of his times; and everywhere bear the mark of a most elegant and accomplished mind. I know you will not take my opinion on Poetry, because I thought my own verses very good, and you find that the public declare them to be unreadable. Show it to Mr. Procter,[25] who is far better qualified to judge than I am. There are certainly passages of great strength and conciseness; indeed the author has sacrificed everything to represent his original truly, in this latter point pray observe the great beauty of the typography; they are the same types as my elegy on Keats is printed from.[26]

When no immediate answer was forthcoming, Shelley wrote again:

> . . . Mr. Taaffe lately requested a commendatory letter from me to you on the subject of his translation of Dante. The comments are certainly very good, but the poetry—however nobody knows what will or will not sell; and I have been so often mistaken in the market value of verses, that I hope for my friend Taaffe's sake I am also mistaken now.[27]

First Medwin and now Taaffe! Such were the writers whose works Shelley recommended to Ollier. From a poet whose own verses were ignored by the public this must have seemed too much to Ollier, who did not reply to either of Shelley's letters.

Word of the death of Keats had reached Shelley in

April, and according to the letter conveying a presentation copy of *Adonais* to Byron, the poem was written "immediately after the arrival of the news." [28] But in a letter of June 5 to the Gisbornes, Shelley said: "I have been engaged these last days in composing a poem on the death of Keats, which will shortly be finished. . . . It is a highly wrought *piece of art*, perhaps better in point of composition than any thing I have written." [29] The completed poem was submitted to Taaffe, as we have seen, for criticism, and Shelley adopted without hesitation Taaffe's advice to delete the passage relating to his own personal wrongs [30] while rejecting Taaffe's objection to the insertion of the name of Christ into the poem. Taaffe was on a visit to Florence when he received Shelley's letter of thanks:

Bagni—. July 4, 1821

My dear Taaffe

I do not wait the slow progress of Rosini [31] before I thank you for your kind letter, & your still kinder attention in bringing me acquainted with the Count Magawly.— [32]

Accept also my thanks for your strictures on Adonais. The first I have adopted, by cancelling in the preface the whole passage relating to my private wrongs.—You are right: I ought not to shew my teeth before I can bite or where I cannot bite. I am afraid that I must allow the obnoxious expressions—if such they are, to which you so kindly advert in the Poem itself, to stand as they are.—The introduction of the name of *Christ* as an antithesis to *Cain* is surely any thing but irreverence or sarcasm.—I think when you read the passage again, you will acquit it of any such tendency. Meanwhile the word *Priest* stands on the proscription list—But be it observed that I speak as Milton would have spoken in defence of the great cause whose overthrow embittered his declining years.—As soon as I get a copy I will send it you; & if you are not discouraged by my liberty in accepting & rejecting your valuable advice, I would pray you to favour me still further with it,—as I consider myself to have been essentially benefited by the adoption of the cancel in the preface.—So much for these trifles.—

How do you like your visit to Florence; and what news is stirring there? We "creep on our petty pace from day to day" as usual. Percy is quite recovered & as gay as a lark. I am amused now and then with news from England of the ridiculous violence of the prejudices which are concieved against me—and as I am interested by the sight of a thunderstorm as a grand tragic ballet of the Heavens; so, at safe distance, I laugh at this comic pantomime which the good people in London exhibit, with my shadow for their Harlequin.—

When may we expect your return to Pisa? Are you still bent upon a journey to Como?—Como is one of the loveliest places in the world; but I should hesitate whether Paradise itself were worth the voluntary exhibition of Passports, subjection to Doganos, squabbling with postillions & inkeepers, which the nature of things exacts between the Apennines & the Alps.—

Pray give my best Compliments to M.r Grainger,[33] & accept from M.rs S & myself our kindest regards for yourself—

My dear Taaffe
Your's very faithfully ever
Percy B Shelley [34]

It was only natural that Taaffe, the orthodox Catholic, and Shelley, the professed atheist, should differ on the propriety of comparing the "ensanguined brow" of Keats to that of Christ. But it must have been plain to Taaffe that no irreverence was intended, and the "sweet nature" to which Taaffe refers was so manifest that Shelley could and did discuss delicate subjects of religion with him without offence. An undated letter of Shelley's to Taaffe in which the subject of damnation is debated was probably written while the Shelleys were at the Baths of Pisa [35]:

Sunday noon

Dear Taaffe

I am not convinced.—If God damns me, even by making me my own hell, (as indeed sometimes when I am in an ill humour, he does in this life) it by no means follows that I *must* desire to be so damned. I may think it extremely disagreable, as I do to be in an ill temper, & wish to God that God would not have damned me either in this or in any other manner—I confess I cannot understand how I should be necessitated to *desire* to be damned under any circumstances; although I can easily concieve [36] that I should be necessitated to be damned; & if your argument is as lucid as my apprehension of it is obscure I am sure I deserve to be damned for my stupidity; though I cannot fancy how I should *desire* to be everlastingly tormented for that or any other of my numerous sins.

Remember that I am predestined to everlasting damnation, merely because I doubt whether either I or any one else will ever be damned, and therefore if I arrive in Hell before you do in Heaven I will endeavour to inform you how far I desire to be punished everlastingly[.]

—It is very *odious* of you not to have sent me your ode [37]: of which however, to speak seriously, I hear spoken very highly—

Yours very faithfully
S.[38]

N.B. I just forgot to say that a man cannot be said to *desire* that which he possesses. How, therefore can *every man his own hell* desire to be damned when he is damned[.]

Mary Shelley had taken advantage of the comparative quiet and freedom afforded by the Baths of Pisa to work industriously on her novel *Valperga*,[39] which she had begun more than a year before. On June 30 she could write to Mrs. Gisborne that "now it is in a state of great forwardness since I am at page 71 of the 3rd vol." [40] This was the last letter that she was to address to Mrs. Gisborne at Leghorn, for the Gisbornes were shortly to return to England and remain there.

On July 23 Claire arrived for a visit. Two days later she and Shelley went to Leghorn, where Claire remained for the benefit of the sea-bathing, which had been prescribed for her.[41] When on the 29th the Gisbornes left for Florence, on the first stage of their journey to England, Shelley accompanied them to look for a house for his friend Horace Smith, who planned to winter in Florence and wanted the Shelleys to do likewise.

In Shelley's absence Edward Williams began the water colour portrait of Mary which she intended as a birthday present for Shelley on August 4. But Shelley was not to spend his birthday with Mary. On his return to the Baths of Pisa, he found a letter from Byron awaiting him; it announced the exile of the Gambas and all of Byron's friends from Ravenna and ended by inviting Shelley to visit him at Ravenna. The invitation was not a complete surprise to Shelley. Discussion of a visit had occurred in earlier letters. On April 26 Byron had written to Shelley, "Could not you and I contrive to meet this summer? Could not you take a run here *alone*?"[42] Shelley, on May 4, had countered by urging Byron to join the Shelleys for the summer, but Byron was too involved, if not too indolent, to leave. Shelley wrote again on July 16 expressing disappointment that he had had no news of a visit from Byron and suggesting that he might visit Byron at Ravenna.[43] The letter which Shelley found awaiting him on his return from Florence was Byron's reply.

Uppermost in Shelley's mind were thoughts of Claire and her child Allegra. If Byron should follow the Gambas, what would he do with Allegra, who had been placed in the convent at Bagnacavallo in the preceding January? Shelley did not hesitate for a moment in deciding to go. On the day after receiving Byron's letter he left Pisa for Leghorn, where he spent the night; then the next day he celebrated his twenty-ninth birthday by rowing in the bay with Claire.[44] Without disclosing to her his destination, he took the night coach for Bologna and Ravenna.

CHAPTER 4

Lord Byron Comes to Pisa

BYRON had first met Shelley in Switzerland in 1816, when by prearrangement with Claire Clairmont—who was with child by him—he had joined Shelley's party in the vicinity of Geneva. Three months later, upon the return of Shelley, Mary, and Claire to England, Byron went on to Italy, first to Milan and Verona and then to Venice, where his dissoluteness for the next two and a half years comprises the most lurid chapter in a life of indulgence.

It was in Venice in April, 1819, however, that he met and formed the liaison with the Countess Teresa Guiccioli that was to stabilize his life until his departure upon the Greek adventure. When a short time later she was forced to return to her home in Ravenna, he followed. The course of that love affair—with its romantic, comic, and tragic aspects—has been fully traced elsewhere.[1] It is enough for our purposes to note that it resulted in a separation of Teresa from her husband by papal decree a year later, that Teresa's father and brother—contrary to what might have been expected—became staunch friends of Byron's, and that their friendship was largely responsible for his involvement in the Carbonarist insurrection of 1820–21. Byron's participation was understandably resented by the government, which, however, was too timid to act directly against him. But with the collapse of the insurrection, it acted indirectly. Among the hundreds of prominent Romagnoles exiled were the Counts Ruggero and Pietro Gamba. And as the Pope had prescribed that Teresa should live under her father's roof, the government assumed that she and Byron would follow. Frightened by a threat to place her in a convent, Teresa did indeed go to Bologna, and when she had lost all hope that the order banishing her father and brother would be rescinded, she yielded to Byron's pleas and joined them in Florence early in August, 1821.[2]

In part because the government wanted him to leave and in part because he hoped to be useful to his unfortunate friends if he stayed, Byron determined that he should not be driven out. "I am so busy here about these poor proscribed exiles, who are scattered about, and with trying to get some of them recalled," he wrote to Murray in July, "that I have hardly time or patience to write a short preface, which will be proper for the two plays." [3] Nevertheless, reluctant though he was to leave Ravenna, of which he had become truly fond, he had made up his mind to do so.[4] There remained the problem of where to go. Florence was objectionable because it was full of "gossip-loving English." One of the attractions of Ravenna was that he did not "see an Englishman in half a year." [5] If not Florence, where?

The Gambas proposed Switzerland, and Byron complied with their wishes so far as to write to a Geneva banker, requesting that two houses on the Jura side of Lake Geneva be engaged for himself and the Gambas. He expected to take Allegra with him.[6] But he was irresolute. His waywardness was never more evident than when trying to pull up stakes and move elsewhere. Now he remembered the proposal that he had made at intervals to Moore—that the two of them go to England and establish a joint newspaper [7]—and wrote nostalgically to Moore: "If you went to England, I would do so still." [8] He could not make up his mind what to do, except that he must leave Ravenna. It was in this state of uncertainty that he had written the letter that was awaiting Shelley on his return from Florence, "earnestly requesting to see him." Shelley, alive to the importance of protecting Allegra's and Claire's interests in any contemplated move, had therefore decided to go to Ravenna at once. At ten o'clock on the night of August 6 he reached the Palazzo Guiccioli, where Byron was conveniently located, and sat up until five in the morning talking to his host.

His visit lasted for about two weeks, during which he slept late hours, talked to Byron, rode in the pine forest, practised pistol-shooting, viewed the antiquities, and talked again until morning. "I don't suppose this will kill me in a week or fortnight," he wrote to Peacock, "but I shall not try it longer."[9] Tita, Byron's Venetian gondolier, "a fine fellow, with a prodigious black beard, who has stabbed two or three people, and is the most good-natured-looking fellow I ever saw," acted as Shelley's valet.[10] The beard was later to get Tita into trouble, and Shelley's friendship was to serve him in good stead. The two poets exchanged confidences, Byron telling Shelley about Teresa while Shelley in turn told Byron what there was to tell about Emilia Viviani. Winter plans also came into discussion. Byron was not committed to Switzerland—indeed, would prefer Pisa or Lucca—and asked Shelley to write Teresa a letter urging her to adopt this view. ". . . An odd thing enough for an utter stranger to write on subjects of the utmost delicacy to his friend's mistress," commented Shelley.[11] "But it seems destined that I am always to have some active part in everybody's affairs whom I approach. . . ." Teresa, who was growing tired of waiting for her reunion with Byron and would probably have agreed to anything that would hasten it, quickly agreed.

With Byron now committed to residing at Pisa, Shelley weighed the relative advantages of Pisa and Florence for himself and Mary. On the one hand were the cultural advantages of Florence and their tentative plan to join Horace Smith there for the winter; on the other were numerous advantages besides the climate in remaining in Pisa:

> The Williams's would probably be induced to stay there if we did—Hunt would certainly stay at least this winter near us, should he emigrate at all: Lord Byron and his Italian friends would remain quietly there, and Lord Byron has certainly a great regard for us—the regard of such a man is worth—*some* of the tribute we must pay to the base passions of humanity in any intercourse with those within its circle; he is better worth it than those on whom we bestow it from mere custom.[12]

As for himself, Shelley would have preferred a solitary island, with only Mary and their child, but he recognized the impracticability of such an idea:

> The other side of the alternative . . . is to form for ourselves a society of our own class, as much as possible in intellect, or in feelings; and to connect ourselves with the interests of that society. Our roots never struck so deeply as at Pisa, and the transplanted tree flourishes not.[13]

As Allegra was Shelley's main concern at Ravenna, he would not leave without having seen her, and on August 14 he paid her a visit. She was tall and slight and much paler, he found, but apparently well treated and certainly improved in character.[14] He naturally hoped, if possible, to persuade Byron not to leave her behind when he left Ravenna. "Is there any family, any English or Swiss establishment, any refuge in short, except the convent of St. Anna where Allegra may be placed?" he asked Mary. "Do you think Mrs. Mason could be prevailed on to *propose* to take charge of her?"[15] In the end he had to leave it unsettled, trusting that when he got back to Pisa some arrangement might suggest itself that would be acceptable to Byron.

His business finished, Shelley wished to leave, but Byron was lonely and prevailed upon him to remain several days longer, during which the old routine continued. When at last he was permitted to leave Ravenna, he was commissioned to find "a large and magnificent house": Byron was coming to Pisa.

On the whole Shelley must have been pleased with the outcome of his visit to Byron. Not only was Byron coming to Pisa, but the chances were good that he would bring Allegra with him. Equally important, Shelley had succeeded in transforming Byron's pet scheme of founding a newspaper with Moore into a scheme of establishing a liberal journal with Shelley's friend Leigh Hunt. The proposal had come from Byron, but Shelley's hand is visible in it. Immediately after his return to Pisa he could write to Hunt:

> He [Lord Byron] proposes that you should come out and go shares with him and me in a periodical work, to be conducted here; in which each of the contracting parties should publish all their original compositions, and share the profits. He proposed it to Moore, but for some reason or other it was never brought to bear. There can be no doubt that the profits of any scheme in which you and Lord Byron engage, must from various, yet co-operating reasons, be very great. As for myself, I am, for the present, only a sort of link between you and him, until you can know each other, and effectuate the arrangements; since (to entrust you with a secret which, for your sake, I withhold from Lord Byron) nothing would induce me to share in the profits, and still less, in the borrowed splendour of such a partnership.[16]

Having leased the Palazzo Lanfranchi, the finest available house on the Lung' Arno, from his friend Vaccà, Shelley informed Byron and asked for further instructions:

> I have taken your house for 400 crowns a year, and signed the compact on your part; so we are now secure. I have as yet bought nothing, guiding myself in that respect by the instructions of the Gambas, who advise me to hear from you, or to wait for Lega before I do anything. They are very much pleased with the house, the Contessa [17] especially delighted.
>
> . . . Pray send me explicit instructions as to what ought to be done about furnishing, etc., the Palace Lanfranchi. I have money enough here, so you need not trouble yourself to restrict me on that head. I am looking out for additional stables, and shall soon have found them.[18]

At Ravenna, Byron was finding that being a lord was costly business at moving time: the price demanded for transporting his possessions to Pisa was outrageous and he refused to pay it. There was nothing to do then but to write to Shelley to make the arrangements at his end:

R.[a] Sep[tr] 8th 1821.

Dear Shelley/

They pretend here to *two hundred Scudi* for the carriage of about *two thirds* of my furniture *only*, & *not for the whole.*—As this seems to me very exorbitant—(and indeed whether it be so or no) I should prefer that *you* sent me from Pisa—*waggons horses* & *drivers* according to the fairest contract you can make with them for me. I will sanction it—be it more or less.—It is the same thing as the drivers &c. must *return* here—and the Tuscans will only have to come here first.—The number of waggons wanted on the whole will be *eight*—the number of *beasts*, what they please—the luggage is heavy—but whether drawn by horses—mules—or oxen, is indifferent to me.—It was for six cars only that the Indigenous masters of horse asked two hundred crowns—i.e. half a year's rent of the house for a transport of chattels.—Send me Etrurians at their own price—for of the two—I prefer being cheated by the new comers to continuing to minister to the antient Scoundrels of this venerable city. — — — — — — When I talked to you about purchase of *other moveables*—I meant such as may be requisite—to complete mine in a new mansion.—Of course I meant things requisite—according to the *premises*—and did not mean to limit the [price?—*word torn by the seal*] to an exact sum or to a few Scudi more or less according to what was wanted.—Of course you have seen *this* house [i.e. at Ravenna]—& *that* house [i.e. at Pisa] & can judge.—You may do it now—or wait till I come—as you please.—

Believe me yours ever & truly

Byron [19]

P.S.

Expedite the Baggage Waggons—we wait only now for those to march.—Make my remembrances to every body I don't know—& my respects to all I do.— — — — — — — — — — — — — —

Whether Byron sent a similar letter to Pietro Gamba is not clear; but somehow the signals got mixed and Shelley narrowly escaped catastrophe:

The moment I received your last letter, I proceeded to send off at the lowest possible price I could get, eight waggons, &c. The Signor Pietro did the same, and the equivoque would have sent sixteen instead of eight waggons to Ravenna, if the same Providence that watches over the fall of a sparrow had not determined that my express should arrive in time at Florence to prevent the departure of the additional number, and save me (for I never should have had the conscience to charge you with the consequences of my bungling) a certain number of scudi. Now, however, all is right, and I hope that before this your caravan will be upon its march.

The real purpose of the letter, however, was less to announce the sending of the caravan than to broach the subject of Allegra again:

. . . My convent friend, after a great deal of tumult, &c., is at length married, and is watched by her brother-in-law with great assiduity. This whole affair has taught me to believe that convents may be well enough for young children, but that they are the worst possible places for them as soon as they begin to be susceptible of certain impressions. . . .

Have you formed any plan for Allegra here? It would be very easy to find a proper place for her in this part of the world; and if you would be inclined to trust to my recommendation, I would of course engage that Clare should not interfere with any plan that you might lay down. Of course, after my experience, *I* cannot say much in favour of convents; but respectable private families might be found who would undertake the care of her. I speak freely on this subject, because I am sure you have seen enough to convince you that the impressions, which the Hoppners wished to give you of myself and Mary, are void of foundation.[20]

Meanwhile Teresa Guiccioli had arrived in August[21] and, with her father and two brothers, Pietro and Vincenzo, who came ostensibly to enroll in the university, occupied at first Casa Finocchietti and later Casa Parra, on the Lung' Arno.[22] Pisa was not to be treated to the scandal of Byron and his mistress living under the same roof. Mary Shelley, making the acquaintance of Teresa, found her "a nice pretty girl without pretensions, good hearted and amiable,"[23] and though Mary was busy completing her novel, she and Teresa exchanged frequent calls.

It was the intention of the Pisan authorities to issue Count Gamba a visitor's card good for two months and renewable, but by mistake it was issued for four. When the mistake was discovered at the end of two months, the police at Pisa wrote hastily to Florence to ask for instructions. Word came back that Count Gamba should be permitted to remain but should be watched.[24]

Byron, lingering at Ravenna, unable to bring himself to leave, was writing *Cain* and fretting over the wretchedly printed third, fourth, and fifth cantos of *Don Juan*.[25] Not all the booksellers' messengers who filled the street in front of 50 Albemarle and forced the harried publishers' men to give out parcels of books through the window[26] could compensate for the nonsense that the printer had made of some of his lines. He wrote Murray a "fierce and furibond letter": "I never saw such stuff as is printed. . . . Desire my friend Hobhouse to correct the press, especially of the last Canto, from the Manuscript as it is: it is enough to drive one out of one's senses, to see the infernal torture of words from the original."[27] But in a few days his fury had subsided into "sullenness," and on September 10, when he sent Murray the MS. of *Cain*, he wrote tractably: "I think that it contains some poetry, being in the style of *Manfred*. Send me a proof of the whole by return of *post*."[28]

To Moore he wrote in September:

> I am in all the sweat, dust, and blasphemy of an universal packing of all my things, furniture, etc., for Pisa, whither I go for the winter. The cause has been the exile of all my fellow Carbonics, and, amongst them, of the whole family of Madame G.; who, you know, was divorced from her husband last week,[29] "on account of P. P. clerk of this parish,"[30] and who is obliged to join her father and relatives, now in exile there, to avoid being shut up in a monastery, because the Pope's decree of separation required her to reside in *casa paterna*, or else, for decorum's sake, in a convent. As I could not say with Hamlet, "Get thee to a nunnery," I am preparing to follow them.[31]

But in fact he did not set out for Pisa. In September and early October he was writing *The Vision of Judgment*, which he took great delight in because of its attack upon the poet laureate, Southey. He had a score to settle with Southey: "With regard to Southey," he wrote to Kinnaird [32] later, "please to recollect that in his preface to *his* 'Vision' [33]—he actually called upon 'the legislature' to fall upon Moore me—& others—now such a cowardly cry deserves a dressing.—He is also the vainest & most intolerant of men—and a rogue besides——"[34] The poem, which paid off Southey handsomely, was finished by the 4th and sent to Murray by next post, but Byron still dallied at Ravenna. The truth was that he did not want to leave, as he made clear to Teresa, whom Moore quotes as follows:

> He left Ravenna with great regret, and with a presentiment that his departure would be the forerunner of a thousand evils to us. In every letter he then wrote to me, he expressed his displeasure at this step. 'If your father should be recalled,' he said, '*I immediately return* to Ravenna; and if he is recalled *previous* to my departure, *I remain*.' In this hope he delayed his journey for several months; but, at last, no longer having any expectation of our immediate return, he wrote to me, saying—'I set out most unwillingly, foreseeing the most evil results for all of you, and principally for yourself. I say no more, but you will see.' And in another letter he says, 'I leave Ravenna so unwillingly, and with such a persuasion on my mind that my departure will lead from one misery to another, each greater than the former, that I have not the heart to utter another word on the subject.' [35]

Shelley, writing to thank Byron for his gift of the third, fourth, and fifth cantos of *Don Juan*, said, "Nothing has ever been written like it in English, nor, if I may venture to prophesy, will there be; without carrying upon it the mark of a secondary and borrowed light." [36] The fifth canto, which Murray's Synod (Byron's name for the hangers on that surrounded Murray) found dull, Shelley thought "gathers instead of loses, splendour and energy." [37] He would have written earlier, he said, except that "I have been led to expect you almost daily in Pisa, and that I imagined you would cross my letter on your road." "The Countess G. is very patient," he continued, "though sometimes she seems apprehensive that you will *never* leave Ravenna." [38]

At length, on October 29, Byron left Ravenna. On the road between Imola and Bologna, he met unexpectedly his dearest boyhood friend, Lord Clare,[39] and for an instant the years between present and past were annihilated as Byron, overcome with emotion, clasped the hand of his friend. "We were but five minutes together," comments Byron, "and in the public road; but I hardly recollect an hour of my existence which could be weighed against them." [40] At Bologna the banker-poet Samuel Rogers had waited a day for Byron and crossed the Apennines with him. ". . . If there was any scenery particularly well worth seeing, he [Byron] generally contrived that we should pass through it in the dark," lamented Rogers.[41] Near Empoli the carriage in which Claire Clairmont was returning to Florence from her visit to the Williamses had to draw aside to let the caravan of the great milord pass.[42] It was the last glimpse that Claire was ever to have of her one-time lover, now her bitter enemy to the death.

Somewhere between Florence and Pisa, Byron composed a poem; its theme, that youth and love are worth more than honour, was prompted by his growing awareness that he was no longer young:

Oh! talk not to me of a name great in story
The days of our Youth are the days of our Glory,
And the myrtle and ivy of sweet two and twenty
Are worth all your laurels though ever so plenty.

What are garlands and crowns to the brow that is wrinkled?
'Tis but as a dead flower with May-dew besprinkled;
Then away with all such from the head that is hoary,
What care I for the wreaths that can *only* give Glory?

Oh! Fame! if I e'er took delight in thy praises,
'Twas less for the sake of thy high-sounding phrases,
Than to see the bright eyes of the dear One discover
She thought that I was not unworthy to love her.

There chiefly I sought thee, *there* only I found thee;
Her Glance was the best of the rays that surround thee,
When it sparkled o'er aught that was bright in my story,
I knew it was love, and I felt it was Glory.[43]

Byron's furniture had preceded him, and thanks to Teresa everything was in readiness for him at the Palazzo Lanfranchi. Williams, who had gone over the house with Shelley on October 27, saw nothing that impressed him enough to comment on except Byron's coat of arms emblazoned on the foot of his bed, with the motto "Crede Byron." [44] Byron himself arrived on November 1, irritable from the inconvenience of moving, the cost involved, and the necessity of adjusting himself to new surroundings. There were other reasons for his irritation too: Murray, who had already exasperated him by playing the stepmother to *Don Juan*, had made no offer for *Cain* but had requested Byron to alter two of Lucifer's speeches in the poem. Byron refused: "The two passages cannot be altered without making Lucifer talk like the Bishop of Lincoln—which would not be in the character of the former." [45] Byron's friend Kinnaird, who had earlier convinced him that Murray was not paying enough for his poems, was also partly responsible for his irritability. With apparent inconsistency Kinnaird had recently advised the acceptance of even smaller sums for such poems as *The Two Foscari*, *Sardanapalus*, and *Marino Faliero*. But a letter from Kinnaird explaining everything satisfactorily and containing good news about his money affairs placated him temporarily. He replied in good humour:

Pisa. No^{r}. 4th 1821.

My dear Douglas/

Your epistle has pacified my wrath—& explained every thing—All the accounts I hear from every body agree in saying that the new *Dons* are liked—but that M[urray] has neither given them nor their predecessors fair play,—from timidity I presume.—Rogers with whom I crossed the Appennines—says—that *M[ur-*

ray] affects *not* to wish to be considered as having any thing to do with that work.—Upon this score I have written him a trimmer.[46] —I rejoice that you accept the dedication—especially as you liked the play.—[47] The most opposite people—Irving—Moore—Hoppner—and yourself for instance—like the Juans & many others—so I suppose that they will do.—The *misprinting* was shameful—such nonsense!—in some of the clearest passages too.—Now you see how people can never pretend to anticipate accurately —Murray and others kept back the Cantos a whole year & more —because they were *dull*—and wanted alterations &c. &c.—I would alter nothing—well—the work appears—with a lukewarm publisher and all these previous impressions against it—& still it succeeds.—I thought it would *not* because it's real qualities are not on the *surface*—but still if people will dive a little—I think it will reward them for their trouble.—Nearly *five hundred* pounds from Sir Jacob [48]—how is this?—it is more than I thought.—As to Marley (?) [49]—you may pay him *ten pounds*—which is double his merit—he is the greatest rascal that ever emptied a brandy bottle. —Pay *him*! quotha! what do you take me for? that I should pay any body?—And of Composition money too!—I presume that you have got *some* account of it from Hanson. — — — — — — — —
Sir Jacob's money must be reserved for *Self*—except deduction of such monies as you have paid away for me already. I hate to bore you—but what can I do?—I have no other active friend—and you always go to the point—with the scoundrels of all kinds. — — — —
I look for a decent sum at Christmas I assure you—but I long to hear that we are out of the funds*—I would sacrifice the interest cheerfully—for a year—to be sure of a safe mortgage at the end of it.—I am in cash sufficiently—as you will perceive—but this changing residences—& removing establishments—has taken a sum out of my pocket as I removed all my furniture &c. &c. We were all obliged to retire on account of our politics—my relations (the Gambas—exiles &c.) are here too lodged about a quarter of a mile from me—the place—and air—&c. are very agreeable hitherto.—
I left Sam Rogers at Florence—& met my old friend Lord Clare between Ravenna—& Bologna—he seemed delighted to meet me —& our meeting was almost pathetic.—Rogers and I abused every body in our journey to Florence—as you may suppose.— — — —
I am glad that you approved of my epistle to Murray—it was become necessary.—But he does not mention it in his late answers.—They are very civil about "*Cain*"—but alarmed at it's *tendency*—as they call it—for my part—I maintain that it is as orthodox as

* *I.e.*, consols or (in American parlance) government bonds.

the thirty nine articles. There is or ought to be—*another* poem now at Murray's.— — — — — — — — — — — — — — — — — — —
Remember me to Hobhouse &c—and believe me ever & most truly

Bnnn [50]

P.S.

I ought to mention to you that Rogers said—that the bruit was that Murray was *ruined* by buying eight & twenty thousand pounds worth of copyrights last year—in Northern & Loo Choo voyages travels &c &c if true it is some comfort that he made no purchases of *me then* but the single drama.—You will be in the way of knowing this—but if true it would form a clue to his costiveness.— [51] I will acquiesce in whatever bargain you make with him—

Whether the purchase of travel books had anything to do with Murray's delay in making an offer for *Cain* or not, Byron was suspicious (probably without reason) that Murray might by-pass Kinnaird and try to negotiate with Byron himself, depending upon distance to cause Byron to agree to whatever was offered.

. . . I think it is fairer for all parties [he wrote to Kinnaird]—that you who are on the spot and can judge at once should pronounce upon all matters of business. . . . Murray has received from me two or three tolerably sharp letters lately—upon the whole of his late conduct and language—which I am not disposed to tolerate much further. . . . To me he talks of the horror—of "Cain" and that Gifford & Moore &c—all place it among the best &c as a composition—but he cants about it's tendency also.—There never was *such cant*—Abel & Adah &c are as pious as possible—but would they have me make Lucifer and Cain talk like two prebendaries—looking out for a step higher in the Church?—"Milton's Satan" is twice as daring and impious—as mine—and what do they say to such lines as these in the "Samson Agonistes?"

In fine
Just and unjust alike seem miserable
Since both alike oft come to evil end

. . . All the people about [Murray] except Gifford—(who I do believe likes me in his heart) hate me—and well they may—for they can only rise by crushing their opponents—at least this is their opinion. . . . I came here [Pisa] not very long ago—the situation on the Arno is very fine—and the air &c—delightful hitherto.——

There are some English—but I never see them in public nor in private—except two or three old acquaintances—& one or two not quite of so antient a date.—I ride out &c as usual—and though Ravenna is quieter—other things are perhaps about equal here—as I have most of my Italian relations near me.—[52]

Because of the size of the Palazzo Lanfranchi, Byron occupied only the first floor, at the top of the staircase leading to which he kept a bulldog on a chain long enough to permit it to bar the entrance of strangers. From the first he liked the great old palace, with its traditions and its sunken basement rooms which he exaggerated into dungeons:

I have got here into a famous old feudal palazzo,[53] on the Arno, large enough for a garrison, with dungeons below and cells in the walls, and so full of *Ghosts*, that the learned Fletcher (my valet) has begged leave to change his room, and then refused to occupy his *new* room, because there were more ghosts there than in the other [he wrote to Murray]. It is quite true that there are most extraordinary noises (as in all old buildings), which have terrified the servants so as to incommode me extremely. There is one place where people were evidently *walled up*; for there is but one possible passage, *broken* through the wall, and then meant to be closed again upon the inmate. The house belonged to the Lanfranchi family, (the same mentioned by Ugolino in his dream, as his persecutor with Sismondi,) and has had a fierce owner or two in its time. The staircase, etc., is said to have been built by Michel Agnolo.[54]

Across the Arno at the Tre Palazzi di Chiesa, to which they had moved at the end of October, were the Shelleys, who had furnished an apartment "out of the fruits of two years' economy"[55]; and a short time later the Williamses took an apartment on a lower floor of the same house.[56] The Pisan circle had now been formed, and thenceforth there was considerable social activity among its members.[57] On the day following Byron's arrival, Shelley called on him, and a few days later Byron, making one of his rare visits, called on the Shelleys with Pietro Gamba and Teresa Guiccioli. Taaffe called several times on the Shelleys, following their return to Pisa, and must have been escorted across the Arno to meet Byron on one of the occasions. Williams, calling on Byron with Shelley on November 5, found that his impressions were quite different from what he had expected:

> In the evening S. introduced me to Lord Byron, on whom we called. So far from his having haughtiness of manners, they are those of the most unaffected and gentlemanly ease; and so far from his being (as is generally imagined) wrapt in melancholy and gloom, he is all sunshine and good humour with which the elegance of his language and the brilliancy of his wit cannot fail to inspire those who are near him. On our taking our leave, he took up a book from the table, saying, "I will lend you others tomorrow; in the meantime you will find something in this *Annuaire Historique Universel* to amuse you, besides the general matter it contains, for at the end it takes infinite pains to prove that I am a devil." Such is ever the reward of exalted geniuses, and an author in the present times may almost be valued in proportion as the abuse of the world increases. S. and L[ord] B[yron] afford proofs of this among those who are living, and among the dead they are numberless.[58]

Taaffe called on the Williamses on November 8, and two days later when they returned his call they met at his house a brother of Maria Edgeworth. Then on November 14 Medwin returned to join the circle.

The Palazzo Lanfranchi was the centre of the Pisan circle; or rather Lord Byron was the centre of the Pisan circle. He accepted almost no invitations, made almost no calls, except on the Gambas. The others came to see him, played billiards at his palazzo, went pistol shooting with his pistols or riding on his horses, dined with him; never he with them. The peculiar composition of the Pisan circle made this possible. At its core it was a masculine circle—Byron, Shelley, Williams, Medwin, Taaffe, and later Trelawny. Occasionally Pietro Gamba or a chance visitor such as John Hay joined the group. Then at the periphery there was a mixed group which included the female members and which carried on normal social intercourse. The Williamses and the Shelleys dined with one another and visited with one another; Teresa and Pietro called on the Shelleys and the Williamses, who in turn called on Teresa. Taaffe and Medwin, unattached, made calls on the various members. But the society at the Lanfranchi was exclusively masculine society, and it was the Lanfranchi which was headquarters for the group. As Mary wrote to Mrs. Hunt, "Our good cavaliers flock together, and as they do not like *fetching a walk with the absurd womankind*,[59] Jane (*i.e.*, Mrs. Williams) and I are off together, and talk morality and pluck violets by the way." [60]

One of Byron's first acts, according to the Austrian spy Torelli, living in Pisa, was to send Taaffe to the Grand Duke Ferdinand, excusing himself for not appearing at Court and kissing the Grand Duke's hand on the score that he had never been presented to any other prince during his stay in Italy.[61] "The Grand Duke laughingly replied," says Torelli, "that Lord Byron could even have been excused from informing him of this since he had not sought out Lord Byron." Whether these were the Grand Duke's actual words or not, they doubtless reflect accurately his thoughts. Byron's reluctance to exhibit his lameness to strangers was responsible for this tactless blunder, but he might have saved himself much of the trouble that finally drove him from Tuscany had he been a little more attentive to the expected formalities.

His mode of life at Pisa was much the same indolent routine as at Ravenna—with minor changes. Upon waking, around noon, he had a cup of strong green tea, without sugar or milk. At two he had a breakfast of biscuit and soda-water.

> Billiards, conversation, or reading, filled up the intervals till it was time to take our evening drive, ride, and pistol-practice [writes Medwin]. On our return, which was always in the same direction, we frequently met the Countess Guiccioli, with whom he stopped to converse a few minutes.
>
> He dined at half an hour after sunset, (at twenty-four o'clock); then drove to Count Gamba's, the Countess Guiccioli's father, passed several hours in her society, returned to his palace, and either read or wrote till two or three in the morning; occasionally

drinking spirits diluted with water as a medicine, from a dread of a nephritic complaint, to which he was, or fancied himself, subject.[62]

Byron kept a stable of some eight or nine horses and could mount his less fortunate friends. "Medwin rides almost constantly with Lord B[yron]," Shelley informed Claire, "and the party sometimes consists of Gamba, Taaf[f]e, Medwin and the Exotic [Shelley] who unfortunately belonging to the order of mimosa, thrives ill in so large a society." [63] Mary attributed an improvement in Shelley's health to a combination of the salutary air of Pisa and the exercise on horseback, though there were times when, because of the excruciating pain in his side, he was unable to ride.

When Byron's application for permission to practise pistol-shooting within the city was refused, a place was found at the Villa la Podera, "an extensive enclosure attached to a picturesque farmhouse—part garden, part farm, part vineyard—situated in Cisanello, some two miles outside Pisa beyond the Porta alle Piagge." [64] It belonged to the Castinelli family, friends of Vaccà, through whom the necessary permission was arranged.[65] Byron was proud of his pistols, made by Manton, Wilkinson, and other famous makers, and usually had eight or ten pairs carried by his courier.[66] They were always discharged, however, before the party returned to the town. Pistol practice consisted of placing a half-crown piece in a slit on a cane stuck into the ground and firing at a distance of fourteen paces. Byron, though his hand was unsteady, was an excellent shot, and Shelley, whose hand was quite steady, was almost as accurate. After each of the party had fired about a dozen rounds, Byron pocketed the battered coin, which he saved as a souvenir, and presenting the owner of the podere with a good half-crown piece, mounted his horse and, with his friends, rode back to Pisa.[67]

Once a week the male members of the Pisan circle were

invited to dinner at the Palazzo Lanfranchi. When Byron was alone, he dined frugally, but on these occasions he provided his guests with choice wines and delicacies of the season that excited Medwin's admiration. Shelley, less impressionable, wrote sardonically to Horace Smith, "Lord Byron unites us at a weekly dinner, when my nerves are generally shaken to pieces by sitting up contemplating the rest making themselves vats of claret, etc., till three o'clock in the morning." [68]

Yet Shelley, at least in the beginning, enjoyed the intercourse with Byron. "Lord Byron is established now, and we are constant companions," he wrote to Peacock; "no small relief this after the dreary solitude of the understanding and the imagination in which we past the first years of our expatriation, yoked to all sorts of miseries and discomforts." [69] The effect of Byron upon Shelley was nevertheless unfortunate in one respect: Shelley's admiration for Byron's poetry, in which his impeccable judgment selected the great poetry from the second-rate, Byron's enormous popularity, and his own consistent failure to find an audience overwhelmed him. The repressive influence of Byron, first visible at Geneva, when Shelley's only composition had been his *Hymn to Intellectual Beauty*, became painfully apparent at Pisa. "I despair of rivalling Lord Byron, as well I may," Shelley had written at Ravenna, "and there is no other with whom it is worth contending." [70] Now in dejection he confessed to Claire: "I am employed in nothing—I read—but I have no spirits for serious composition—I have no confidence, and to write in solitude or put forth thoughts without sympathy is unprofitable vanity." [71] Still later he was to write to Horace Smith: "I do not write—I have lived too long near Lord Byron and the sun has extinguished the glow-worm; for I cannot hope with St. John, that '*the light came into the world, and the world knew it not.*'" [72]

In describing her new apartment at the Tre Palazzi

di Chiesa to Mrs. Gisborne, and its proximity to Lord Byron, Mary Shelley concluded by saying: "So Pisa, you see, has become a little nest of singing birds." [73] The statement was literally true. All members of the Pisan circle were poets or writers of some description. Williams, though his play was rejected, continued to write, with Shelley's encouragement. Medwin, whose aspirations soared above his accomplishments, had published *Oswald and Edwin* and *Sketches in Hindoostan* and was to give to the world two valuable though not always accurate books on Byron and Shelley. Trelawny, not yet arrived in Pisa, later wrote his autobiographical *Adventures of a Younger Son* and his books on Byron and Shelley, and even Pietro Gamba made translations of Byron's poetry and was to chronicle his friend's last days in a modest little book. And we have already seen that John Taaffe was the author of *Padilla*, *A Tale of Palestine*, as well as of occasional verse, and that Shelley had interested himself in the publication of Taaffe's *Comment on Dante*, though without success.

Byron had not been long at Pisa before he also lent his influence to Taaffe, as evidenced by the following letter to Moore:

> There is here Mr. Taaffe, an Irish genius, with whom we are acquainted. He hath written a really *excellent* Commentary on Dante, full of new and true information, and much ingenuity. But his verse is such as it hath pleased God to endue him withal. Nevertheless, he is so firmly persuaded of its equal excellence, that he won't divorce the Commentary from the traduction, as I ventured delicately to hint,—not having the fear of Ireland before my eyes, and upon the presumption of having shotten very well in his presence (with common pistols too, not with my Manton's) the day before.
>
> But he is eager to publish all, and must be gratified, though the Reviewers will make him suffer more tortures than there are in his original. Indeed, the *Notes* are well worth publication; but he insists upon the translation for company, so that they will come out together, like Lady C——t chaperoning Miss ——. I read a letter of yours to him yesterday, and he begs me to write to you about his

LORD BYRON
As he appeared after his daily ride at Pisa and Genoa
(*From a silhouette cut in paper by Mrs. Leigh Hunt*)

Poeshie. He is really a good fellow, apparently, and I dare say that his verse is very good Irish.

Now, what shall we do for him? He says that he will risk part of the expense with the publisher. He will never rest till he is published and abused—for he has a high opinion of himself—and I see nothing left but to gratify him, so as to have him abused as little as possible; for I think it would kill him. You must write, then, to Jeffrey to beg him *not* to review him, and I will do the same to Gifford, through Murray. Perhaps they might notice the Comment without touching the text. But I doubt the dogs—the text is too tempting.[74]

Nothing came, or could very well have come, of this rather vague proposal, but Byron knew how to be persistent.

In spite of his attempts to aid Taaffe, Byron could not resist a certain amount of good-natured jesting about his versification. Mary Shelley, an untrustworthy witness where Taaffe is concerned, refers to him as Byron's butt at Pisa,[75] but her statement is contradicted by Teresa Guiccioli, who says that his "sincerity won for him grace and compassion."[76] Though Mary's statement is not quite fair, it is nevertheless true that Byron, who seldom spared his own friends, quizzed Taaffe on two scores—his versification and his horsemanship. Taaffe bore the jesting at the expense of his verses in good spirit, but Byron's low opinion of his horsemanship cut him to the quick and was in part responsible for his behaviour in the affair with the dragoon.[77]

Taaffe had at least his share of vanity, and Byron could not have touched him at a more sensitive point than on his horsemanship. At the age of four he had been given a Shetland pony by his maternal grandfather, and his father had decreed that he must learn the rudiments of good riding from that early age by riding without a saddle. A lover of horses, he rode constantly while growing up and, during his three years at Smarmore before going to Edinburgh, rode to the hounds a great deal. By his own testimony he was a skilful and even reckless rider. In Pisa he was so much in the saddle that he feared the townspeople would regard him as lame, like Byron. "Even to go to the printing office twenty times a day during the printing of my *Comment* . . . ," he records, "I used to mount my horse and traverse the streets at full gallop." [78]

At Tangier he had first come in contact with pure-bred Arabian horses and with the Turkish school of manage riding, in which the reins flow freely and the horse is turned by pressure of the heel, the bridle being used only for pulling the horse in. It may have been the adoption of this mode of riding that accounted for the occasional spills at which his English friends jested. Byron's laughter hurt the more as Taaffe regarded Byron as only a mediocre horseman; but, says Taaffe:

> . . . I forgave even his witticisms and (as appeared to me) ill-timed jokes on that most delicate and momentous of subjects, horsemanship, when I recollected that he called my horse "*a really beautiful horse*." Little did I heed his other words—what I thought his improper liberties with myself and his aspersions of an art in which I considered him very ignorant. When he attacked my riding, I held him an incompetent judge. He seemed to me to know how to ride, as all men know how to ride, even a little better; but that not for this he was much advanced in equestrian lore; any more than a correct writer of unpretending prose were fit to pronounce on one of his Lordship's splendid poems or compose it, *Manfred* for example. . . . Most cordially did I overlook everything else for Lord Byron's just eulogium of my fine Pole. He was indeed a horse, as there are few.[79]

Throughout the autumn of 1821 the little colony pursued their pleasant social intercourse and devoted themselves with varying degrees of diligence to the task of composition. Shelley, who had been inspired by the revolution in Greece to write a dramatic poem called *Hellas*— "a sort of imitation of the Persae of Æschylus, full of lyrical poetry" [80]—put the finishing touches on it in late October and turned it over to Williams early in November for him to make the fair copy. Thereafter he worked sporadically on a play on the uncongenial subject of Charles I, which he never completed and of which he said "a devil of a nut it is to crack." [81] With Williams he was also translating Spinoza, "that is to say," explains Williams, "I write while he dictates." [82] Mary, having finished copying out her novel, rewarded herself by resuming her study of Greek. Byron alone, having sent off *Heaven and Earth* to Murray on November 14, was idle, though Williams, who heard Shelley read the poem aloud on the evening of December 14, was under the impression that it had been finished the evening before.[83]

The weather was ideal: cold, but not uncomfortably so, by night, and balmy by day, so that one might dine with open windows without a fire.[84] Shelley and Williams both found themselves in greatly improved health, the relations between the various members of the circle were pleasant, Hunt (mistakenly) was expected to arrive almost any day, and life withal held as much of hope for the members of the little colony as men and women who had learned by experience that its stages are inevitably marked by suffering dared anticipate.

CHAPTER 5

The Winter of 1821–22

THE high winds of late December, ushering in the winter, had not yet arrived when an incident occurred which, though it later turned out to be compounded of more rumour than fact, greatly excited the Pisan circle and brought characteristic reactions from the several members. It began with a story which Medwin picked up in a bookshop and which Shelley also heard while out walking. Medwin tells the tale thus:

> One day when I called at the bookseller Moloni's, I heard a report that a subject of Lucca had been condemned to be burnt alive for sacrilege. A priest who shortly after entered, confirmed the news, and expressed himself in the following terms:—"Wretch!" said he, "he took the consecrated wafers from the altar, and threw them contemptuously about the church. No tortures can be great enough for such a horrible crime; burning is too light a death. I will go to Lucca, I would go to Spain to see the infidel die at the stake." Such were the *humane* and *charitable* feelings of a follower of Christ. I left him with abhorrence, and betook myself to Lord Byron. "Is it possible," said he, with shuddering, "do we live in the nineteenth century? But I can believe anything of the Duchess of Lucca. She was an Infanta—is a bigot, and perhaps an advocate for the Inquisition. But surely she cannot venture in these times to sign a warrant for such an execution! We must endeavour to prevent this *auto da fé*. Lord Guilford [1] is here. We will move heaven and earth to put a stop to it. The Grand Duke of Tuscany will surely appeal against the consummation of such a horrible sacrifice, for he has not signed a death-warrant since he came to the throne." [2]

Shelley and Mary were out walking with the Williamses when Shelley, who separated from the others, heard the same rumour and immediately went up to the Palazzo Lanfranchi.[3] Medwin's narrative continues:

> At this moment Shelley entered. He had also heard that the offender was to be burnt the next day. He proposed that we should arm ourselves as well as we could, and immediately ride to Lucca, and attempt on the morrow to rescue the prisoner when brought to the stake, and then carry him to the Tuscan frontier, where he would be safe. Mad and hopeless as the plan was, Lord Byron, carried away by Shelley's enthusiasm, declared himself ready to join in it, should other means fail. We agreed to meet again in the evening, and in the meanwhile to make a representation, signed by all the English at Pisa, to the Grand Duke, then with his Court at Pisa.[4]

Sometime before the evening meeting at the Lanfranchi one of the group learned that the *auto da fé* was not to take place on the following day; hence they had a little more time in which to investigate or make plans.[5] Apparently only Medwin and Shelley were with Byron at the second meeting: Williams remained at home writing, and Taaffe was indisposed. In his autobiography he says that he was not well, but Byron, writing to Moore, gives a different explanation:

> The consummation you mentioned for poor Taaffe was near taking place yesterday. Riding pretty sharply after Mr. Medwin and myself in turning the corner of a lane between Pisa and the hills, he was spilt,—and, besides losing some claret on the spot, bruised himself a good deal, but is in no danger. He was bled, and keeps his room. As I was ahead of him some hundred yards, I did not see the accident; but my servant, who was behind, did, and says the *horse* did not fall—the usual excuse of floored equestrians. As Taaffe piques himself upon his horsemanship, and his horse is really a pretty horse enough, I long for his personal narrative—as I never yet met the man who would *fairly claim a tumble* as his own property.[6]

In spite of Taaffe's condition it was decided, during the deliberations of the evening, to draft him for service because of his extensive acquaintance at Lucca. Although it was long past midnight, a note, probably composed by Shelley, was despatched to him by one of Byron's servants, apprising him of the rumour and requesting his aid. Taaffe's reply, which has been lost, was apparently delivered unsealed to Byron, who read it and then sent it on to Shelley, now returned home, with this accompanying note:

December 12, 1821.

My dear Shelley,—

Enclosed is a note for you from [Taaffe]. His reasons are all very rue, I dare say, and it might and may be of personal inconvenience to us. But that does not appear to me to be a reason to allow a being to be burnt without trying to save him. To save him by any means but *remonstrance* is of course out of the question; but I do not see why a *temperate* remonstrance should hurt any one. Lord Guilford is the man, if he would undertake it. He knows the Grand Duke personally, and might, perhaps, prevail upon him to interfere. But, as he goes to-morrow, you must be quick, or it will be useless. Make any use of *my* name that you please.

Yours ever, etc.
[Byron] [7]

Before going to bed, Byron also wrote to Taaffe, as follows:

Dec.r 12th 1821.

My dear Taaffe—

Your reasons may be good and true—but ought not to weigh against the possibility even of saving a human creature—from so atrocious an infliction.—However without compromising *you*, I could wish you (as a personal favour to *me*) I not having any acquaintance with the Sovereign or his ministers to apply to any of the *latter* in *my name* only—and say that I will and would do any thing either by *money* or *guarantee* or otherwise—to have this man's punishment commuted;—(*saved* if possible) at least for some less cruel mode of destruction.—As to the Government I appeal to the whole of my conduct since I came here to prove whether I meddle or make with their politics.—I defy them to misinterpret my motive—and as to leaving their states—I am a Citizen of the World —content where I am now—but able to find a country elsewhere. —I only beg of you to take any steps in *my name* that may even have the possibility of being useful in saving the World from another reproach to it's Annals.—I am willing to make any sacrifice—of money or otherwise—I could never *bribe* in a better cause than that of humanity.—

Yrs ever & truly
Byron [8]

P.S. Try the *priests*—a little cash to the Church might perhaps save the man yet. *You* know *Lucca* well—I wish you would try there—always *without* compromising *yourself*.—

Nothing aroused Byron so quickly and thoroughly as tyranny, and in this letter we see his best qualities—his compassion for the victims of oppression and the generous spirit almost certain to appear whenever his sympathies were touched.

From the beginning Taaffe felt that the rumour was either false or exaggerated. "I who know the Lucchese to be utterly incapable of such cruelty or of suffering it to profane their town even if their Sovereign desired it (which indeed she did not) . . . was anxious to set his mind at ease on the matter," Taaffe wrote later.[9] Accordingly he sent the following letter to Byron:

Two o'clock, Tuesday Morning.[10]

My dear Lord,—

Although strongly persuaded that the story must be either an entire fabrication, or so gross an exaggeration as to be nearly so; yet, in order to be able to discover the truth beyond all doubt, and to set your mind quite at rest, I have taken the determination to go myself to Lucca this morning. Should it prove less false than I am convinced it is, I shall not fail to exert myself *in every way* that I can imagine may have any success. Be assured of this.

Your Lordship's most truly,
[J. Taaffe, Jr.] [11]

P.S.—To prevent *bavardage*, I prefer going in person to sending my servant with a letter. It is better for you to mention nothing (except, of course, to Shelley) of my excursion. The person I visit there is one on whom I can have every dependence in every way, both as to authority and truth.

On receiving Byron's letter, Taaffe directed his servant not to return to bed, but to awaken him in an hour and have his horse ready. At daybreak he set out for Lucca, imagining that there must be at least some slight foundation for the tale—that perhaps the hand of a corpse or an entire corpse had been condemned to the flames. Meanwhile Byron, whose note to Shelley leaves the impression that he expected Shelley to apply to Lord Guilford, himself wrote to Guilford. Moore received a brief account of the affair from Byron, together with Taaffe's and Shelley's [12] notes to Byron:

> You must really get Taaffe published—he never will rest till he is so. He is just gone with his broken head to Lucca, at my desire, to try to save a *man* from being *burnt*. The Spanish ***, that has her petticoats over Lucca, had actually condemned a poor devil to the stake, for stealing the wafer box out of a church. Shelley and I, of course, were up in arms against this piece of piety, and have been disturbing every body to get the sentence changed. Taaffe is gone to see what can be done.[13]

At Lucca, Taaffe learned to his surprise that decapitation was the only form of capital punishment recognized by law and that the story was pure fabrication so far as the mode of punishment was concerned. The crime, however, had been committed, and the wretch,[14] who turned out to be a Florentine, either surrendered to the Tuscan authorities or was handed over to them for punishment. Before Taaffe's return Shelley had already picked up the information that the burning was not to take place and so informed Byron:

> Thursday morning
>
> My dear Lord Byron
>
> I hear this morning that the design which certainly had been in contemplation of burning my fellow serpent has been abandoned & that he has been condemned to the gallies. Lord Guilford is at Leghorn, & as your courier applied to me to know whether he ought to leave your letter for him or not, I have thought it best, since this information, to tell him to take it back.
>
> Ever faithfully yours
>
> P.B.S.[15]

Byron turned Shelley's note over and wrote on the back of it:

> Dear M[oore]
>
> I send you the two notes [*i.e.*, Taaffe's and Shelley's] which will tell you the story I allude to of the Auto da Fe.—Shelley's allusion to his "fellow Serpent" is a buffoonery of mine—Goethe's

Mephistopheles [16] calls the Serpent who tempted Eve "*my Aunt the renowned Snake*" and I always insist that Shelley is nothing but one of her Nephews walking about on the tip of his tail—

B [17]

Taaffe returned to Pisa during the course of the day, and Mary's journal contains the following entry: "Thursday, Dec. 13 . . . Edward and Jane in the evening. Shelley at M. Mason's. Mr. Taaffe calls. We find the burning story to be all false." Medwin, who in his *Conversations* reported that the culprit was condemned straightway to the galleys, corrected his statement in his later *Life of Shelley* and said that the man "delivered himself up to the [Florentine] police, who had not made him over to the Lucchese authorities, but on condition that he should be tried by the statutes of Tuscany."[18] Taaffe, also writing years after the event, says that "he was not to be tried in the Lucchese territories at all, but had been already delivered up to the Tuscans as a Florentine."[19] Williams, writing at the time, says that the criminal fled to Florence "for protection [and] was there detected, but the Grand Duke, hearing of the cruel punishment that awaited him refused to give him up."[20] He adds: "It is reported that it was actually the Queen of Lucca's intention (who is an Infanta of Spain) to burn the culprit alive, not so much for the theft of the sacrament cup itself as for having spilt the most Holy Eucharist upon the road."[20] In the face of this contradictory evidence it may be reasonable to hypothesize that the offender was a Florentine who, for that reason, fled to Florence for protection and that the Florentine authorities refused extradition and dealt with him themselves.

Though the high winter winds made sailing hazardous, Shelley and Williams continued at intervals to sail on the Arno; once, running into a storm, they made shore just in time. Christmas passed quietly, with the men of the Pisan circle dining with Byron and leaving the women to console themselves as best they might. It was on the occasion of the Christmas dinner that Byron wagered Shelley £1,000 that Lady Noel would outlive Sir Timothy Shelley,[21] but when, less than two months later, word of Lady Noel's death reached Pisa, Byron said nothing about the bet. According to Medwin, Williams was so indignant that he never afterwards crossed Byron's threshold.[22] Medwin is mistaken; on the contrary, though news of Lady Noel's death reached Pisa on February 16, Williams called on Byron on February 24, when he beat him at billiards, called again on March 3,[23] and dined with him on March 8, after which he recorded in the friendliest possible fashion: "It is a singular circumstance that this personage should be so insensible to his real merit."[24] And still later, as we shall see presently, Williams acted for Byron following the affair of the dragoon when Trelawny caused difficulties between Byron and Taaffe. So much for this canard.

Three days after Christmas Count Ruggero Gamba and Pietro, who had been absent for a month on a hunting expedition to the Maremma, returned with only a single wild boar to exhibit as their kill.[25]

With the new year Shelley continued to struggle at intervals with the unrewarding theme of Charles I; then on January 26 he sent Williams some "beautiful but too melancholy" verses—*The Serpent is Shut Out from Paradise*,[26] in which he speaks of his "cold home" and is apparently explaining Mary's objection to his intimacy with the Williamses. In another poem of his about this time, *The Magnetic Lady to Her Patient*, Jane Williams, who used magnetism to relieve Shelley's attacks of pain, tells her patient that she does not love him but feels compassion for him because a hand not his had to charm his agony. We are not to jump to the conclusion that Shelley had made advances to Jane: "as to real flesh and blood," he had written to John Gisborne when Emilia was his attraction, "you know that I do not deal in those articles;

you might as well go to a ginshop for a leg of mutton, as expect anything human or earthly from me."[27] But when his own cold hearthside failed to provide the warmth essential to his nature, Jane's good humour and beauty were strong attractions. Shelley asked Horace Smith to buy a pedal harp, to cost perhaps 75 or 80 guineas, for her, but when Smith refused, he had to be content with a guitar, which was accompanied by the verses, *With a Guitar: to Jane*. To Jane Williams also were addressed the beautiful lines entitled *To Jane:*

The keen stars were twinkling,
And the fair moon was rising among them,
Dear Jane!
The guitar was tinkling,
But the notes were not sweet till you sung them
Again.

As the moon's soft splendour
O'er the faint cold starlight of Heaven
Is thrown,
So your voice most tender
To the strings without soul had then given
Its own.

The stars will awaken,
Though the moon sleep a full hour later,
Tonight;
No leaf will be shaken
Whilst the dews of your melody scatter
Delight.

Though the sound overpowers,
Sing again, with your dear voice revealing
A tone
Of some world far from ours,
Where music and moonlight and feeling
Are one.

Williams, hearing on January 9 that his play had been rejected, cast about for another subject. He consulted Taaffe about the lives of Celestine V and Boniface VIII as possible themes for a tragedy and then selected the latter. Shelley, to whom he read a sketch of it, praised it but warned that it would not perform. Undeterred, Williams began combing historical authorities and continued to confer with Taaffe.

As Moore had done nothing—was in position to do nothing—about Byron's proposals that he get Taaffe's *Comment* published, Byron adopted more practical measures in sending the *Comment* and translation to Murray with the following note:

Pisa, J^y^ 22^d^ 1822.

The enclosed letter,[28] with the annexed packet, will explain its object. I can only say that the work appears a desideratum in literature (especially in English literature), and with a lift in the *Quarterly* would be likely to go off well. Foscolo can tell you this better than I. Taaffe is a very good man, with a great desire to see himself in print, and will be made very happy by such a vision. He was persuaded to add his translation, which is *not* good; but the Comment is really valuable. If *you* will engage in the work, you will serve him, and oblige me: if not, at least recommend it to some of the other publishers, as I should feel sorry to disappoint a very good natured man, who is publishing an useful work. He stipulates for no terms: at any rate, let us have an answer.

Yours sincerely,

B.[29]

His politics and religion are all in your own damned way, so that there will be no dispute about that.

The requested answer did not come promptly, and Byron tried to jog Murray. "What is to be done about Taaffe and his Commentary? He will die if he is *not* published: he will be damned, if he *is;* but that *he* don't mind. You must publish him."[30] And again: "You must really get something done for Mr. Taaffe's Commentary. What can I say to him?"[31] Already so irritated by Murray's treatment that he was threatening to transfer to another publisher, Byron wrote the following postscript on a letter of March 8 to Moore:

Do tell Murray that one of the conditions of peace is, that he publisheth (or obtaineth a publisher for) Taaffe's *Commentary on*

Dante, against which there appears in the trade an unaccountable repugnance. It will make the man so exuberantly happy. He dines with me and half-a-dozen English to-day; and I have not the heart to tell him how the bibliopolar world shrink from his Commentary;—and yet it is full of the most orthodox religion and morality. In short, I make it a point that he shall be in print. He is such a good-natured, heavy ** Christian, that we must give him a shove through the press. He naturally thirsts to be an author, and has been the happiest of men for these two months, printing, correcting, collating, dating, anticipating, and adding to his treasures of learning. Besides, he has had another fall from his horse into a ditch the other day, while riding out with me into the country.[32]

Murray, yielding to the conditions of peace rather than exercising his independent judgment, one suspects, published the first volume of Taaffe's *Comment* later in the year. The actual printing was done in Pisa from the types of Didot, as with a few copies of Shelley's *Adonais*, and Murray merely announced the book for sale and acted as half-hearted distributor.[33] The public reception of it was such that no second volume was ever issued.[34] Taaffe bore his failure philosophically. Looking back upon his disappointment in later years, he could say:

. . . All this gave me small vexation as likewise the criticisms and taunts of the Reviews. My vanity is of a consolatory nature. I always feel more pleasure at praise, than displeased at blame or sneers. In three days I usually get over the worst. I should never have been murdered by an article, as they say Keats was. . . . I dwelt much more on Lord Byron's laudatory opinion of my Comment, than on his disparagement of my verses. This favourable judgment of his in calling my Comment "*excellent*" seemed to me more than an equivalent for the censure of others. That the Comment came out without the verses is a clear proof that I was not so wedded to them as his Lordship imagined.[35]

As the *Comment* was to have extended to eight volumes, Taaffe took what consolation he could from the fact that the unflattering reception of the *Comment* by the public saved him from a labour that would have occupied ten to fifteen years of his life and distracted him from what he had set his heart on—the fulfilment of his promise to his parents to write a great poem that would make them proud of him.

On a lower floor of the Tre Palazzi lived Dr. Nott,[36] a prebend of Winchester, who conducted chapel services on Sundays for some fourteen or fifteen English who attended. Just after Christmas he had christened the Williamses' daughter, Mary Shelley standing as godmother,[37] and on several occasions during the winter Mary attended the services, more to be neighbourly than for any other reason. Once when she attended by invitation and Dr. Nott preached on atheism, all the while apparently directing his gaze at her, the intent seemed so obvious that Mary wrote him a letter asking whether he meant any personal allusion and received his assurance that he did not.[38] Though Mary was satisfied and attended services at least once thereafter and called on his daughter,[39] the incident, as she wrote to Mrs. Gisborne, "made a great noise" among the English residents of Pisa. "The gossip here is of course out of all bounds," she added, "some people have given them something to talk about——" [40] But she held no ill-will against Dr. Nott. When Medwin published the incident in his *Conversations*, Mary wrote to Hobhouse, "Medwin could also have mentioned that as soon as Dr Nott heard that he was accused of the impropriety of preaching against Shelley, he paid us a visit to exculpate himself from the charge." [41]

Throughout the months of November and December Williams was in frequent correspondence with Edward Trelawny, as the unpublished portions of his journal show. Late on the afternoon of January 14 Trelawny himself arrived in Pisa and, after putting up his horse and dining at the Ussero inn, hastened to the Tre Palazzi, where the Williamses received him cordially.[42] With much to talk about, the conversation was naturally lively; but Trelawny was suddenly disturbed by observing, in the passageway opposite him, a pair of glittering eyes fixed steadily on his own. Jane Williams, comprehending the situation, went to the door and said laughingly: "Come in, Shelley, it's only our friend Tre just arrived."[43]

Shelley came in, blushing, and Trelawny looked at him in astonishment:

> . . . I could hardly believe as I looked at his flushed, feminine, and artless face that it could be the Poet. . . . I was silent from astonishment: was it possible this mild-looking, beardless boy, could be the veritable monster at war with all the world?—excommunicated by the Fathers of the Church, deprived of his civil rights by the fiat of a grim Lord Chancellor, discarded by every member of his family, and denounced by the rival sages of our literature as the founder of a Satanic school? I could not believe it; it must be a hoax.[44]

In response to a question by Jane, Shelley said that he was translating Calderon's *Magico Prodigioso*, from which he read aloud a few passages with utmost ease and about which he talked brilliantly. Then suddenly he disappeared as noiselessly as he had appeared, returning presently with Mary, who welcomed Trelawny to Italy and asked eagerly for news of the rest of the world. So passed Trelawny's first evening in the company of his Idol.

Next day at two o'clock Shelley and Trelawny crossed the Ponte Vecchio and went along the Lung' Arno to the Palazzo Lanfranchi.

> We entered a large marble hall [relates Trelawny], ascended a giant staircase, passed through an equally large room over the hall, and were shown into a smaller apartment which had books and a billiard-table in it. A surly-looking bull-dog (Moretto) announced us, by growling, and the Pilgrim instantly advanced from an inner chamber, and stood before us. His halting gait was apparent, but he moved with quickness; and although pale, he looked as fresh, vigorous, and animated, as any man I ever saw.[45]

Ill at ease among strangers, Byron tried to conceal his uneasiness by an affectation of ease. Presently he invited Trelawny to play billiards, but it was clear that he cared nothing for the game and everything for the opportunity it gave him of relating anecdotes of his earlier travels. The anecdotes were insignificant and unedifying. Expecting more in Byron, Trelawny was disappointed:

> I had come prepared to see a solemn mystery, and so far as I could judge from the first act it seemed to me very like a solemn farce. I forgot that great actors when off the stage are dull dogs; and even the mighty Prospero, without his book and magic mantle, was but an ordinary mortal. At this juncture Shelley joined us; he never laid aside his book and magic mantle; he waved his wand, and Byron, after a faint show of defiance, stood mute; his quick perception of the truth of Shelley's comments on his poem transfixed him, and Shelley's earnestness and just criticism held him captive.[46]

Yet Trelawny was struck with Byron's mental vivacity and wonderful memory, conceded him a nobility of appearance, and read his genius in his eyes and lips.

> In short [he concludes], Nature could do little more than she had done for him, both in outward form and in the inward spirit she had given to animate it. But all these rare gifts to his jaundiced imagination only served to make his one personal defect (lameness) the more apparent, as a flaw is magnified in a diamond when polished; and he brooded over that blemish as sensitive minds will brood until they magnify a wart into a wen.[47]

At three o'clock a servant announced that the horses were at the door, ending a discussion between Byron and Shelley. At the door Trelawny found three or four "very ordinary-looking horses," [48] with holsters on the saddles and other trappings such as appealed to the Italian rather than the English taste. Trelawny had his own horse, but Shelley and Taaffe, who had just come in, mounted two of Byron's "sorry jades." Byron, as usual, rode in a *calèche* until the party reached the gates of the town; in his morbid sensitiveness he could not bear to mount in sight of the "d——d Englishers" who had the habit of congregating about his palace.[49]

> After an hour or two of slow riding and lively talk,—for he was generally in good spirits when on horseback [continues Trelawny],—we stopped at a small *podere* on the roadside, and dismounting went into the house, in which we found a table with wine and

cakes. From thence we proceeded into the vineyard at the back; the servant brought two brace of pistols, a cane was stuck in the ground and a five paul-piece, the size of half-a-crown, placed in a slit at the top of the cane. Byron, Shelley, and I, fired at fifteen paces, and one of us generally hit the cane or the coin: our firing was pretty equal; after five or six shots each, Byron pocketed the battered money and sauntered about the grounds. We then remounted.[50]

With Trelawny thus initiated into the group, the Pisan circle was now complete, though Captain Hay was to join its ranks for a short time a little later and to play an important role in the affair with the dragoon. "At Pisa we were all under thirty except Byron," Trelawny recalled many years later. "Such hearts as ours united under the sunny clime of Italy, such scenes and events no time can fade; their glowing colours can never be dimmed. To try even to forget them is as vain as to expect their return." [51] Two days after his arrival he was introduced, along with the sculptor Bertolini, who was doing a bust of Byron, to one of Byron's weekly dinner parties, the guests as usual sitting very late.[52] In the mornings he frequently went to the Palazzo Lanfranchi to play billiards; in the afternoons he was usually one of the riding and shooting party; and in the evenings he dined out, attended the opera, paid visits, and once even escorted Mary Shelley to a ball at Mrs. Beauclerk's.

From the moment of Trelawny's arrival there was much talk of boat-building. In fact the subject had begun in the correspondence between Williams and Trelawny before the arrival of the latter. "I shall reserve all that I have to say about the boat until we meet at the select committee, which is intended to be held on that subject when you arrive here. Have a boat we must, and if we can get Roberts [53] to build her, so much the better," Williams had written.[54] With him Trelawny brought "the model of an American schooner, on which it is settled with S. and myself to build a boat thirty feet long," Williams says, "and T. writes to Roberts at Genoa to commence on it directly."[55] Nevertheless nothing was settled until more than two weeks later (Feb. 5), when Trelawny wrote "definitively" to Roberts, specifying a small undecked boat seventeen or eighteen feet long for Shelley—"a thorough *Varment* at *pulling* and *sailing*"[56] —and confirming the order of a large roomy yacht, with iron keel, copper bottom, and four brass guns for Byron. This letter followed a conversation between Trelawny and Shelley, as they returned from a trip to Leghorn, on the subject of forming a colony on the Gulf of Spezzia. The proposal originated with Trelawny, who said: "You get Byron to join us, and with your family and the Williams', and books, horses, and boats, undisturbed by the botherations of the world, we shall have all that reasonable people require."[57] The idea enchanted Shelley; he begged Trelawny to propose it at once to Byron, who was always most influenced, he said, by the latest arrival. Trelawny continues:

> The following morning I told Byron our plan. Without any suggestion from me he eagerly volunteered to join us, and asked me to get a yacht built for him, and to look out for a house as near the sea as possible. I allowed some days to pass before I took any steps in order to see if his wayward mind would change. As he grew more urgent I wrote to an old naval friend, Captain Roberts, then staying at Genoa, a man peculiarly fitted to execute the order, and requested him to send plans and estimates of an open boat for Shelley, and a large decked one for Byron.[58]

With plans actually under way the boat talk grew warmer. Two days after his "definitive" letter of February 5 Trelawny sent Roberts the model of the American schooner from which hints might be taken for the Williams-Shelley boat; and again taking up the subject of Byron's boat, he wrote:

> It will not be possible will it to have any sort of water closet in so small a vessel as Lord B! Let the cabin be most sumtuously fitted up: with all kind of conveniences for provisions, wine, Books, tables, sofas, hooks for pistols, riffles, beautifully painted, but not gaudily! What think you of blue & white—she is to be named (a

damned curious one youl [*i.e.*, you'll] say) Guiccioli? it is the name of a favrite mistress of his who is here—and will be at the Bay with him who is certainly a lovely girl? Lord B will most likely Build a yactht next year—and the boat you are now building Shelley will have? [59]

There was more about sails, anchors, a pennant, and two sets of flags for signalling. On the outside of the letter Trelawny wrote: "her name to be The Countess Gamba Guiccioli." To be sure that it was quite legible, he wrote it again, this time more legibly than before, and boxed it off with lines: "The Countess Gamba Guiccioli." In Teresa's unpublished *Vie de Lord Byron en Italie* the Marchesa Origo found—and could hardly believe—Teresa's statement that it was Byron's first intention to name his boat for her and that only a fear of compromising her and of annoying her father caused him to change his mind.[60] That such was his intention Trelawny's letter to Roberts makes clear beyond question. Exactly when he changed his mind is not known, but when next we hear of the boat it is renamed the *Bolivar*.

Trelawny had ample opportunity, as the days passed, to form an estimate of Byron's character. If that judgment, as recorded later in his *Recollections*, was not very favourable, we must not forget that it was highly coloured by Byron's attitude toward Trelawny and by Trelawny's strong sympathy for Claire, to whom he later wrote love letters. It was unfortunately true that each brought out the worst in the other's character. Trelawny, expecting to find Byron the hero of his own romantic poems, found instead the exact opposite:

Here was not an arch-Manfred but a Thersites, not a hero but a jester, not a crusader but a cripple, not a Childe Harold but a supercilious man of the world, full of prosaic poses and affectations at utter variance with what he [Trelawny] conceived should have been his [Byron's] true character. Instantly he recoiled, in distaste, in bewilderment, in dismay.[61]

And what of Byron? How could he possibly have

regarded Trelawny with complete approval? In the first place Trelawny was the very opposite of the man-of-the-world type that Byron so much admired: on the contrary he was an illiterate,[62] half-civilized pirate with neither address nor social standing to recommend him. And then his strength—unmarred by any physical deformity; his superiority over Byron as a swimmer, Byron's own specialty (had he not swum from Sestos to Abydos and proclaimed the feat to the world for years thereafter?); his extravagant manner; his arresting tales of his own romantic adventures, partly fact, partly fiction—all combined to repel Byron. The pose that Byron affected in Trelawny's presence was always that of a man of the world, not "a mere sing-song driveller of poesy"[63]—a pose that was accentuated, no doubt, by Byron's perception of Trelawny's disillusionment and his consequent desire to appear the opposite of what Trelawny expected. And though Trelawny saw that the pose was based on the false assumption that the world had not progressed beyond the vulgar manners of the Regency, to one who affected such a pose the blunt and unpolished Trelawny could only have inspired a certain amount of good-natured contempt. Years later Claire Clairmont, musing over the past and its phantom figures, remarked, "Well, Byron snubbed him, you know: he said, 'Tre was an excellent fellow until he took to imitating my *Childe Harold* and *Don Juan*.' This got to Trelawny's ears, and he never forgave Byron for it."[64] Whether he forgave Byron or not, it could not help colouring his attitude toward him. Yet, when John Murray asked Trelawny in after years to write an estimate of Byron, the sting of Byron's treatment of him was so far forgotten that he could write with fairness:

> Lord Byron was nothing in conversation, unless you were alone with him, but then he was rich as a gold mine, in every direction you bored into him you could extract wealth, and he was never exausted—

People may say what they like of their Moore, their Campbell—their Southey, and their Rogers, Byron was the master spirit of the age the force and vigour of his writing was unequalled—and his style unlike anything that has appeared in our English literature—Eminently remarkable for its splendour—ardour—and consiseness—which is a very rare combination? . . .

Byron when he put forth his strenth soared—above this 'our dingy Earth' with the might of an Eagle—and gained by one flight—a height—which he maintained with unveried wing—leaving all his rivals—at an immesurable distance beneath him.[65]

Byron admitted Trelawny to his company, made him his agent in various transactions, and finally invited him to go to Greece with him, but underneath it all there was little of the real sympathy that is the basis of genuine friendship. And because Byron delighted in making Trelawny feel inferior in his presence, Trelawny turned unerringly to the Tre Palazzi, where in Shelley he "found those sympathies and sentiments which the Pilgrim denounced as illusions believed in as the only realities."[66] Shelley, whose intellectual powers Trelawny regarded as far greater than Byron's and whose unaffectedness and unworldliness were firmly rooted in character, fitted Trelawny's conception of a poet much better than Byron affecting the role of a decaying Regency buck.

To Mary Shelley, bored by Medwin and Taaffe,[67] largely deprived of the companionship of her husband by his habits and literary pursuits, Trelawny was almost a godsend. Of all the Pisan circle she came nearer than any other to accepting him at face value. She recognized his extravagance but thought it suited him well; his air of good nature she interpreted as goodness of heart; his romantic tales she accepted as fact when she looked at his half-Arab appearance. ". . . Tired with the everyday sleepiness of human intercourse," she wrote in her journal, "I am glad to meet with one, who, among other valuable qualities, has the rare merit of interesting my imagination."[68]

With Trelawny in charge of the details of getting

Byron's boat built, Byron had nothing to do but pursue his customary routine and fret over literary and financial matters. Murray added to the catalogue of his offences by omitting the dedication of *Sardanapalus* to Goethe[69] and showing increasing reluctance to publish Byron's poems. Though *Cain* eventually appeared on December 19, with *Sardanapalus* and *The Two Foscari*, Byron had heard nothing (and was to hear nothing for more than a year) about *The Vision of Judgment*, which he had sent to Murray on October 4.[70] Mildly he wrote to Kinnaird on January 18: "But I wish you would let me know why 'The Vision' is not published—or whether it is to be so or no—and by whom." [71] Three weeks later he wrote again: "'Try back the deep lane,' till we find a publisher for the *Vision*; and if none such is to be found, print fifty copies at my expense, distribute them amongst my acquaintance, and you will soon see that the booksellers *will* publish them, even if we opposed them. That they are now afraid is natural; but I do not see that I ought to give way on that account." [72]

Then there was Kinnaird's obstinate refusal to share Byron's alarm over the state of England and transfer Byron's capital from government securities—"the funds."[73] From Ravenna he had written to Kinnaird, shortly before leaving: "It is fit that you should be informed that up to this present writing—I have *not* received the half year's fee of mine stocks.—And it is also fitting that you should extract me from the said stocks—which sit very heavily upon my slumbers of secure property." [74] His uneasiness was based largely upon the feeling that there would be a war which would cause the funds to decline sharply. "Do not, my dear Fellow, fidget about the Funds," replied Kinnaird—"we are looking out for mortgages—we will sell the instant we can find them—I am confident the Funds will rise within a couple of months—even tho' there be a Turkish war. . . . You shall never wait again for your circulars—I see it fidgets you—& you like your payment to be punctual—"[75] But Byron was not altogether reassured: "The fee is arrived—There 'will be a Turkish war'—and yet you tell me not to be disturbed 'about the funds'?—It may be a very good jest to you 'a prosperous Gentleman' but for one who thinks as I do—and is situated as I am—it is not so agreeable a landscape.—I shall certainly (as I have always told you) never be easy (but who is?) in my mind till we are out of the Stocks.—"[76] Again, on October 9, he wrote: "I pray you in your prosperity to think of the *funds* and of those therein and am yours ever."[77] Kinnaird felt sure that the funds would rise and thought it foolish to sell out at a loss; he therefore disregarded Byron's instructions. Writing again in November, Byron assured Kinnaird that he would never take him to task for selling out at a loss. "My confidence in your skill is as great as in your integrity," he wrote—"and though I hope that *I* am an honest man too—I am a mere child in business—& can neither count nor *ac*count.—"[78] And to a letter of January 18 he added a postscript: "The *funds*! What not *yet*?"[79]

With Byron any matter that he was concerned over was likely to remain uppermost in his mind until another came along to drive it out. So it was with the funds. In the early part of the winter it seemed unlikely that the death of Lady Noel * would be the occasion of his forgetting at least for a time his worries over the funds. Reports of Lady Noel's failing health had reached Byron more than once, but each time a contradiction or a report of recovery followed. "As to what Sir Henry Halford said to your friend of Lady Noel's health," Byron wrote to Kinnaird in December—"it is little to be depended upon—old ailing women are eternal,—he gave her over before—and she got well—and so she may now."[80] But

* Lady Noel was of course Lady Byron's mother, at whose death Byron, by right of his wife, according to the terms of the marriage settlement and the separation agreement, would inherit her estate.

in February news arrived that Lady Noel was not immortal after all; she had died on January 22, and Byron had inherited the property for the duration of Lady Byron's life. Thereafter he busied himself with the details of the business as well as he could at such a distance. By the terms of the separation agreement signed in 1816 arbitrators were to be appointed, one by each of the principals, to determine how the income from the property should be divided. Byron wrote at once to Kinnaird naming Sir Francis Burdett as his referee. Subsequently the referees decided that the income should be divided equally between Byron and Lady Byron.

The addition of about £3,500 a year to his income should have ended all of Byron's money worries; but as his interest in the estate was only a marital life-interest he began to have nightmares about what would happen if Lady Byron should die before him. He wrote post-haste to Kinnaird:

> . . . *Immediately insure Lady Byron's* life for me—for *ten thousand pounds*—or (if the expense seems too great to you) for *six thousand* pounds—that, in case of her demise—as the *Marital* is only a *life* interest—there may be some provision to compensate for the diminution of income, and provide for my children. . . . Do *not* neglect *this*; but act *immediately*.[81]

The letter was signed "Yours most affectionately and (since it must be so) Noel Byron." [82] Three days later he added the following postscript to another letter to Kinnaird: "*Above all do not forget or omit to insure* Lady Byron's life for me for ten thousand pounds *immediately*." [83] And in an undated postscript: "If we have upon the whole a *good* year—I should be inclined to encrease the ensurance even to £25,000—but that will depend on so many contingencies.—" [84]

From the moment that word of Lady Noel's death reached him, Byron showed eagerness to assume the name of *Noel*, and two days after receipt of the news he wrote to his attorney, Hanson: "Send me out a Seal and directions about the Noel arms, and how I am to adopt or quarter them." [85] Hanson, in fact, had not waited to hear from Byron before acting: "I lost no time in taking the necessary measures to procure the Crown License for ye assumption of ye Noel Name & Arms without waiting for your Lordship's particular directions . . .," he wrote to Byron, adding virtuously, "I could not allow your Lordship in this Instance to appear to be merely passive, and I dare to say there are some Persons who did not like it." [86] A few days later he wrote again: "I now enclose the gazetted Notification of the License for your Lordship's assuming the Name & Arms of Lord Wentworth,* the grant is making out at the Herald's office and when it has been exemplified with all its quartered Blazonings, I will not fail to get a Seal engraved from it and forwarded to your Lordship as desired—" [87]

The prospect of adding several thousand a year to his income stimulated Byron's growing avarice. In his early days Byron had learned niggardliness at the hands of an excellent teacher—his mother. During his college days and immediately afterwards he had spent money recklessly, only to have to pay a heavy penalty in debts, usurious rates of interest, and personal embarrassment, particularly during the year of his marriage. Symbolical of his reform in this respect is his facetious suggestion in *Don Juan:*

> So for a good old-gentlemanly vice
> I think I must take up with avarice.[88]

This was autobiography; and nurtured, the tendency to pinch pennies grew. Kinnaird, observing it disapprovingly, had rebuked Byron sharply in a letter which concerned the publication of *Don Juan:* "You could not crave money with more avidity, were you one of Alcibiades his whores—You cannot eat it—Famine is a great way off—and yet you will print your poeshie for the sake of the

* Lady Byron's uncle, from whom Lady Noel's wealth derived.

fee—"[89] A little over a year later Byron confessed to Hobhouse: "I have quite lost all personal interest about anything except money to supply my own indolent expences; and when I rouse up to appear to take an interest about anything, it is a temporary irritation like Galvanism upon Mutton." [90] Still later when Murray was shilly-shallying about *The Vision of Judgment*, Byron wrote to Kinnaird: "I wish . . . you would come to an agreement with Murray —because though I have a decent sum of monies in hand —yet I love Monies—& like to have more always.—I have no dislike to anything so much as to paying anybody.—" [91] He repeated the last sentence in even stronger words in another letter of about the same time: ". . . Don't speak to me of paying—it makes me so very unwell." [92] After the death of Lady Noel he paid his debts—reluctantly—but showed no lessening of his concern over money.

> . . . As my notions upon the score of monies [he wrote to Kinnaird] coincide with yours and all men's who have lived to see that every guinea is a philosopher's stone—or at least his *touch*-stone—you will doubt me the less when I pronounce my firm belief that Cash is Virtue.—I have been endeavouring to square my conduct to this maxim—which may account for my late anxieties upon all topics of L.S.D. . . . My only extra expence (and it is more than I have spent upon myself) is a loan to Leigh Hunt of two hundred & fifty pounds—and fifty pounds worth of furniture I have bought for him—and a boat which I am building for myself at Genoa—which will cost a hundred or more.
>
> With regard to L. Hunt—he stuck by me through thick & thin —when all shook, & some shuffled in 1816.—He never asked me for a loan till now.—I was very willing to accommodate a man to whom I have obligations.—He is now at Plymouth—waiting for a ship to sail for Italy.
>
> But to return—I am determined to have all the monies I can—whether by my own funds, or succession—or lawsuit—or wife — or M.S.S. or any lawful means whatsoever.—— [93]

Byron's quarrel with Southey, dating back to 1817 when Southey had returned from Switzerland and Byron suspected him of originating a scandalous report that Byron had been living incestuously at Geneva in "promiscuous intercourse with two sisters," reached a climax in the winter of 1821–22. Byron had intended to dedicate the first canto of *Don Juan* to Southey but refrained when he decided to publish it anonymously. Southey, however, learned of his intention and attacked Byron in the preface to his *Vision of Judgment*, published on April 11, 1821. Calling Byron and other corrupters of the public morals "men of diseased hearts and depraved imaginations," Southey coined for them the phrase "the Satanic school."

The phrase stung, and in Canto III of *Don Juan* (published August 8, 1821) Byron labelled Southey a "turncoat," a "Pantisocrat," and a "renegade." Moreover in a note in the Appendix of *The Two Foscari* (published in December) he referred to the calumnies which Southey "scattered abroad on his return from Switzerland" and branded him an "arrogant scribbler of all work." Answering the charge in *The Courier*, Southey denied scattering the calumnies and asserted that the real cause of Byron's charge was the wound inflicted by the term "Satanic school." Nor was he a scribbler of all work; he had not, for example, published libels on his friends, expressed sorrow for the libels, and then reissued them later; he had never used his power to wound the character of a man or the heart of a woman; he had never published an anonymous book; he had never "manufactured furniture for the brothel." As for the things he had done: "I have sent a stone from my sling which has smitten their Goliath in the forehead. I have fastened his name upon the gibbet for reproach and ignominy, as long as it shall endure. Take it down who can!" He concluded with a word of advice to Byron: "when he attacks me again let it be in rhyme." [94]

Medwin, with whom Byron had been discussing his note to *The Two Foscari*, saw Southey's letter before Byron did—at Mr. Edgeworth's [95]—and mentioned it to Byron on their afternoon ride later in the day. "His anxiety to get a sight of it was so great," says Medwin, "that he wrote me two notes in the course of the evening, entreating me to procure the paper." Obtaining a copy, Medwin took it to the Palazzo Lanfranchi at eleven o'clock at night. Byron had left Teresa earlier than usual and was "waiting with some impatience." Taking the paper, "he glanced rapidly over the contents. He looked perfectly awful: his colour changed almost prismatically; his lips were as pale as death. He said not a word." [96] The date was probably February 5, for on that day Byron sat down and wrote a long reply—eight folio pages—to the editor of *The Courier*. As for Southey's denial of spreading calumnies, he wrote truculently, "I can only say that my authority was such as I have no reason to doubt—and that authority—as well as any other sort of Satisfaction shall be at Mr. Southey's service whenever he pleases to call for it." He denied that his "present exacerbation" was produced by the preface to *A Vision of Judgment*. He denied being the founder of a Satanic school of poetry: "I have no school nor Scholars . . . that I know of—my poetical friends are poets upon their own system not on mine.—As far as I recollect I have had no imitators—& certainly no coadjutors." Several pages of analysis of Southey's letter, point by point, followed.

It was a lame reply—for a Byron to make—and he must have been conscious of its impotence, for he concluded with a challenge:

> Mr. Southey declares that he "abhors personalities"—so do I—can not we settle our little affairs without troubling the public further?—I am as tired of this war of words as he can be—and shall be happy to reduce it to a more tangible decision—when—where—and how he pleases. —It is a pity that we are not nearer—but I will reduce the distance—if he will only assure me privately that he will not decline a meeting.—To any one but himself such a hint would be unnecessary. [97]

Even with the blustery challenge at the end it was weak; and he himself must have realized that this was true, for he never made a fair copy of it, never mailed it. But next day he sat down and wrote to Kinnaird, stating his intention of challenging Southey and asking Kinnaird to be his second. The duel never came off, however, for Kinnaird refused to convey the challenge. Thus far the honours rested decidedly with Southey. But the time-bomb—written in verse—that was to blow Southey to smithereens was already at 50 Albemarle Street, and the fuse was lighted: it was Byron's own *Vision of Judgment*. True, Murray finally declined to publish it, and it had to come out in the first issue of *The Liberal* (October, 1822), but the explosion was not weakened by the delay. Though Southey ungallantly reopened the controversy upon the publication of Medwin's *Conversations* in 1824, he was silenced for the remainder of Byron's lifetime.

As it was necessary to make plans for the summer, when the heat of Pisa became intense, Shelley and Williams left on February 7 on a househunting expedition in the vicinity of La Spezia, but made no final arrangements. Williams, with the seriousness which characterized him after his meeting with Shelley, settled down to work on a new tragedy, *Gonzago, Duke of Mantua*, having decided that Shelley was right about Boniface. When he read part of the first act to Shelley, Shelley found some faults in it but gave it his general approval.[98] Byron offered to write a prologue and an epilogue for it and advised Williams to change the name to *The Secret*.

From Roberts at Genoa came word that the boats he was building for Byron and Shelley were progressing as expected. Meanwhile those indefatigable sailors, Williams and Shelley, had to content themselves with the small boat, in which they could sail more frequently as February gave way to March. But an incident which occurred on March 14 almost caused them to lose the boat. As they returned from a sail and passed the bridge, they were hailed by customs officers, to whom they paid no heed, as ordinarily they were not bothered by customs officers. This time, however, their boat was seized, their servant was threatened with imprisonment, and the boat was returned only after Shelley had written to the minister of police.[99] Occasionally they made fairly long expeditions, as on March 23 when they sailed to Leghorn by way of the canal, the boat running swiftly before a strong gale.[100]

Sometime in March Byron's old friend John Hay came to Pisa for a visit and became a temporary member of the circle and, by chance, the chief victim of the most exciting event of the Spring. Hay had been hunting in the Maremma, the wildest portion of Italy, in which game of various sorts was supposed to abound, and on January 20 the Williamses, Medwin, and others dined with the Shelleys on the side of a wild boar that he had sent to Byron.[101] Byron had apparently agreed to join Hay in the hunt and then had reneged, as his letter of thanks implies:

Pisa. Fy. 6th. 1822.

My dear Hay/

I am really overpowered by your caccia[102]—which is too splendid—and I shall distribute it amongst our friends—with yr. remembrances. I am sorry that I must decline my *own* proposition—and your kindness about the shooting at Bolgheri [103] as I have got a little world of business on my hands from England &c.—but I shall be more glad to see you again—than I could have been in any success in sporting. —— [name missing] is not much improved in practice—and still less in health—he has had bilious attacks partly owing I believe to waltzing with Mrs. —— [name missing] and partly to my screwing him up with blue wines (?)—(at Midnight—) after a foundation of Madeira & Claret at dinner one day —He hath left off wine—but still sticks to elderly gentlemens—— [word missing].

Excuse haste—& believe me ever & truly

Yours

Byron.[104]

The recipient of this letter and Byron were old friends and (by courtesy) distant relatives. As he has puzzled the biographers of Byron and Shelley,[105] let us identify him before we proceed further.

A Scotchman, a resident of Kelso, Roxburghshire, Hay had known Byron as early as 1809 (if Medwin, quoted below, can be trusted) and perhaps earlier. He was related, though distantly, to Byron's youthful love, Mary Duff,* and, through a connection with the Gordons, even more distantly to Byron himself. Byron had once purchased a pony from Hay at a pretty stiff price and in 1809 or thereabouts had made two unusual bets with Hay. Medwin gives us the circumstances of one of them:

> I called to mind [Byron told Medwin] a friend of mine, who had married a young, beautiful, and rich girl, and yet was miserable. He had strongly urged me against putting my neck in the same yoke: and to shew you how firmly I was resolved to attend to his advice, I betted Hay fifty guineas to one, that I should always remain single. Six years afterwards I sent him the money.[106]

The other bet (or really forfeit, for Byron collected his guinea at the time it was made, agreeing to forfeit fifty guineas if the event should prove him wrong) was "respecting the French being in possession of Spain," and in a letter of December 22, 1811, Hay wrote to Byron claiming the forfeit, which he asserted to be in the amount of 100 guineas.[107] Byron, who had made no memorandum

* It will be remembered that Byron, when about eight and living in Scotland, conceived a youthful passion for Mary Duff. She had dark brown hair and hazel eyes, and Byron's feelings for her defied even his own explanation. "I certainly had no sexual ideas for years afterwards," he confessed; "and yet my misery, my love for that girl were so violent, that I sometimes doubt if I have ever been really attached since" (Moore, p. 9).

Byron was sixteen when, one day, his mother announced to him the marriage of Mary Duff. Byron received the news in most unexpected fashion; he almost had convulsions, frightening his mother so much that she never dared mention the subject to him again. Byron himself was puzzled by his reaction: ". . . Hearing of her marriage . . . was like a thunderstroke—it nearly choked me—to the horror of my mother and the astonishment and almost incredulity of every body." Seventeen years after his childhood acquaintance with her he could not dismiss her from his mind and wondered whether she had the least remembrance of their acquaintance or of him. "I should be quite grieved to see *her now,*" he declared; "the reality, however beautiful, would destroy, or at least confuse, the features of the lovely Peri which then existed in her, and still lives in my imagination, at the distance of more than sixteen years" (Moore, p. 9).

of the forfeit, remembered it as £50 and on Kinnaird's advice suggested referring the matter to Martin Hawke,[108] with whom Byron had made a similar bet, and Scrope Davies,[109] who was supposed to have been present on the occasion. Hay agreed to the proposal, but as Hawke could not be found at the time, Hay let the matter drop for the time being. It was not revived until more than three years later. Then on January 18, 1815, Hay wrote to Byron: "Mr. Hawke shewed me yesterday a letter he had received from you announcing an event on which I beg leave to congratulate you & wish Lady Byron & yourself all the happiness the marriage state affords."[110] In the letter to Hawke Byron had acknowledged a forfeit of £50 to Hay; but Hay, after looking up his betting book and showing it to Hawke, with the forfeit duly entered, asserted as on the previous occasion that the amount was a hundred guineas and reminded Byron that the earlier forfeit was still unpaid. In the end, however, he agreed to accept Byron's view of the amounts involved; in a letter of January 23 he wrote: ". . . I regret that I should have made any mistake in the Spanish business, if it was a bet of an even fifty between you & Hawke I certainly can have no claim on you as what I find in my Book is by way of forfeit & not bet."[111] And then in conclusion:

> It is not quite correct to mention old acquaintances I believe to new married men however there is a Cousin of mine (M. Duff that was) whom I have had much conversation with about your Lordship She is a very nice woman I had not seen her from an infant till I came to this country about two years back & found her to be the same that you spoke of to me at Brighton I believe you know she married a Mr Colbourne——[112]

Byron, remitting the hundred guineas in payment of the two forfeits a few days later, took up the subject of Mary Duff:

> Pray tell me more, or as much as you like, of your cousin Mary. I have some idea her family is related to my late mother's. I believe I told you our story some years ago, and thank you for recollecting

it. It is now nearly—I know not how many years; I was 27 a few days ago, and I have never seen her since we were children, and *young* children too. But I never forgot her, and never can,—if it is no impropriety in a "married man," who may very possibly never see her again, and if he did, we are both out of harm's way. You would oblige me by presenting her with my best respects and all good wishes.[113] . . . It may seem ridiculous, but it is at any rate, I hope, not offensive to her nor her's in me to pretend to recollect anything about her at so early a period of both our lives, almost, if not *quite*, in our nurseries. But it was a pleasant dream which she must pardon me for remembering. Is she pretty still? I have the most perfect idea of her as a child; but Time, I suppose, has played the devil with us both. . . . [114]

Hay, in answering Byron's letter, wrote:

With regard to *our Cousin Mary* (as I shall make appear presently) I will reply to your questions as well as I can but although I have been returned to my Native Country between two & three years I am not sufficiently reclaimed to be able to trace relationships accurately. Your Mothers Family & the Gordons of ours are related but excepting in Scotland I suspect it would be difficult to point out exactly in what degree of affinity Mary & yourself stand to each other however in this country whenever we are at a loss we always say Cousin & thus Mary & your Humble servant both aspire to the honor of being one of your Lordships sixteenth Cousins & they will go in Scotland as far as 116th sometimes—

Mary is still handsome (tho she is breeding fast) & carries her age extremely well her disposition is sweetness itself but you would be dispointed in her appearance altogether at least I think so however I am not an admirer of my own Countrywomen they are greatly behind in my opinion their neighbours on both sides the water—Mary has been lately with her Husband in Portugal & I know not if they are returned to this Country there can be no impropriety in my making known your respectful good wishes to her & when I have an opportunity I will do so—if you like to send me a copy of your last Poem & write with the authors respectful Compts to Mrs. Colbourne I am sure it will be recieved most gratefully & read with delight I will deliver it at the same time I do your other commission & if you have more than one copy by you don't forget me I shall receive it as a mark of your friendship & esteem it accordingly.[115]

This, then, was the John Hay who came to Pisa in March, 1822, and joined briefly the activities of the Pisan circle. He was a link with the old halcyon days when Byron's star was at its zenith, and Byron made him welcome. "There is no pleasure in life equal to that of meeting an old friend," Byron remarked later to Medwin. "You know how glad I was to see Hay." [116] But neither Byron nor Hay could know, when he arrived, that Misfortune lay in wait for him on a dusty country road outside the Porta alle Piagge on a Sunday afternoon.

TITA

From a drawing by Daniel Maclise, R.A.

CHAPTER 6

The Affair with the Dragoon: the Afternoon of March 24, 1822

On the Sunday afternoon of March 24, Byron, Shelley, Trelawny, Pietro Gamba, and the visitor, Captain Hay, set off for the customary afternoon's ride and pistol practice. Williams, absorbed in his tragedy, did not join them, and Medwin had left Pisa two weeks earlier. As usual, Byron rode in his carriage to the city gate, where he was met by his courier, Giuseppe Strauss,[1] with horses, and the servant Tita took the carriage back. The direction taken by the riders was the familiar one to the *podere*, where they dismounted for pistol-shooting practice. There is no record of who shot well in the presence of Captain Hay that afternoon, for before the day was over the journal keepers had something of greater importance to record.

Between five and six o'clock the horsemen were cantering back toward Pisa along the road to the Piagge gate, at the eastern end of the town. Up ahead of them, in Teresa's small carriage, were Mary and Teresa, who had come out for a drive an hour later than Byron and his friends and had taken the road to Cisanello in the hope of seeing their cavaliers. The carriage was driven by Byron's coachman, Vincenzo Papi, and Teresa's servant Antonio Maluccelli[2] was behind it. Half a mile from the town Byron and his company met Taaffe, who had not accompanied them but had gone out for some "equestrian diversions" (as he expressed it) with his Turkish friend Mehemet Effendi.[3] His horse being heated, Taaffe allowed his friend to return alone and was continuing on, walking his horse "slowly and alone, not to bring him back into the stable in that agitated state and dreadful perspiration" when he encountered Byron and his companions. After an exchange of greetings, Taaffe turned his horse and accompanied them, the group proceeding at a walk.[4]

The riders now fell into three unequal lines: in the front line were Taaffe (riding on Byron's left, between him and the ditch), Byron, and (on Byron's right) Shelley and Trelawny. Hay and Gamba formed a second line, and the courier, Strauss, brought up the rear. So engrossed were Byron and Taaffe in conversation that they did not observe a rider in a hurry who had turned in from a side road and was rapidly overtaking them about a quarter of a mile outside the Piagge gate. Though they did not learn his name until later, they were to have occasion to remember it well: he was Stefani Masi, a sergeant-major in the Tuscan Royal Light Horse, who had been dining with friends in the country and now had to get into the city in time to answer roll call. The four riders in the front line occupied nearly all of the road, and they gave no sign of drawing aside to let Masi pass. Measuring nicely the distance between Taaffe and the ditch, Masi did not check his horse but galloped through without warning, just missing the ditch and just brushing or seeming to brush Taaffe in passing.[5] Taaffe's horse, startled by the unexpected appearance of horse and rider at such close quarters, reared, bumped Byron's horse, and plunged out of control. Masi's sudden dash past them all caused the horses of the other riders to jump also, but Taaffe's, being nearest, was naturally the worst frightened.

"Have you ever seen the like of that?" cried Taaffe to Byron in great agitation.

Byron did not answer, but putting spurs to his horse, he started in pursuit of the dragoon. As the dragoon was well mounted, well dressed (with a good deal of gold braid and epaulettes), and well armed, Byron thought him an officer and a gentleman and was pursuing him for the purpose of calling him to account for his rudeness. Shelley and Trelawny, guessing from Taaffe's agitated expression and the behaviour of his horse that the man had insulted him, followed Byron's example and joined in the pursuit. Instead of quieting, Taaffe's horse (the beautiful spirited one that Byron admired) became the wilder as the others galloped away. Taaffe consequently had to give his full attention to the management of his horse; and though he succeeded in keeping his seat, his hat fell to the ground. When he had brought his horse under control, he addressed with an embarrassed smile one of two old female peasants who were passing and complaining of the galloping horses:

"As you see, good woman, I at least restrain my horse and it is out of consideration for you; therefore I pray you to give me my hat."

The woman obligingly retrieved Taaffe's hat and handed it to him covered with dust. Conscious of his reputation as a sorry horseman—a reputation that he regarded as most unjust—and half-fearful that he was the victim of some trick inspired by Byron to get the laugh on him, he spent a few minutes in carefully brushing the dust from his hat lest Byron think that he had been thrown from his horse. When he looked up again, a turn in the road had hidden his companions from view, but according to his own testimony he did not hasten to join them.

Shelley's and Trelawny's horses were fleeter than Byron's, and they soon passed him in pursuit of the dragoon. All of the riders, pursued and pursuing, passed the carriage with Mary and Teresa, who had to put up the glasses in order to keep out the swirl of dust. Seeing that he was pursued, Masi slowed his horse and permitted himself to be overtaken about thirty paces short of the city gate. Shelley, whose almost white horse was the swiftest, was the first to come up with the dragoon and crossed in front of him, blocking his way.

"What do you want of me?" asked Masi.

As Trelawny, who was just behind Shelley, did not speak Italian, Shelley replied civilly: "Please explain what you mean by your conduct."

According to Masi's testimony, he replied that the road was free and that he would pass over it at will; according to Shelley he answered only with curses and insults. Whatever his words, there was no doubt about the rudeness of his manner, which Shelley accounted for on the score of drunkenness, but Trelawny was probably more accurate in describing Masi as not drunk but heated by wine.

Byron, followed by Pietro Gamba, Hay, and the courier, now came up, and as the group surrounded the dragoon, the man placed his hand on his sabre threateningly.

"Why have you insulted us in this manner?" demanded Byron.

The dragoon's answer, Byron testified, was another string of insults in Italian and French.

"This man is very insolent," said Byron to Trelawny.

At the Piagge gate were a number of loiterers, whose attention was attracted by the altercation. Among them was an artilleryman named Tommaso di Marco, who was on leave from Pietra Santa and who now strolled up to the scene of the argument. Others of the loungers drifted nearer and were in time to hear a demand by one of the Englishmen for Masi's name in order that he might be called to account on the following day. Still under the impression that Masi was an officer, Byron reached into his saddle bag, got a card, and handed it to di Marco to deliver to Masi.

"Give us your card," someone insisted.

"I have no card, but my name is Masi," Masi replied, according to his own testimony, "and I am ready to fight you all, one at a time." [6]

Trelawny also gave di Marco a card to pass on to Masi, and Shelley, who had no card, told Masi his name, which Masi "without saying a word accepted . . . with a still more insulting attitude." Taaffe, approaching in time to see from a distance the passing of the cards, played an inconspicuous part in what followed. Speaking in French, Trelawny challenged Masi to fight on the following day, and Byron likewise issued a challenge—both of which they understood to be accepted. Hay seems to have been the only person present who was not under the delusion that Masi was an officer.

"Let him go; he isn't an officer," he told his companions.

Masi testified later that during the course of this argument he was shoved about by the English group with their hands, and one of them—almost certainly Pietro Gamba, though Masi thought it was the courier Strauss—struck him smartly on the chest with a riding whip, at the same time calling him "Ignorante."

Masi was enraged. "You are all madmen," he cried; "you are not sane." He wheeled his horse and rode off toward the gate, followed by Byron and his companions and di Marco.

"Why don't you arrest them?" di Marco called out, adding abusive language. "Command us to arrest them!"

Reaching the gate, Masi turned back toward Byron and his companions. "If I liked," he exclaimed, "I could draw my sabre and cut you all to pieces, but as it is, I only arrest you," and he called out in a loud voice to the guards, "Arrest them! Arrest them all!"

"Arrest us indeed!" laughed Byron scornfully. "Let us ride on," he added to Pietro Gamba and Trelawny, who were nearest him; and spurring his horse forward, he rode through the gate, followed by Gamba. Byron thought that one of the armed foot-soldiers attempted to block his way, and indeed di Marco may have done so, but it is clear from subsequent testimony that the guard at the gate did not respond to Masi's order.

Trelawny, who was close behind Gamba, found his way blocked by Masi, who shook his fist in Trelawny's face and, when Trelawny tried to pass him, drew his sabre. In an account written next day Trelawny described what happened next:

> Two dismounted men in soldiers habits with swords came to his assistance one seased [seized] on my horse rein at this moment the Dragoon made a violent blow at me with his sword—I put out my arm to arrest his when the foot soldier made a cut at me—I forced my horse on through the gates and escaped being wounded although both the swords struck me.[7]

One of the foot-soldiers was certainly di Marco, and whether or not there was actually a second is disputed in the testimony. But Shelley thought there were two and adds the detail that one of them (di Marco) caught Trelawny's bridle and struck Trelawny about the legs with the flat of his sabre.

Masi had taken up a position in front of the toll office, just under the gate, from which he struck out savagely to left and right, first at Trelawny and then at Shelley, Hay, and the courier.

"Do you have any pistols?" Trelawny yelled to Shelley.

Feeling in his saddle bags, Shelley found them empty. Seeing Masi attacking Trelawny, he attempted to come between the two, only to have Masi turn on him and slash furiously at him with his sabre. Hay, who carried a light walking stick, tried to parry the blow, which cut his cane in two. The weapon was deflected, but Shelley was struck on the back of the head, not with the blade but with the hilt of the sabre, and knocked from his horse to the ground, where he lay senseless for some minutes. Masi now aimed a blow at Hay, and this time the sabre, though deflected by striking the gate first, slashed through Hay's hat and cut him across the nose, from which blood flowed freely. The courier, whom Masi attacked next, received a staggering blow in the chest with the hilt of the sabre which caused him to spit blood for weeks thereafter; and di Marco joined in, striking the courier about the thighs and the groin with the flat of his sabre.

Only the fact that the action was at such close quarters saved both Shelley and Hay. "If my head was not chopped off or rather cloven in two," Hay told Taaffe later, "it was from my being too near for the weapon to have its swing; and so it struck me close to the hilt." [8]

In the carriage behind, Mary and Teresa were bewildered and horrified witnesses of the swift pursuit, the argument that they could not hear, and the cutting and slashing that felled Shelley and wounded Hay. Teresa's active imagination even conjured up a shot from a gun that was never fired, and later she swore positively that she saw the flash from it. "I have no words," she testified eloquently, "in which I can express the fear with which I was overwhelmed."

When Shelley recovered his senses, he was sick at his stomach and had to vomit. His head hurt violently, but he succeeded in remounting his horse and riding on through the gate unmolested. He now joined Trelawny, who had already got through, and the two started into the town, followed by the carriage, when they discovered that Hay was missing.

Taaffe had seen Masi's lifted sabre and Shelley's rearing white horse regularly charging the dragoon as he slashed about him; but so quickly did the action occur —or so slowly did Taaffe ride—that he came up just as Masi was sheathing his sword. Seizing Masi by the arm and shaking him roughly,[9] he said: "Aren't you ashamed of having made such use of a sabre against unarmed people?" And thinking he recognized Masi, he added, "It seems to me that I have seen you before, and I took you for a man of honour. I know your captain, and you would be severely punished if I reported what you have done."

Masi did not reply, but as he rode off toward town, Taaffe thought that he had cooled off and that the affair had ended. Taaffe remained behind to address the guard and the numerous bystanders, whom he admonished to witness that arms had been used against unarmed individuals and to whom he declared that he would swear that the holsters of the Englishmen contained only unloaded pistols. Meanwhile Masi had gone only a short distance before he met Trelawny and Shelley returning to search for Captain Hay. Trelawny was in advance, for Shelley had stopped for a moment upon meeting Teresa and Mary in the carriage.

"*Sta tranquile*," Shelley said to Teresa, seeing the terror written in her face. But it was beyond Teresa's power to calm herself.

Riding up to Trelawny, Masi shook his fist in Trelawny's face and began his abuse all over again. "I have knocked down two of your companions," he said in French, making a threatening gesture as if to draw his sabre. "Are you satisfied? You seem to me from your moustaches to be an officer."

"We are not satisfied," replied Trelawny. "I have given you my card, and tomorrow I expect satisfaction."

To this Masi assented or seemed to Trelawny to assent, but nevertheless continued making insulting gestures with his hands to his face and urging his horse nearer Trelawny. But when Shelley came alongside and some of the crowd at the gate began to shift over to the new scene of action, Masi put an end to matters by riding off in the direction of the Lung' Arno.

Shelley and Trelawny, with the departure of Masi, once more started back to look for Hay. They found him, dismounted and bleeding profusely, just outside the gate. Faint from shock and loss of blood, he was unable to proceed unaided; but with the assistance of his two friends he was presently able to make his way slowly toward the Palazzo Lanfranchi.

Once through the gate, Byron had directed Pietro

Gamba to gallop ahead to the Palazzo Lanfranchi and order Lega to go at once to the police and report the altercation. Riding on ahead of Byron, Pietro had found his father, Count Ruggero Gamba, Lega Zambelli, and the Gambas' agent or clerk, Giacomo Batuzzi, at the entrance of the palace and had despatched Lega on his mission.

Byron's doorman Tita, who is not mentioned as being at his post when Pietro Gamba arrived, testified that he first heard of the danger to his patron from a passer-by. If this is true, it suggests that he had wandered away from the Palazzo Lanfranchi, perhaps to exchange a few words with a servant from a neighbouring palace. The news was confirmed a moment later with the approach of the courier, Strauss, at a full gallop.

"Tita, Tita! Hurry, hurry!" Matteo Giuntini, keeper of a fruit-stand beside the Palazzo Lanfranchi, heard Strauss call out.

Without further explanation Strauss ran up the steps and into the palace, while Tita, who saw Byron riding up the Lung' Arno, remained to attend his patron. Numerous witnesses later testified that Byron dismounted from his horse in front of his palace; equally numerous witnesses testified that he did not. Byron testified that he did not dismount; Pietro Gamba testified that he did dismount, adding that he removed the empty pistols from his saddle bags. In response to Byron's question, various ones assured him that Lega had gone at once to the police.

Strauss now came down the steps with a black sword-stick, which Byron took and then turned his horse back in the direction of the Porta alle Piagge to look for his companions. Strauss remounted and followed him. Tita, hurrying inside the palace, caught up a pair of cavalryman's sabres and, with one slung over his shoulder and the other in his hand, again hastened outside. So great was his hurry that he did not observe the arrival of the carriage with Mary and Teresa as he ran down the steps and started after his master. Though the sun had set and darkness was coming on, Tita, with his great black beard and his distinct livery, was a conspicuous figure in what followed.

Byron, meanwhile, had gone only a short distance before he saw Masi opposite the Church of St. Matthew coming up the Lung' Arno. At the sight of Byron, Masi put his hand on his sabre.

Giuseppe Bisordi, a key witness in the subsequent investigation, heard Byron say: "Don't draw," and heard Masi's reply, "I shall not draw, but I want satisfaction." But Masi himself testified that he said: "Are you content now that I have beaten you all?"

"No," answered Byron; "I must know your name and rank, that I may require satisfaction of you." [10] Williams, though not an eye-witness, is probably accurate in reporting that as Byron said this, he half-drew his sword-stick to show that he was armed; for Masi, instead of answering Byron immediately, put out his hand and caught hold of Byron's, the two continuing to ride slowly on toward the Palazzo Lanfranchi in this fashion. His purpose in taking Byron's hand, Masi testified, was to prevent Byron's drawing of the sword-stick.

"My name is Masi," he said, "and I am a sergeant-major."

"We shall see each other tomorrow," said Byron.

The dragoon now sharpened his pace, still holding on to Byron's hand. At this moment Tita, with his two sabres, came running up. With his right hand he caught hold of Masi's bridle, pushing Masi away from Byron and placing himself between them, while with the left he offered Byron a sabre. Byron refused the sabre and commanded Tita to release the bridle; and as Tita obeyed, the dragoon put spurs to his horse and rode swiftly off through a large crowd that was collecting.

The Palazzo Lanfranchi was only some thirty paces or so ahead of him, and conscious of possible danger as he approached it, Masi kept to the left or river side of the street. Suddenly he heard a voice cry out "No, no!" and looking up, he saw a man on the steps of the Lanfranchi Palace pointing a pistol at him. Masi testified that the man was dressed in Byron's livery, but as Pietro Gamba was also seen on the steps of the palace armed with pistols, it is possible that the person Masi saw was he.

Matteo Giuntini, who had been an interested spectator of all that had happened up to this point, had a grandstand seat for the next episode, but unfortunately the crowd now swarmed about his fruit-stand and he found himself so busy guarding his merchandise that he missed the climax of the action. Even so some of his fruit was stolen.

Masi, intent only on getting away from danger, spurred his horse hard and managed to get past the Palazzo Lanfranchi without being fired upon. But he had failed to see a second figure lurking on the steps of the palace with a long lance in its hand; and as he drew abreast of the palace, this figure ran out and from a position slightly behind Masi thrust violently at him with the lance. Even as his assailant launched himself at him Masi did not see him.

"I hit him! I hit him!" he heard a voice cry out and in the same split-second realized that he had been struck in the right side. He reeled in the saddle for an instant; then, recovering himself, he rode on. A little way down the street his casque fell off and then his *berretta*, freeing his mass of red hair to stream in the wind. The blood drained from his face, his strength ebbed away, and with an awful cry, "Alas, I am killed!" he pitched from his saddle into the street in front of a café. Though severely wounded, as it turned out, he was nevertheless able to stagger to his feet, walk through the café, and reach the house of a jeweller named Barletti, in the Via dei Mercanti, from which the Misericordia later carried him on a litter to the hospital.

Masi's assailant, his bloody work done, was in no hurry to escape from the scene. Ranieri Figi testified that he lingered on the steps of the palace and that when others would have pursued Masi he said, "I beg of you, let him go." Someone else, speaking in a foreign accent, said, "That's enough," and then the two went into the palace together.

Byron, who was some distance away from the point of the attack—Dr. James Crawford, a Scottish physician who chanced to be looking out of a window upon the scene below, says forty paces, Byron says about thirty—swore that he did not see the attack. Because of the fading light and the intervening crowd it is probable that he was telling the truth. "I could observe," he testified later, "that his casque fell off, a thing that surprised me greatly as I was unable to conceive the reason why, [but] the man went on." Byron, followed by Tita, now came up to the palace steps, and he ordered the casque and *berretta* to be picked up and taken inside the palace for future evidence if needed. A peasant who had picked up the *berretta* found himself seized roughly by Tita, who attempted to take it from him by force. The peasant resisted, and in the ensuing struggle the *berretta* was torn. Tita got most of it, but the peasant retained a scrap, which he later deposited with the Tribunal.

"Quick, quick, into the house," Matteo Giuntini heard Byron say, and Byron, Tita, and others entered the house.

When Mary and Teresa, terrorized by what they had seen, arrived at the Palazzo Lanfranchi, Antonio Maluccelli, who had been riding behind the carriage, opened the carriage door, put down the steps for them, and offered them his arm. Both of the ladies, he observed, had been weeping. Tita was just leaving the palace as they drove up, but as he did not see them, it remained for Gaetano Forestieri, Byron's Ravennese cook,[11] to open the palace door for them. When he had done so, Teresa ran quickly up the stairs, crying out, "Oh God! Oh God!" Her father followed her, but Mary remained behind to give an order to Antonio.

"Go to Mr. Williams," she directed—"you know where he is—and tell him he can help his friends. Tell him what has happened." Then she entered the palace, where she found Pietro Gamba in the drawing-room. She remained first to talk with him; then she went to try to calm the hysterical Teresa, for whom Forestieri had already fetched a glass of water from his master's table.

She was thus occupied when Byron entered, followed a few minutes later by Shelley and Trelawny, supporting the bleeding Hay, who, of course, instantly became the centre of attention. Byron ordered Forestieri to bring a basin of water and a flask of vinegar, and Hay, while awaiting Forestieri's return, asked Byron what he thought of the wound and whether or not he thought it would leave a disfiguring scar.

Taaffe, the next arrival, found a large crowd gathered about the entrance to the palace, while inside all was confusion. Hay was washing his wound, and everyone was talking at once. The talk was all of the encounter at the city gate, the insolence of the dragoon, and Hay's wound. For, surprisingly—unless every one of the group lied—word of the wounding of Masi had not yet reached them. Mary stated positively in her testimony that at first none of the gentlemen knew of the wounding of Masi. This would seem to be the fact, since there would have been little point in lying about the time when the news reached them. Shelley says that after about an hour, "someone came in, I do not remember who, and said that the dragoon had been wounded." Trelawny and Taaffe both testified that they first heard the news two hours after they assembled at the Palazzo Lanfranchi. As Byron first heard the story, it was so fantastic as to be incredible. "I remember having heard from the adjutant of Mr. Foscarini [a surgeon who was called to attend Teresa] that this man had been wounded," Byron testified at the investigation, "and he stated with a pistol—that is what he said, and added, that the wound was in the shoulder, and I answered that it seemed impossible since none of us had had loaded pistols." Taaffe picked up the story of Masi's wounding as he left the Palazzo Lanfranchi to wait on Governor Viviani and make a report of what had happened. On the way he encountered someone going to inform Captain Bini, the governor's adjutant, and learned the story from him.

Williams, who with Jane had been engaged to dine with the Shelleys that evening, had gone up to the Shelleys' apartment around six o'clock and had found nobody at home. Familiar with the informality of the Shelleys' housekeeping, they thought nothing amiss at first and sat down to await the return of their host and hostess; but presently they became concerned over the growing lateness of the hour. After a considerable wait on their part, Trelawny arrived to tell them what had happened. He had just finished his story when the rest of the group entered. It had been decided to bring Teresa to the Shelleys' apartment because of its proximity to the surgeon Vaccà, who was sent for to attend Teresa. As Williams describes the scene:

> Trelawny had finished his story when Lord B. came in—the Countess fainting on his arm—S. sick from the blow—Lord B. and the young Count foaming with rage—Mrs. S. looking philosophically upon this interesting scene—and Jane and I wondering what the Devil was to come next.[12]

Vaccà, who may have been attending Masi at the time, could not be found, but a surgeon named Foscarini came and looked at Teresa, who had gone into convulsions. He gave it as his opinion that she should be bled and advised that she be taken to her own house. Byron's coachman, Papi, drove her home, escorted by Byron and

Mary; and when the surgeon came, Byron left Mary with her and returned to the Palazzo Lanfranchi.

At the Governor's palace Taaffe found the Governor indisposed, but he made a full report to Captain Bini, "concealing nothing of what had happened to the dragoon two hours earlier." When a little later he returned to Byron's palace with a long face to say that he had heard that Masi could not live out the night, the effect of the announcement upon the group was consternation. Byron now requested Pietro Gamba, Hay—his wound still not completely stanched—and Shelley to go to the Governor's palace and make a report of what had happened. Lega, whose earlier mission had been unsuccessful as he had been unable to find any of the proper authorities, was ordered to accompany them. Just why Byron himself and Trelawny did not go is not clear. "All now again saley'd forth," records Edward Williams—"to be the first to accuse, and according to Italian policy not wait to be accused—All again return mutually recriminated and recriminating."

It was not until Shelley, Hay, and Gamba had made a report to Captain Bini, who promised to inform the proper authorities, that Hay was seen by Dr. John Todd, an English physician residing in Pisa whom Hay had known earlier, and his wound stanched with cold water and sticking plaster. It was probably upon Lega's return from the Governor's palace also that Byron ordered him to go to Foscarini, with the request that Foscarini take care of Masi at Byron's expense.

By nine o'clock the earliest of the fantastic rumours of the affray that were to spread over Pisa had made its appearance:

> The report already in circulation about Pisa [writes Williams] is that a party of peasants having risen in insurrection made an attack upon the guard headed by some Englishmen—that the guard maintained their ground manfully against an awful number of the armed insurgents—that they were at length defeated—one

Englishman whose name was Trelawny left dead at the gate, and Lord B. mortally wounded, who is now telling me the tale—and I drinking brandy and water by his side— [13]

At eleven o'clock the assembly at the Palazzo Lanfranchi, having refought the battle of the Piagge gate with the strategy of hindsight and deliberation, dispersed, exhausted, to their several homes.[14]

CHAPTER 7

Reverberations of the Dragoon Affair

NEXT morning Taaffe, the first of the English group to be out and about, made inquiries into the wounded dragoon's condition and then wrote encouraging reports —too encouraging as it turned out—to Hay and Byron. The note to Hay was naturally solicitous about Hay's own condition:

Monday morning March 25
Casa Mostardi, Lung' Arno

I hope you are better this morning, my dear Sir. As for the scoundrel himself, his wound is a mere flesh scratch; notwithstanding all the rumours. That being the case, we ought still to have him, if possible, punished. Your cuts [*some words missing*] I hope not. Pray let me know how you have passed the night.

I am dear Sir
Yours truly
J. Taaffe Junr. [1]

To Byron he wrote:

Monday morning [March 25]

My dear Lord,

Mountains (as usual) are delivered of mice. The Nun who aided to dress the wound last night and this morning lets me know it is a mere trifle—not more than an inch deep and that there is *only one wound*. That it were in a dangerous place if deeper; but as it is so shallow, and the man fat, it's a slight flesh wound. The report of the guard last night appears to have been not incorrect; and if the fellow had not been sent to the hospital there was enough to have had him severely chastised. There seems no ground for further anxiety on our part; except it be to see to have the rascal punished otherwise, if this turn out such a mere scratch.

I have the honor to be
Your's truly
J. Taaffe, Junr. [2]

The physicians who examined Masi—Drs. di Giuseppe of the Santa Chiara Hospital, Foscarini, and Vaccà—found a shallow, irregular wound between the third and fourth ribs, evidently made by a steel implement thrust upward and from the back, missing the liver. As Masi passed a calm night, they were unduly encouraged; hence Taaffe's report. But toward the end of the following morning, he grew alarmingly worse, exhibiting symptoms that caused the physicians to fear that a lesion had been made in the liver. During the course of the morning Dr. Todd was sent by Byron to see Masi, who, however, objected to being seen by him.[3]

By twelve o'clock, when Shelley called on Williams, it was known that Taaffe's hopeful report was inaccurate; the dragoon was reported much worse. At two o'clock when Williams called on Byron, he heard that extreme unction had been administered to the dragoon, and at four o'clock the man was reported to be dying. The affair had taken on a grave aspect indeed.

The police having asked for a statement about the affray from the English group, Byron drew up an individual report and requested the various principals in the affair to do likewise; then a joint report, signed by all of the English except Taaffe, who may have demurred on the score that he had not originally been one of the group or that he had not been a participant in the action at the gate, was drawn up. Nevertheless, he agreed to write an individual statement and place it in Byron's hands. As might be expected, there was a good deal of collaboration in the preparation of the reports.

Though Captain Hay was better and Teresa Guiccioli had recovered her self-possession, they were almost forgotten in the atmosphere to which the multitude of wild tales and fantastic rumours contributed. "A report is now abroad that Taaffe is the assassin," writes Williams, "and is now confined in Lord B's house guarded by bull-dogs, &c., to avoid the Police—This he overheard himself

ignoriamo come, e da chi, poichè ognuno di noi tro=
vavasi o in Casa, o in dietro. Solamente fù recato in Casa
di Milord il Boné di questo Sergente.
È da notare innoltre, che il Capitano Hay si trova in Ca=
sa obbligato per la ferita ricevuta, e che il Corriere ha
sputato sangue per i Colpi avuti nel Petto, come si può
assicurare per relazione di Chirurghi. Questo è il Rapporto
preciso di ciò, che è passato fra noi, e il Sergente Mag=
giore Masi coi soldati &:-
In fede di che noi sottoscritti compromoviamo. &.

Noel Byron

Edwd. J. Trelawny

Percy B. Shelley

John Hay Captn.
H.M.S.

DEPOSITION TO THE POLICE AT PISA

Signed by Byron, Trelawny, Shelley and Hay

while walking down the Lung Arno—S[helley] and T[relawny] think it necessary to go armed. A skaite strap is therefore substituted for a pistol belt and my pistols so slung to T[relawny]'s waist."[4] Another report was that Byron and all his servants, with four English gentlemen, were captured in the Palazzo Lanfranchi and that forty brace of pistols and numerous stilettos were taken with them.[5] Captain Hay heard that Williams was the Englishman wounded, that his nose had been cut off, and that Byron and Williams had fled from Pisa with as many horses as could be put to Byron's carriage.[6] These and other garbled or exaggerated stories no doubt increased the nervous tension within the town, already such that Shelley received a note from a lady, probably Mrs. Beauclerk, warning him not to venture near her house after dark because friends of Masi were on the watch for him, although they did not regard him as most to blame.[7]

At 4:30 on the day following the incident the usual riding party mounted and rode forth according to their custom—only this time well armed with sword-sticks and pistols. A considerable crowd assembled about the Lanfranchi to see them dismount, and some of the crowd removed their hats respectfully. According to Torelli, Byron turned to young Prince Schubalof and remarked, "Since yesterday the Pisans have become more respectful," a speech which, whether made or not, was communicated to the police.

At the Palazzo Lanfranchi a message from Hay awaited Byron, to which he immediately sat down and wrote the following answer:

March 25th 1822

My dear Hay

We are just returned from riding—well armed of course—as the wounded man was a favourite bully of the students and soldiers. —No interruption has yet been experienced.—I am sorry for the fellow—& should have been wretched but for the gross and murderous provocation he had given—but people are not to be cut down unarmed without some retaliation.—He is said to be in danger but with what truth in this country of fiction it is not easy to discover—I trust that you will only suffer a temporary inconvenience from this assassination.—What are the books you want—I did not know that you were visible or I should have called upon you[.]

Yours truly
N. B.[8]

Tuesday was another day of tension, the anxiety of the members of the Pisan circle betrayed by an unusual amount of visiting among themselves. Williams's journal records most of the activity:

Jane's music master comes and informs us that the report is the dragoon is better; but raves like a mad man against the English—

11 o'clk. Called on S. previous to going to Capt. Hay's—met there Vacca who had just quitted his patient the Dragoon—V. thinks him better but not out of danger—The man's story is that he was held by one of Lord B's servants while the other stabbed him—and that he should not have drawn his sword had he not been horsewhipped by some one of the party—this was strongly denied by us to V who seems to view the thing in a most unfavourable light—and declares that in any court of justice he could swear conscientiously that the wound was given with a stiletto having three sides like a bayonet—

Called on Captain Hay with S. Found him doing well but his face is much cut and bruised—On our mentioning to him what we considered a falsehood in the dragoon's having said he was struck, Hay confirmed the fact by saying the young Count Gamba cut him with his whip as he passed—The affair consequently takes a serious turn in the man's favour.

3 o'clock. Called on Lord B. The police had only proceeded so far as to require the evidence of his courier—Suspicion as to the person who really stabbed the dragoon much excited—Nothing else new—They ride as usual.

7 o'clock. The wound neither better nor worse—Trelawny dined with us & Mary passed the evening— [9]

Taaffe, who is missing from all the accounts of this day, was possibly engaged in working on his statement during the course of it. The following cryptic note, written to him by Byron, may have had something to do with his statement but more probably relates to the condition of the dragoon.

March 26th 1822.

Dear Taaffe/

I write a word of haste in answer let me know the truth as soon as possible—

Yrs truly
N. B.[10]

On Wednesday the dragoon was reported to be better, and hopes for his recovery were entertained. "It is S's opinion that on recovery this man will demand the *satisfaction of a gentleman*—and some of the *most respectable Italians* think that it ought not to be refused to him," writes Williams.[11] Later reports in the day were that the dragoon's condition remained the same. As Williams and Shelley went to the post, they encountered Pietro Gamba, who in some manner had procured Dr. Crawford's deposition, which he handed over to Byron.[12] Shelley and Williams had a midday sail up the Arno and then at four o'clock called on Byron.

The police moved so slowly in the affair that Masi's assailant might easily have left Pisa and gone into hiding had he wished. Two days after the wounding they had done no more than require statements of the English group and examine Byron's courier, Strauss, who provided one of the highlights of what developed into a pretty dull routine. Asked if he had struck the dragoon, he replied forthrightly, "No, but if I had had a pistol I should have shot him." As, however, Strauss had been seen, mounted and hovering about Byron during the second encounter with Masi, he was adjudged innocent and released.

On Wednesday the police made two more arrests—those of Byron's coachman, Vincenzo Papi, and the doorman, Tita. The lieutenant himself went to Byron's palace and made the arrest, apparently an unusual procedure. "They were examined by Coadiutore Carloni before the

Auditor, whose presence indicates a capital offence," reports Torelli, "and both were shut up in secret confinement."

The arrest of Tita was perhaps to be expected. A familiar figure about Pisa, he was widely hated for his proud and arrogant bearing. According to popular legend he had slain two in his native Venice, and it was well known that during the preceding Carnival he had driven away the police officer posted near the Palazzo Lanfranchi and that a warning transmitted to him by Lega Zambelli made no perceptible change in his ways. Although the testimony of both Byron and Masi that Tita was with Byron some thirty paces or more from the point of the wounding would eventually establish his innocence, there was no lack of witnesses willing to come forward and swear that he was Masi's assailant. His unpopularity and his great beard and ferocious appearance were enough to warrant his arrest; but when it was discovered that he had come to the examination armed with a brace of short English pistols and a stiletto more than a foot long, his guilt was at first regarded as certain.

Other witnesses were found who cast suspicion on Vincenzo Papi[13] as the assailant. Giuseppe Bisordi, for example, deposed that the coachman had come out of the palace, armed with a sabre slung across his shoulder and a lance with a triangular steel head in his hand, just prior to the wounding of Masi. The evidence of Domenico Landrini, who saw on the steps of the Palazzo Lanfranchi a servant in the livery of Lord Byron armed with a weapon the length of a garden implement, likewise pointed to Papi. Pietro Gabrielli, who had returned from the Baths of Pisa just after the wounding, told Maluccelli that he had heard Papi spoken of as the wounder and so informed the Court. As the examination of Papi went on until late Wednesday night, he was locked up until Bisordi and Landrini could be brought forward to identify him.

Shelley, Trelawny, and Williams learned of the arrest

of the two servants when they called on Byron during the course of the evening. They found Byron engaged in writing a letter about the affray with the dragoon to the British chargé d'affaires at Florence. A manuscript note in Trelawny's hand relating to the occasion is both illuminating and amusing:

Lord Byron had occasion to write a letter to Mr. Dawkins secretary of Legation at Florence[.]

he asked me if he was an Honble & how he was to be addressed —I said—'a Monsieur—Monsieur Dawkins Secretary of Legation'—No no said Byron that wont do—"dress—and address is everything"—he then concluded his letter—with Honour to be & very Humble obedient &c &c &c & addressed it to his Excellency —the Honble &c &c and smiling observed—"with as little a web as this—will I ensnare as great a fly as Cassio." [14]—I must here remark—that there can be no greater proof of Byron's admiration of Shakespeare than his *involuntary* habit of quoting him continually—[15]

The letter which Byron wrote to Dawkins was as follows:

Pisa, 27 March 1822.

Sir

I take the liberty of transmitting to you the statements as delivered to the Police of an extraordinary affair which occurred here on Sunday last. This will not, it is to be hoped, be considered an intrusion, as several British subjects have been insulted and some wounded on the occasion, besides being arrested at the Gate of the city without proper authority or reasonable cause.

With regard to the subsequent immediate occurrence of the aggressor's wound, there is little that I can add, to the enclosed statements. The testimony of an impartial eye-witness, Dr Crawford, with whom I had not the Honor of a personal acquaintance, will inform you as much as I know myself.

It is proper to add that I conceived the Man to have been an *officer* as he was well dressed, with scaled Epaulettes, and not ill-mounted; and *not* a Serjeant Major (the son of a washerwoman, it is said) as he turns out to be.

When I accosted him a second time, on the Lungharno, he called out to me with a menacing gesture—"Are you content?" I, (still ignorant of what had passed under the Gate-way, having ridden through the Guard to order my steward to go to the Police) answered "No; I want your name and address." He then held out his hand, which I took, not understanding whether he intended it as a pledge of his hostility or of his repentance, at the same time stating his name.

The rest of the facts appear to have been as within stated, as far as my knowledge goes—Two of my servants (both Italians) are detained on suspicion of having wounded him. Of this I know no more than the enclosed papers vouch; and can only say that, notwithstanding the atrocious aggression (of the particulars of which I was at the moment ignorant) the act was as completely disapproved of by me as it was totally unauthorized either directly or indirectly. . . .

I have the Honor, &c.,
Signed/ Noel Byron—[16]

With the letter to Dawkins, Byron enclosed copies of the statements made by the various members of the Pisan circle and by Dr. Crawford. He also enclosed Taaffe's letter of March 25 (*supra*, p. 107), across the top of which he wrote, "It is proper to observe that the following note proved incorrect the man being *dangerously* wounded (and still said to being so) but this does not alter his previous behaviour. N.B."

None of the English group felt that Taaffe had acquitted himself well in the affair, though as might be expected it was Mary who blamed him most.

You have no notion what a ridiculous figure Taaffe cut in all this [she wrote to Mrs. Gisborne]—he kept far behind during the danger, but the next day he wished to take all the honour to himself, vowed that all Pisa talked of him alone, and coming to Lord Byron said, "My Lord, if you do not dare ride out today, I will alone." [17] But the next day he again changed, he was afraid of being turned out of Tuscany, or of being obliged to fight with one of the officers of the sergeant's regiment, of neither of which things there was the slightest danger, so he wrote a declaration to the Governor to say that he had nothing to do with it; so embroiling himself with Lord Byron, he got between Scylla and Charybdis, from which he has not yet extricated himself. . . . [18]

Shelley, though less severe, wrote to Claire:

. . . The fault of the affair, if there be any, began with Taaffe, who loudly and unfortunately asked Lord Byron if he would submit to the insult offered by the Dragoon. Lord B. might, indeed, have told Taaffe to redress his own wrongs; but I, who had the swiftest horse, could not have allowed the man to escape, when once the pursuit was begun. . . .[19]

Withal, Taaffe's behaviour so resembled that of another great braggart but timid warrior that, in a moment of wit, Jane Williams coined for him the name "False Taaffe."[20] Williams, an impartial observer, felt that Taaffe's conduct was "highly blameable" and that his "very deposition damns him." The deposition to which Williams refers was not immediately forthcoming. The reason Byron did not include it with the other papers sent to Dawkins was that he did not have it to send at the time. Pressure had to be exerted to get the statement out of Taaffe or at least to hasten its appearance. The following undated note was probably written by Byron in the earlier part of March 28:

Dear Sir/

I have not sent the papers to England but to the B^h^ Minister at Florence by *express.* I beg leave to observe that your deposition is absolutely necessary & not to be dispensed with & must add my wonder that you should wish to recall your word upon the occasion.

Yrs.
&c.
N.B.[21]

This note had the effect of prying the statement out of Taaffe; it was probably delivered to Byron during the course of the day by Taaffe's servant, but when Byron read it he was greatly displeased. Denying that the dragoon had touched him in passing or that he had taken offence at the dragoon's behaviour, it exculpated Taaffe from initiating the affray, participating in any part of it, or even observing any consequential part of it. Some days later when Byron forwarded a copy of the statement to Kinnaird, he wrote at the end his own opinion of it:

This being Mr. Taaffe's testimony as to his own impressions I cannot and do not wish to controvert them—as he must be the best judge of his own feelings.—But I must declare that the impression of the moment on my mind—from the *words*—the *tone*—the *starting* of his *horse*—and the nearness and rapidity with which the dragoon rushed past him—was—that he had received and *felt* that he had received an insult. With regard to the rest as I saw no more of him till some time after the close of the whole business—I have nothing to observe.—[22]

Byron not unnaturally felt that if Taaffe cleared himself of all responsibility in the matter, such responsibility as must be assumed by the English party would fall upon him alone. Wishing to discuss Taaffe's statement with him and perhaps hoping, since it was not yet sworn, to get it modified, he wrote the following note to Taaffe without so much as a salutation:

March 28th 1822.

If you can make it convenient to see me this evening I am at home & will state to you my opinion on your note & the enclosed paper—[23] Of course you are the best judge of what concerns yourself.—

Yrs &c

N. B.[24]

P.S. One of the Servants [*The Coach Man* struck out] has been released at least for the present—

At the meeting with Byron, Taaffe's attitude was evidently unsatisfactory, for relations between him and the rest of the group, especially Trelawny and Byron, grew strained. Mary was probably right in thinking that Taaffe was afraid of being turned out of Tuscany. Some two years earlier he had been a principal in an incident that had involved him with the police, and he may have feared that the authorities would exile him as a chronic troublemaker.[25] Such a penalty may have seemed of little consequence to a bachelor, as Taaffe appeared to be, but tied to Tuscany as he regarded himself by the arrangement he had made for his children and having now no home to return to, expulsion would have been a serious matter to him.

Taaffe had been disturbed to learn from Byron that

the letter of March 25, which he had written hastily and without consideration, had been sent to Dawkins and had thus become a sort of official document. Taaffe had known Dawkins at Florence well enough to send him a copy of his *Elegy on the Death of Prince Clement*,[26] in return for which Dawkins had written a gracious acknowledgment, and he now seized upon the pretext of this kindness to send a copy of his statement to Dawkins and to write confidentially to him:

Private
Wednesday Night [March 27]
Pisa

My dear Mr. Dawkins,

Allow me to address you, not officially so much as in confidence; to which your few kind expressions in answer to my formal transmission of the little *Elegy* engages me—at least no further officially, than as in your prudence you may think it necessary. Lord Byron wrote you an account of the unfortunate transaction here the other day. That account he did not show me. Not considering myself any way more implicated than as a casual spectator of part of the fray, I should not have thought it necessary to trouble you about it, were it not that his Lordship tells me he sent you a note of mine; by which it appears he has used my name as freely as he chose. I must then tell you that when I come to be juridically examined my oath must be the inclosed. You will thus see that in fact I was but a spectator of an inconsiderable part of the business and a real actor in none of it. My expression at the Dragoon's going at full gallop past "*did you ever see anything like that?*" however his Lordship may have interpreted it, was a mere pettish exclamation at my horse's being made jump. I saw the dragoon was not an officer—and even if he was, would never have considered his act as an insult—and when it was an insult I would have resented it myself & sought no gratuitous interference. I am little inclined to a quarrel myself and totally incapable of trying to engage others in one. In fact were I quarrelsome, it would be a far more legitimate cause for one to have such misconduct attributed to me than the galopping by of any one, much less of a Sergeant of Dragoons. You will perceive, my dear Sir, that in all this I neither used nor underwent an improper word, nor gave nor received a blow, nor was present aiding or abetting any such doings—so that I have nothing either to ask or be asked satisfaction for. What may be in my note to his Lordship I know not. It was a confidential one which

I never imagined would have passed into other hands. I have confidence however enough in my own honor to know well I can answer for it in *substance*. Its *manner* indeed may require this explanation. It was written ere I had begun to suspect the possibility of the Dragoon's having had any provocation: so that I though[t] him most barbarously wrong. It is now said generally that one of the Gentlemen struck him with a whip—he adds it was not Lord Byron. Who it was or whether the fact be true I know not. It must at least have occurred ere I came into sight. But to a man of my sentiments it makes all the difference in the world if he had a stroke of a whip. I did not begin to suspect it for two days after I wrote that note. Lord Byron is not accused of striking the man neither did he receive any sabre blows—so that expect [*i.e.*, except] he used hard words or gave or accepted a challenge he might consider himself as little engaged otherwise than juridically on account of the stab supposed given by one of his Servants; and herein his innocence will be proved. But he seems (whether on account of words or a challenge which he may have given) to consider himself as principal and I suppose those gentlemen who gave or received blows are glad enough he should. But as to me, I certainly disclaim any participation in a matter where I might have trouble & vexation without end without the possibility of gaining any credit. This was my own firm conviction: but I had occasion also to consult a most respectable nobleman [27] whom you will shortly see at Florence and who gave me his decided advice to the same effect.

Forgive the long letter dear Sir. Pray let me know you have received it. You will use both it and the inclosed deposition (which is not yet sworn, but I suppose will be so as soon as the dilatory police come to my name) as your judgment dictates; but yet with necessary caution, for his Lordships Society is made up of curious heads.[28] I will tell you more on that score whenever we have the pleasure of meeting. In the mean time I have the honor of being, dear Sir,

Your ob[t] hum[e] Serv[t] &c &c

J. Taaffe Jun[r] [29]

Dawkins now found himself engaged in a two-way correspondence, with Taaffe wishing Byron to be as little aware of his side of it as possible. It was of course Dawkins's duty to do whatever he could do legitimately for his own nationals, and Trelawny was probably right in guessing that he was not a little flattered at the opportunity to be of service to one who was both a peer of the realm and a famous poet. Byron's letter was sent to Florence the day after it was written, and Dawkins answered it the same day:

Florence 28 March 1822

My Lord

I have had the Honor to receive Your Lordship's letter and the Statements which accompanied it, and I have communicated them to the Grand Duke's Minister.

I understand that the Government sent a Law officer to Pisa yesterday to take the depositions of the Soldiers and of Your Lordship's Servants; and I fear it will be deemed necessary to detain the latter untill the Examination of both parties is closed: but I cannot discover the slightest suspicion of Your Lordship's having approved or having authorised, either directly or indirectly, the Act of which one of them is accused.

Your Lordship will always find me ready to do you every service in my power; and should any thing occur at Pisa on this occasion which savours of partiality, Your Lordship will confer an obligation upon me by communicating it to me immediately.

I have the Honor to be with great respect

My Lord
Your Lordship's most obedient
Humble Servant
E. J. Dawkins [30]

The
Lord Byron—

To Taaffe, Dawkins wrote reassuringly:

Florence 29 March 1822

My dear Sir

. . . I see no immediate occasion for making use officially either of [your letter] or the Deposition which accompanied it, but I am very glad you sent them, as Florence is full of unkind & absurd reports which the information I have derived from Lord Byron & yourself enables me to contradict—When you have made your affidavit before the Police you will oblige me by sending me a signed copy of it.

I have made no *use* of your Note to Lord Byron which came to me in His Lordship's letter, as he has told you—I sent all the other Enclosures to the Grand Duke's Minister for Foreign affairs with as strong an appeal as I could write, and he has forwarded them to the proper Department. . . .

Believe me &c
EJD [31]

Taaffe's peace of mind could not have been long-lived, however, for Trelawny was engaged in making trouble between him and Byron. The following undated, unaddressed note in Trelawny's hand is, from its context, clearly directed to Byron:

Lord Blanford [*i.e.*, Lord Bradford] came here from Lucca two days back purposely to ascertain the truth of the Row he requested Mrs. Beauclerk to introduce him to one of the gentlemen concerned. She send for False-taff—who made up such a garbled roundabout tale—that L B[radford]—could not understand it—and requested Mr. Taff to procure a statement from you—which Taff declined—but wrote one himself for Lord B[radford]—to disseminate and said he had nothing to do in occasioning the row pleaded ignorance as to its commencement and altogether—left a very bad impression from having given a very false statement which he Lord B[radford] is to promulgate in England Mrs. Beauclerk states that she has received a letter from a lady of the Tuscan court to say that the Grand Dutchess is most anxious to ascertain the facts— [32]

Thoroughly aroused by such a piece of knavery and duplicity as this must have seemed, Byron wrote icily to Taaffe:

Sir/

I have been informed that you thought proper without consulting me or any of the party to give to Lord Bradford a written statement of the late affair here at the same time declining to comply with his Lordship's request to apply to *me* for one.—

Did you do this or not?—

An early answer will oblige

Yr obedt Servt

Noel Byron [33]

April [*i.e.*, March] 29 1822

Not content to leave it at that, Byron requested Williams to call on the unhappy Taaffe and ask for an explanation of his conduct. Following this conference, Taaffe wrote a stiffly formal reply to Byron's note, also without salutation:

Your Lordship is quite misenformed. Lord Bradford so far from wishing me to apply to you for a statement expressly and preremptorily forbade me to do so. Mrs. Beauclerk, it is true, introduced me to Lord Bradford but he had already twice brought me letters from Lucca and called upon me—and by mere accident I was neither times at home. I dont deserve to be cross questioned by persons to whom I have ever acted to the best of my judgment as a true friend.

I have the honor to be Your Lordship's
Ob[t] Serv[t] and (if you will but believe it)
Most sincerly
J. Taaffe Jun[r] [34]

Captain Williams asks me whether I told Lord Bradford something that implies I had not as much to do with the affair as was the fact. I can only answer that what I told Lord Bradford answers exactly to what is contained in my deposition as I gave it to your Lordship —anything else would prove *me perjured*[.]

All of this was bad enough, but without consulting his associates, Taaffe made the mistake of calling on Captain Chiesi, Masi's commander, requesting guarantees for the English group against a hostile act by Masi's fellow-soldiers. Chiesi, according to Torelli, replied that his troop was too honourable to be capable of an unworthy act even to the assassin of their wounded comrade. Taaffe assured Chiesi that the assailant of Masi was not one of the English, but when he wished to enter into details of the affair, Chiesi told him that if he had any evidence to give he should give it to the tribunal. When Byron and Trelawny learned of Taaffe's action, they expressed their disapproval, as might be expected, in strong terms.

On Thursday Dr. Todd, who despite Masi's statement above [35] had seen the wounded man, pronounced him better. Papi, meanwhile, had been exposed to the view of the witnesses Bisordi and Landrini (who, according to the custom of the time and country, occupied places of concealment), but neither was willing to identify him as the assailant. Another witness, Francesco Frassi, moreover, who had promised to identify the assailant, proved to be useless. He confused Strauss and Papi and ended weakly by admitting that he was not standing in a position that would enable him to describe the assailant. Papi himself stuck staunchly to his story of having driven the carriage to the stables as soon as the ladies alighted and of having remained there unhitching the horses and polishing the carriage until summoned to drive the Countess Guiccioli home at a later hour. Persistent cross-examination failed to shake his testimony, and when it was corroborated by the two grooms, Giovanni Vichi and Giovanni Vannuzzi, there was nothing to do but free him, which was done on Thursday.

With the freeing of Papi, the angry public denounced Teresa's servant, Antonio Maluccelli[36]—"the meekest fellow in the world," according to Mary—and his arrest followed. When Bisordi and Landrini both identified Maluccelli as the servant with the lance whom they had seen just prior to the wounding of Masi, things looked black for him indeed. Moreover he proved as bad a witness for himself as Papi had been excellent. At first he swore that he had entered the hall behind his patroness, following the return of the carriage, and that he had remained there until informed by Count Ruggero Gamba that his patroness had returned home. Examined again later, he told a very different story. This time he said that upon his arrival at the Palazzo Lanfranchi he had been ordered by his patroness to go to Signor Williams and that on the way he had met his Lordship and the sergeant in conversation near the Church of St. Matthew, had heard Byron ask Masi his name, had seen the two shake hands, but had gone on to do his errand. At the Tre Palazzi di Chiesa he found nobody at home and thereupon returned to the Palazzo Lanfranchi and so informed his patroness. Although Williams deposed that no one was at his house except one servant with the baby in a back room where she could not hear a knock at the door, Maluccelli's case was weakened by the testimony of Teresa and Mary that he did not report to them his inability to carry out Mary's order. By common consent he was now regarded as guilty.

On Friday, the 29th, it was reported that the dragoon was much better and was likely to recover. By Saturday the minds of the Pisan circle were at ease about the wounded man: "The dragoon considerably recovered and doing well," Williams records.[37] Thereafter they ceased to worry about him, and on April 7 Trelawny thought he met Masi walking abroad leaning on the arms of two comrades.[38]

Writing an account of the affray to Hunt after it was known that Masi was recovering, Mary Shelley concludes by saying: "So much, my dear Friend, for this business to which Lord Byron attaches considerable importance, although to us, ever since the convalescence of the soldier it has been a matter of perfect indifference." [39] What she says is true: Byron did attach considerable importance to it.[40] If the Italian courts and the efforts of Mr. Dawkins did not secure the ends of justice—*i.e.*, the absolving of the English party from blame and the punishment of the dragoon—Byron intended to appeal to the British Parliament itself, though it is difficult to see what Parliament could do. In a postscript to the chilly letter of March 29 to Taaffe,[41] Byron wrote: "That Mr Dawkins will see justice done to both sides—I do not doubt—but even if he should not—I will have the business brought before parliament.—I should like to know if unarmed men are to be cut down at City gates with impunity.—Now that the fellow is recovered he ought to be looked to.—" [42]

Aside from Byron's anger at the indignity he and his party had suffered, the main reason for his exaggerated view of the whole affair was his sensitiveness to public opinion in England and his experience with the abuse of the press, which caused him to fear outrageous distortion of the incident in English newspapers. To prevent or at least to counteract such distortion, Byron requested Mary Shelley to send copies of all the depositions to Hunt and to ask him to print a true account in the *Examiner* in the event that inaccurate accounts appeared in the conservative press. She also sent copies of the documents to Medwin in Rome. Byron himself sent copies of the depositions to Kinnaird, Sir Walter Scott, and Hobhouse; but it was Kinnaird upon whom he depended to take whatever action should be necessary. The documents to Kinnaird were accompanied by the following letter:

Pisa. March 28th 1822

Dear K/

To prevent mistatements I send you authentic copies of some circumstances which occurred on Sunday last.—You can use them according to the circumstances related by others;—if there is anything stated incorrectly in the papers these will serve to rectify them by.—You must get them translated by a very careful hand.—They are the same papers directed to the Government here & an Ambassador at Florence. The Aggressor is dangerously wounded & still in danger—(they say)—two of my Servants both Italians are arrested on suspicion—I need hardly add that *I* neither approved nor sanctioned directly nor indirectly—their summary mode of acting—notwithstanding the atrocious brutality of the Dragoon's whole conduct—of part of which (his sabring those arrested at the gates) I was ignorant having rode through the guard to send my Steward to the police—I did not dismount but rode back to the Gate with only a stick in my hand—and expecting merely to find the party detained—On my way I met the Aggressor—the papers enclosed will inform you of the rest.—

Yrs truly & ever
Noel Byron [43]

The documents were not sent, after all, until April 4, following Taaffe's advice to submit them to Dawkins in order that they might not form a part of an *ex parte* statement. Kinnaird's reply, received in due course, should have relieved all of Byron's fears of the newspaper treatment of himself and the affair:

Pall Mall May 3—1822

My dear Byron,

I receiv'd all your documents—I made out a statement from them & had it inserted in the Observer whence it was copied on the following day into the Times & the M. Chronicle—The misstatements appeared the *preceding day* in an extract from the Courier

Français [44]—& on that day your last packet reached me—All this was very pat—& I hope will be satisfactory to you. . . . I have engaged for £46000 on mortgage at $4\frac{1}{2}$ per cent—not 4—I hope you are well satisfied with this—Let me know—for I think it wise —I am sincerely rejoic'd you are out of the Scrape with the rascally Dragooners—a pretty gentleman your Irish friend—He is a pretty backer? I am endeavouring [?] to persuade Hobhouse to accompany me to Rome in August—Where shall we find you?

Yours ever faithfully
Douglas Kinnaird [45]

Byron's concern over public opinion in the affair and his determination to press for an investigation of Masi's conduct in order that the man should be punished are evident in his second letter to Dawkins, which Hay delivered in person:

Pisa. March 31st 1822.

Sir

I beg leave to acknowledge your very obliging letter—the more so—as I have not the honour of your personal acquaintance—and have no great claim to the favour of diplomatists from my political opinions.—It is indeed necessary for me that this business should have a full & free investigation—for I have no pretensions to popularity abroad or at home—and I know not what story the Public in the first confusion—may be pleased to make of it.——— Two servants have been detained—one since released,—and a Servant of the Countess Guiccioli's confined in his stead—the rest of my Servants and various others have been examined—but I am rather surprized that they have not yet called upon Dr Crawford whose evidence is essential—but who probably will not remain much longer at Pisa—To the steps which the Government have taken I have nothing to object—but I wish to allude to some that they have *not* yet taken. — — — — —

The Man is pronounced out of danger (as far as I can learn) and I employed an English physician Dr Todd to visit him & report upon his progress towards recovery; this being the case is it not proper that they should investigate the conduct of this person as well as the consequence of that conduct? — — —

He is not an officer or a Gentleman—though his dress differed from that of the former only by the bars on his sleeve—which as I am no great Connoisseur in uniforms I did not recognize or distinguish, —and had he been either of the above—he forfeited all pretensions to the name by his conduct in sabring those who were already arrested by the Guard, & unarmed and defenceless.—I should wish to know whether—delivering a card to a man who insults you justifies *him* in arresting you—or your companions—or whether I broke any law in resisting that arrest—which I did not do by any violence—but merely by riding through the Guard when they surrounded me with arms in their hands.—But even had they cut me down—was that any reason to assault those who had *not* opposed their detention?—With regard to what passed afterwards the evidence is before your Excellency.—I do not present these *questions* to be answered by *you*—but merely as suggestions upon which you will form your own judgment—whether this Man was or was not grossly culpable in the first instance. I gave him no ill language—nor menaced him by gesture or threat—I merely asked him his name (which he did not give till I met him on the Lungarno the second time) and I neither saw nor heard such from the others.—When I gave him my address—always ignorant that he was not an Officer—I certainly did not expect him to call out the Guard in reply. But I am troubling you at too great a length—and what vexes me is that I fear that I must trouble you still further. I had at first thought of sending the enclosed accounts to England—but as this would appear an ex parte statement—I could wish that whatever account is to be given came through your Excellency—that it [*sic*] is to say—if my request is not improper. Of course the Statement must be what appears just to you, I have no wish that anything as far as I am concerned should be modified or concealed.—I add a testimony of Mr. Taaffe's—upon which you will form your judgement also.—There is a note of mine appended to it.[46]—I have the honour to be most respectfully your Excellency's obliged and obed[t] Ser[vt]

Noel Byron [47]

Dawkins's reply, written on the day that he received Byron's letter, shows that he needed no prompting to do everything in his power to assist his countrymen:

Florence 1 April 1822

My Lord

. . . Your Lordship suggests the importance of examining the Sergeant who gave rise to the subject under investigation, and D[r] Crawford whose Deposition I sent to the Tuscan Gov[t]. The Grand Duke's Minister told me this morning that the Sergeant had already undergone one examination, and that another more minute will take place as soon as his health will admit of it: and that D[r] Crawford will be called upon immediately to give his evidence. . . .

I must say that all that has passed at Florence leads me to believe that altho' the investigation may be more dilatory than we could wish, the strictest impartiality will be observed. . . .

It has always been my intention to send to England the Documents relating to this business as soon as I could announce it's Conclusion—The greater part of them (I mean the two Depositions and Your Lordship's first letter to me, with the omission of the paragraph reflecting on Italian testimony) [48] is already in the hands of this Government & has moreover been shewn by me to many, both English & Florentines, who have expressed in my presence a desire to be well informed: I took this step without Your Lordship's sanction and ought perhaps to offer an apology for it; the best I can adduce is that it appeared to me the shortest & surest way to contradict many absurd reports which had been circulated in Florence. . . . [49]

The precariousness of a position between Scylla and Charybdis and the hostility of certain members of the Pisan circle are pathetically revealed by Taaffe's next letter to Dawkins:

Private

[Pisa] Monday Evg. [March 31, 1822]

My dear Sir

I thank you for your letter of the 29th, which I had the honor of receiving yesterday. His Lordship sent you a copy of the same declaration of mine which you had already had from me. He sent it you the day before yesterday. The fact was this. Having asked me to call upon him I found him making up a parcel for England in which he wished to put my deposition too: on which I represented to him that anything coming from him without any legal verification would have the appearance of an ex-parte statement. He then determined on sending those papers first to you; which I supported with my *opinion—my opinion* however, as I thought necessary to write to him afterwards, for fear of being held responsible in any way. The fact is, such circumspection is more requisite than I could have imagined. I have acted to his Lordship with the most devoted friendship—so devotedly, as to incur the risk by my strong representations of having the public odium fall upon myself, though in the affair itself I had no real part whatever: nevertheless the greatest vexation I have had has been occasioned by the captious suspicious way in which my friendly exertions have been canvassed by him. Instead of being thanked cordially, I have been invariably cross questioned as if it was suspected I had some secret;—which to an open-hearted candid man is highly painful. His Lordship is excuseable (and I pity him) from the manner in which his head has been heated. All this was the cause, why on his proposing to send the papers to you I did not at once say you already had my deposition. . . . He knows however I have written to you, but *not officially*. . . . You see the matter of the thing is the same: but as there might seem something superfluous in letting him send you the copy of the same deposition, it might be as well not to mention your having had the first—or at least only to say generally Taaffe already let me know he had seen only what the deposition forwarded by your Lordship says, and by means of your relation, as well as what I learned from him, I have been able to contradict the false ill-natured statements abroad. The part I have had is so trivial, that any one who reads must see it is of no moment. Yet his Lordship thinks my testimony of high consequence and wishes to publish the whole in England immediately. . . . Again I thank you dear Sir and beg of you to be circumspect with regard to me in your letters to his Lordship; for I perceive he does not much appreciate my true kindness because I am not as warm-headed as some that surround him, and who are cause why I am obliged to refrain from waiting on his Lordship as sedulously as I wish and as my feelings towards him personally would engage me to do. I have the honor dear Sir to remain with the most distinguished Sentiments

Your very faithful Servant
J. Taaffe Jun[r] [50]

The saying nothing at all about me in England in the affair would be what would please me most. I fortunately saw little but would to heaven I had not seen even that little. I would that my name should appear for the first time in almost any other affair.

Three days later, without awaiting a reply to this letter, Taaffe made a second appeal to Dawkins to keep his name out of the affair, especially in writing to Byron :

Private

. . . In fact [he continues] the consequences of the slightest word may be very serious; for you have, you can have no idea of the captiousness that surrounds me. I had endeavoured to act as kind a part as I could—as to what I saw, I must swear to it without change or shuffling—yet, instead of thanks, I have been repaid with more Cross-questioning and annoyances than I can recount; so that at last I am become sick. My Lord Bradford had been here, who without choosing to have any direct correspondance with Lord

B[yron] was yet desirous to have means of contradicting the scandalous reports abroad, (taxing his Lordship with assassination &c &c) and I thought I did a most friendly act by giving him those means effectually: yet behold my so doing has exposed [me] to a load of vexation. I had a letter from Lord Bradford from Genova; he tells me he will be shortly in Florence and speak to you confidentionally about all this. He will be astonished at learning that his interview with me has been represented in very false colours and that the note I gave him has [been] divulged and been denounced to Lord B[yron] as calumniatory instead of justificatory of him. He will wonder by what strange breach of common prudence and confidence his (Lord Bradfords) name has been mentioned at all. But these are most thoughtless vain, not to say intriguing wicked people.

In the next sentence he makes clear that he suspects Mrs. Beauclerk of having played the part of mischief-maker by talking of Lord Bradford to Trelawny, and as she is to leave Pisa for Florence on the following day, he warns Dawkins against her as "a dangerous person" who "has been off and on with Lord B[yron] in various little matters, and (without attributing any evil intention to her) I am afraid she is sometimes indiscreet." [51]

But seeing her in Florence, pray be reserved about this affair [he concludes]. She cannot be half as well informed on it as you: for at least up to yesterday she knew it principally from me. . . . I am going to take leave of her & will beg of her to be circumspect without however mentioning about Lord Bradford; for if she has been guilty of the indiscretion, she might fall into another in endeavouring to remedy it. I would suggest to you not to say any thing about my suspecting her either to her or Lord Bradford; for I merely notice it in order to let you know my reasons for putting you on your guard. If I write to you at such length give me leave to assure you it is that I find my situation most delicate and trying and one that requires the utmost prudence.[52]

Williams, still acting for Byron, called on Taaffe later in the same day "to learn further of the business," and Byron, who had received from Mrs. Beauclerk a letter "requesting his interference with Trelawny, and enclosing all the notes that had passed between them," professed to be satisfied and was "willing to give his hand to Taaffe as usual." [53] "All right again," concludes Williams, adding "devil of an affair—all parties quarrelling—and everybody defaming everybody—" Nevertheless, the breach once made was never healed completely. There was still Taaffe's deposition, which continued to rankle with Byron, and except for visits which Taaffe made to Byron on April 4 and April 6, when Trelawny appears not to have been present, Taaffe's name virtually disappears from the journals of Williams and Mary Shelley.

Hay, his nose now almost healed, departed for England on April 4. As he was going by way of Florence, he requested Byron to give him a letter of introduction to Dawkins, which Byron, despite the fact that he had never met Dawkins himself, obligingly did.

Pisa. April 4th. 1822.

Sir/

Captain Hay has requested me for the honour of a letter of introduction to your Excellency.—It may well be deemed a liberty in me—who have not had that honour myself, to venture on the presentation of another.—But as he is the most injured party in the late business—& can give any details which may be further necessary for it's elucidation—I hazard being deemed intrusive or perhaps worse.—I have to acknowledge the receipt of your second letter—which is quite satisfactory as far as the business has hitherto gone.—I have no objection to any use you think proper being made of my letters.—I shall forward the returned documents by post to London tomorrow—as you say that you have no objection.—I have the honour to be with great respect & obligation

Your most obedt.
very humble. Servt.
Noel Byron [54]

To H. E.
E. W. Dawkins Esqe.

Having some money matters to arrange in Leghorn, Hay went there first, and bad weather caused him to stay longer than he had intended. He arrived in Florence on April 10 and "lost not a moment" in presenting Byron's letter to Dawkins, whose family he had known in former years. Writing next day to Byron, he said:

. . . [Mr. Dawkins] is disposed & desirous of doing every thing in his power to serve your Lordship & indeed he has already done a great deal in as far as relates to our own Countrymen in doing away false impressions occasioned by the multiplied & exagerated reports that followed each other from the scene of action & he took the straightforward way . . . of putting into the hands of the English & also the Italien's the Deposition sent by Your Lordship signed by yourself & the Gentlemen of your party. . . . More he has written in a letter to Lady Burgersh [55] the exact statement sent by your Lordship which in all probability will as it has been made confidentially *& to a Woman* find its way to the publick before any of the other accounts get currency—

Mr Dawkins has not sent in Taaffs statement nor will he without you should desire it & I must own on reading it over again I agree with M^r D—that it would do more harm than good to our cause he has formed a most perfect idea of the whole of Mr Taaff's conduct & has a most contemptible opinion of that Gentleman who I understand intends coming to Florence & as he is a recieved guest at the Countess of Albany's [56] as well as at some Italien Houses it might be as well to school him a little before he leaves Pisa otherwise he may do a great deal of harm here—

I mentioned to M^r D—that your servants were still in custody & that they were deprived of most of the necessaries of life he will if you wish it make a remonstrance to the Minister Fossombroni. . . . Mr Dawkins thinks he could get it all terminated & get your servants liberated but then he thinks it would appear in England that there must have been blame on our part if the proceedings are abandoned should you decide on the thing going on you must have patience & great patience for to use M^r D—s own words—if we live to see the termination of it—requires your making up your mind to deprive yourself of the service of your servant for a length of time. . . .[57]

Byron's reply was sent under cover to Dawkins with this accompanying note:

Pisa. April 12th 1822.

Sir,

I have received a letter from Capt. Hay—who requests me—(I presume with your permission) to address my answer under cover to you.—As the letter is entirely upon the late squabble—I send it open—if you think it worth the trouble of your perusal.—Indeed, it refers to matters which must be submitted to your attention.—I have the honour to be with great consideration and esteem

Your obliged
& obedt
humble Servt
Noel Byron [58]

To E. Dawkins Esqe.
&c &c &c

The letter to Hay was as follows:

Pisa. April 12th 1822

My dear Hay/

I received your dispatch early this morning.—Many thanks to Mr. Dawkins and to yourself.—The detenees are treated with great rigour—they wont even allow them to receive anything to eat but the prison allowance.—The Judge appears to have a better table, as he is allowed three Scudi a day—during the process—which is *thus* likely to be soon terminated!! Now—these poor devils are innocent, and I really believe that the Count [Court?] knows that neither of them was the suspected person.—It is a question—(as you say Mr Dawkins thinks that he could have the affair terminated) whether I to save any unjust surmises—should dissent from the steps being taken to liberate these men.—With regard to my own conduct—I have given them all time (it is now three weeks) to examine & investigate hundreds of witnesses—and am willing to undergo any investigation they please—and at their own length—Nobody has evaded or withdrawn from the pursuits of their process.—I cannot contemplate the probable duration of the detention in the harshest confinement of these two innocent men—without great uneasiness on their account.—Every body says—& believes that it was another man who harpooned the Scoundrel—& yet upon this they have not acted.—I will give you an instance of their Spirit of Justice—the Procaccino [59] was taken ill last night—the Priests told him that it was a judgment on him for having foresworn himself—What he has sworn or foresworn I do not know—nor am I aware of the person of the man—but believe him to be the same who goes to Leghorn.—The Man is better—& says this himself of the priests, so Fletcher [60] tells me.—I will agree to whatever Mr Dawkins thinks proper—my own opinion inclines rather (& naturally) to the wish that these poor fellows should be out, for two things are sure—one—that they are innocent—& the other—that they have not fair play granted them.—I write in haste to save time—make my best respects to the Minister Mr. D. & believe me yours ever

N. B. [61]

P.S. Mr. Taaffe's Statement can (I think) hurt no one but himself—a pretty fellow he is!—The Officers defend their Serjeant (I am told) upon this principle—"that Mr. Taaffe declared that he exculpated the Man—as he had not been even slightly moved by his original aggression"—Now his *own* statement contradicts this—for he admits that his horse was startled—and that he appealed to me upon the subject of the *rush* past him!—He also substantially [?] [62] adds that the dragoon was all in the wrong.—Besides I sent his first note *in English* (the morning after) to Mr. Dawkins which is decisive of his *then* opinion.

At all events I hope that these men will be allowed some victuals & decent treatment.

As an afterthought Byron added on a separate sheet of paper:

April 12th 1822.

Dear Hay/

I forgot to say in my letter—that I agree with you about the paper you wish to draw up—& will do what you like about it.—No introduction to Douglas K[innair]d will be necessary—except mentioning my name to him—you will find that sufficient—& I had already written to him on the subject.

Yrs ever & truly

N. B. [63]

Dawkins now wrote to Byron suggesting that he place the legal management of the affair in the hands of a well-known Florentine lawyer who, it later turned out, did not quite deserve Dawkins's high recommendation:

Florence 15 April 1822

My Lord

I did not answer the letter Your Lordship did me the Honor to send by Mr Hay, because I knew he was in correspondence with you: and we appeared to agree so perfectly on the measures to be adopted, whether this tiresome business stops or advances, that I should probably have sent you a duplicate of his letter. We think you should name some lawyer of this Country to advise your Servants whilst the present examinations are going on, and to conduct your cause if you think proper to bring an action hereafter against the Sergeant of Dragoons—I know no man better qualified for such an office or more likely to please Your Lordship than the Avvocato Collini, to whom, I find, you brought a letter of introduction from Lord Holland. I would therefore propose that you should allow me to send him immediately to Pisa; and that, after shewing him every document you possess and telling him every thing you know, you should put the business into his hands—You may depend upon him thoroughly. He will give the business a proper direction & save Yr. Lds time & patience. . . .

The Minister desires I will give him the names of Your Lordship's Servants that he may recommend them to milder treatment; altho' he says the forms of this country require that they should be detained for the present. Mr Hay does not know their names—Your Lordship will therefore have the goodness to send them to me—

I am convinced I had better make no use of Mr Taaffe's papers, and Mr Hay perfectly agrees with me—Mr Taaffe cannot complain of their detention, for he is aware of it and has not called upon me to bring them forward; which I may do of my own accord when he has sent a signed deposition to the Police. I beg leave to take this opportunity of removing from Your Lordship's mind an impression which I fear exists there, that I have sought a separate & confidential correspondance with Mr Taaffe—That Gentleman has my leave to shew Your Lordship or any one else every line I have ever addressed to him.

I enclose a letter to Your Lordship from Captain Hay [64] who leaves Florence immediately. He put off his journey 24 hours in order to see Collini and make his deposition—

I have the Honor to remain, with great respect
My Lord
Your Lordship's most obedient humble Ser.
E. J. Dawkins [65]

Byron lost no time in furnishing the names of the servants and in welcoming the suggestion that Collini be employed to see to his interests. Having learned by experience that English legal costs were crushing,[66] he showed a natural curiosity to obtain advance information about Collini's probable fee:

Pisa. April 16th 1822.

Dear Sir,

Enclosed are the names of the Servants detained, as required.—I shall be delighted to know Collini to whom I had the letter which he mentions, though I little thought that the first occasion I should have of availing myself of the introduction would be on an affair of carnage and cutting of throats.—Whenever he comes he will find an apartment prepared for him in my house—where I hope that he will make himself at home.—Could you have the goodness to favour me with the account of proper and highest *fees* of Tuscan Counsel in such affairs?—I do not ask this from motives of economy or a wish to limit our friend's emoluments, but from actual ignorance, and a fear of perhaps falling short of what is right—from that ignorance.—This is of course "*entre nous.*" With regard to "*my time and patience*" the one is about as little worth as the other —God help me!—but that is no reason why yours should be further abused.—I trust that Collini's retainer will at least render further trouble to yourself unnecessary.—I believe that I need hardly repeat my acknowledgements and those of my countrymen for your extremely kind and handsome conduct throughout this business.—If I were insensible to it—(which I trust that I am *not*—) I should not have the plea of ignorance for ingratitude—for besides what has occurred to my own knowledge—I hear of nothing else from Florence—(not only from Capt. Hay—but from several others) but of the highly zealous and effective conduct for which we are indebted to Mr. Dawkins.——With regard to that illustrious deponent John Taaffe Jr. Esqe.—whose head is more Irish (apparently) than his heart—he did not *directly* give me to understand that he had a separate correspondence with you—and still less that *you* had sought it.—He merely said that you were his friend, in general, & that he had written to you on this subject.—To this nor to any other mode of communication—I could possibly have no objection—leaving his deposition to make it's proper impression upon a Man of honour.—What he means or meant I cannot pretend to guess—I can only judge of his paper from it's contents—and as a party I am not a competent Arbiter.——His whole language changed upon one morning—about three days after the event.—He came to me with a Cock and a Bull Story—about his having been to the Captain of the wounded man—*(totally without* the knowledge of and with the fullest disapprobation on it's being known—of *all* concerned) to speak about the Soldiery &c. —as they had threatened to besiege the house, and such like magnanimous menaces.—He added something to me—about the Man's (the Serjeant's) being ready to ask satisfaction if he got well —and if not—somebody or other for him.—Upon this—I immediately spoke with my friends—and we agreed that we would either give *singly* satisfaction to any *officer* of the regiment—or as we were *six* in number (including Mr. Taaffe the original Cause of the Scene—and an Italian Gentleman whose name I kept out of the paper as he is an exile on account of politics) would meet any *six officers* of the regiment—whichever they chose.—I said to M[r] Taaffe "I suppose you would choose to make one."—To this he answered that he would make no such thing,—neither *singly* nor *sixthly*—that *he* was *not* offended—*never* had been—&c. &c. &c.—though before he had used a different tone.—He became so tiresome and tedious & contradictory of *himself* & his *first* accounts—that if I had not interfered—M[r] Trelawney who is somewhat warlike in his notions—would have furnished matter on the spot for a fresh action of battery.——Repeating my sense of our obligations to you—I beg you to believe me, dear Sir—with every sentiment of esteem

Your faithful
& obliged Serv[t]
Noel Byron [67]

Dawkins, though he was uninformed about lawyers' fees, had had ample opportunity to observe the length of legal processes, about which he wrote amusingly in his prompt reply to Byron's letter of the day before:

Florence 17 April 1822

My Lord

I have received Your Lordship's very kind and flattering letter of the 16th—a most liberal reward for having told what I knew of an event in which every body takes an interest. Woe be unto your purse if you pay Collini half as well. With respect to his fees I can tell you nothing for the present, for they are never paid in this Country untill a law suit is closed; and it usually lasts so long that I almost doubt a lawyer's ever being able to claim them, as the profession is not hereditary. He need not remain at Pisa above a day or two, whether the matter is compromised or not—but we shall in either case feel the advantage of his having been there—I will write to Your Lordship again by him— [68]

By the time Your Lordship receives this you will have permission to supply your Servants with food and clothes at your own expense. I have heard the right to refuse you doubted, & shall mention it amongst other things to Collini.

All your depositions, & that of the Countess Guiccioli will be taken in your own houses—I shall write to M[r] Taaffe tomorrow on the subject of his, and if I find it in the style of the Draft he sent me I shall beg the Government to make his Note which begins "Mountains as usual produce mice" a part of the evidence—I have lived in dread of his provoking chastisement—However well he may deserve it it would have put the operator in the wrong & raised an unsurmountable prejudice against you both here & in England, for the public never takes the trouble to understand the whole of a subject—

. . . With many thanks for Your Lordship's good wishes & the highest sense of your good opinion Believe me

Your Lordship's very faithful Servant

E. J. Dawkins [69]

Meanwhile Byron's servant Tita had been examined on three different occasions, but in spite of the eagerness of many witnesses to implicate him the fact remained clear that he had not struck the wounding blow. On April 17 a deposit guaranteeing the fine for illegal possession of firearms having been made, the Cancelliere decided that there was no basis for holding him longer and so notified the local authorities. But Tita was not to be allowed to resume his arrogant manner at the door of Byron's palace. On the advice of Auditor Pazienza and Governor Viviani, both of whom were active against Tita, President Puccini of the Buon Governo (State Police) decreed that if the evidence in the dragoon affair were insufficient to warrant holding him in prison further, "there shall be handed to him a formal decree of banishment from the whole Grand Duchy with the customary warnings in case of failure to observe, and [he shall be] accompanied to the frontier in that direction which shall be indicated by him."

Byron, who was of course in the dark so far as the activities going on behind the scenes were concerned, no sooner learned that Tita was free of criminal charges but was being held on technical grounds than he notified Dawkins.

Pisa. April 18th. 1822

Dear Sir,

My Servant is I understand exculpated from all suspicion of being art or part of the principal fact.—He is also released from the penalty of having carried arms by the fine being paid, which it was yesterday.—But now they are detaining him under some pretence either because he wears a *beard* or for some other weighty reason—referring to the police only—& not to the Criminal tribunal.—Now—I can find securities for his good conduct if necessary—and I should be glad to know why this man (the best servant I have) is still detained after absolution from the two primary pretexts of his detention.—I hope if it is only a mere affair of police and the man is actually absolved that they will not continue to retain him for their own absolute pleasure. Would you have the goodness to avize Collini of this—& if he could do anything before he sets out—but I forget he will be here—before this letter is at Florence.—

A thousand thanks for your letter—I can assure you that there is no expression of regard in it—but what is more than reciprocal.— Do not *bore* yourself to answer my scrawls—which are merely suggestions—& don't require regular answers or answers at all.— Excuse haste & believe me ever & truly

with great esteem
yr obliged
& faithful Servt
Noel Byron [70]

P.S.

The Man was allowed yesterday to see his friends—to-day they have shut him up again in "Secret" as they call it in their jargon —and be d——d to them—excuse the phrase which is neither diplomatic nor decorous—but these fellows make me [lose] all patience with their shuffling—which was to be borne with while the man was *really accused*.

Dawkins's next letter, though dated April 19, was written before the arrival of Byron's letter of the preceding day and is really a continuation of his letter of the 17th.

Florence 19 April 1822

My Lord

Monsieur Collini takes charge of this letter—He declines Your Lordship's kind offer of an apartment in your house, as he requires more attendance at night than can be conveniently afforded by strange Servants—He will remain two days at Pisa to look into the pending examination and to collect materials for an action against the Dragoon, which I have threatened in Your Lordship's name—I have told him that a case of perjury may be proved hereafter against several of the witnesses and he says he shall take advantage of it. . . .

Your Lordship will see that no Italian is mentioned in Mr Hay's deposition—We stated the difficulty to the Notary public who drew it up, and I have mentioned it to Collini—They are both of opinion that [it] is not necessary to introduce any more names.

The Dragoon officers still maintain amongst their friends that the Soldier was struck with a whip before he drew his Sword. Indeed the Lieutenant of the troop quartered at Pisa affirms that two pistol shots, fired by one of Your Lordship's Servants, was hardly sufficient to make him unsheath it. The report of them has not reached the Captain, who by the bye has the reputation of being a good officer. The self elected deputation [71] which called upon him three days after the event was ill timed & ill judged. I had heard of it before I received your last letter and had contradicted it flat.

I have told Mr Taaffe in a note of which Collini is the bearer, that if the evidence he is about to give resembles his later [earlier?] production I shall inevitably be called upon by his companions to produce the Note he wrote Your Lordship, and to make it evidence —Madame d'Albany is the only person whom I have heard undertake his defense and She is notorious for praising people in proportion to the court they pay her. She goes to Paris on the 1st of next month.

Do not suppose My Lord that I named Collini from a desire to avoid either trouble or responsibility—All my cares and difficulties vanished the moment Your Lordship felt I could be trusted—I shall continue to do what I can, and if ever I do less than you expected it will not be from a want of inclination to serve you. . . .

I have the Honor to remain,
Your Lordship's most faithful Servant
E. J. Dawkins [72]

Tita was a favourite not only with Byron but with all of the Pisan circle. Of him Mary Shelley wrote to Mrs. Gisborne: "He is an excellent fellow, faithful, courageous, and daring. How could it happen that the Pisans should be frightened at such a *mirabile mostro* of an Italian, especially as the day he was let out of *secreto*, and was a *largee* in prison, he gave a feast to all his fellow prisoners, hiring chandeliers and plate?" [73] But strong forces were working against him, and his case was hopeless (though Byron had no way of knowing this) from the beginning. As a matter of routine Governor Viviani asked Cancelliere Lapini for a formal release of Tita from charges of wounding Masi and when it was given, on April 20, requested the Buon Governo to issue the requisite instructions for carrying out the order of exile. On April 22 Tita received notice of the decree and was asked in what direction he wished to proceed. He replied that he would give an answer after consultation with his principal (Byron) or Byron's house-master (Lega Zambelli).

Byron learned of the decree of exile on the same day that he received the unexpected news from Bagnacavallo of the death of Allegra from a fever. Collini, returning to Florence, where all appeals had to be made, carried with him the following letter from Byron to Dawkins:

Pisa. April 22ᵈ 1822.

Dear Sir/

An order has come from Florence to exile my Servant.—The Advocate Collini is of opinion that this must be protested against for various reasons which he will state in person.—It is entirely a measure of police and has nothing to do with the tribunals or the process.—It is also a gross injustice to *me*—because sending away the man in the *middle* of the *cause*—leaves always a suspicion.—But I will not plague you with further details as Collini will inform you of all that is necessary.—He is of opinion that the man should pass through Florence to appeal.—The Man is absolutely innocent of every thing relating to this affair and is allowed to be so.——I write in great haste for Collini is just starting and I have only time to repeat—how truly I am

Yʳ obliged
& faithˡ Servᵗ
Noel Byron [74]

Acting under instructions, Tita declared his intention of going to Bologna, "passing through Florence, where he intends to present himself to the President of the Buon Governo, to whom he needs to talk," and requested a safe conduct and a delay of fifteen days in which to order his affairs. The delay was granted, but the safe conduct was refused.[75] Byron, who received the news on the same day as Tita, communicated it to Dawkins, with the suggestion of a new line of appeal:

Pisa. April 24th 1822.

Dear Sir,

The answer to the request of Tita (the Barbone) is—fifteen days of delay *granted*—passage through Florence—*granted*—Salvo Condotto—*refused*. I should certainly very much wish to have his exile repealed if possible—as he has not deserved it in any respect.—He is a young [76]—good natured man—& an excellent servant—a little vain of his person—and somewhat *bavard*—but far more *harmless* in every respect than the Sbirri [77] who—I understand are his accusers on the plea of their fears. — — —

As I am going to reside for the Summer near Leghorn—perhaps—you might obtain a commutation for a temporary exile from *Pisa* only—if however they persist in driving him from the Tuscan territory—as I mean to retain him in my service nevertheless;—I could wish him to be sent to Lucca or Genoa—in one of which places I can find means to occupy him in some apparent service near one of my acquaintances.— — — — — — — — — — — — — —

Believe me to be ever &
very faithfully
your obliged St
Noel Byron [78]

P.S.

Excuse anything hurried or abrupt in this—on the night of Collini's departure—I received the intelligence of the death of my daughter Allegra (a natural child) in the Convent of Bagna-Cavallo in Romagna—where she was placed for the commencement of her education.— — — — — — — — — — — — — —

P.S.

I open my letter to add that Tita has been in my service four years and that I paid 1200 francs at Venice upon one occasion when he was drawn for the Conscription—I need hardly add that I should not have done so for a man who was a bad subject—or ill-disposed in any way.——

It is doubtful whether Byron felt the death of Allegra as keenly as he would have had Dawkins—and perhaps himself—think. After all, when she had been but twelve miles away at Bagnacavallo, he had not cared enough for her to pay her a single visit, and he had indifferently left her behind when he moved to Pisa. It may be that he felt her death as much as he was capable of feeling anything; yet his feelings were probably based less upon deep affection than upon a sense of loss of something that belonged to *him* and upon remorse from having acted contrary to the advice of all and having been proved wrong by the event. To Murray he wrote that he was seeking forgetfulness in composition, but if a means of escaping reality was really needed, the fight to save Tita, into which he threw himself with considerable zeal, was a better one than composition. Without awaiting the result of any action by Dawkins to have the sentence commuted to exile from Pisa only, Byron himself applied to Auditor Pazienza for permission to send Tita to Spezia. The move was unsuccessful, however, as he informed Dawkins:

Pisa. April 26th. 1822.

Dear Sir,

I wrote to you by Staffeta [*i.e., express*] this morning [79]—but have a few words to add on the subject of Tita.—I have applied to the Auditor for permission to send to him to *Spezia* (if exiled) to an English family there—which he has *refused* without an order from *Florence*—which unless obtained by you I know not how to obtain.— — — For my own part—if I were not embroiled with the houses which I have rented—and some other affairs which detain me here—I would leave their states tomorrow—and if they will permit me to retain the man in his service—I will quit them at any given period they choose to assign;—I wished to have nothing to do with Tuscany beyond it's climate—and as it is, I find myself not allowed even *that* in quiet. — — — — —
Excuse my adding this much to the letter of this morning & believe me ever & truly yrs.

N. B.[80]

Dawkins, who believed that there was a possibility of obtaining permission for Tita to remain in Tuscany, considered Byron's petition to the Auditor a tactical blunder, as indicated by his reply:

29 [error for 27] April 1822

My Lord

I had written the accompanying letter [81] when I received your last by the post—I am sorry you said any thing about Spezia before I hear the result of my last request; for if they think you will be satisfied by an alteration in Tita's route, which you have a right to demand, they will never allow him to remain at Leghorn, which they consider as a matter of favor. If I find the latter alternative to be hopeless I will not lose a moment in endeavouring to secure the former.

I would not upon any account appear to foresee even a possibility of their assigning a period for your quitting this [state]. If you should ever determine to take that step it should be by your own free will; but I hope that when once this tiresome business is over, your very natural inclination to leave Tuscany will be forgotten with it. A party has been raised against you in Pisa by the professors who flattered them selves with the hope of being admitted to your intimacy and of appearing in appendices to your future works. If you live at Monte Nero their Mortification will cease, and none of your Neighbours will presume to intrude upon you uninvited. I can answer for one resident in Tuscany who will always be at Your L^ds^ command, without the most distant intention or idea of founding a claim to Y^r^ L^ds^ private acquaintance—& he is Y^r^ L^d's^ most faithful Servt & sincere well wisher

EJD [82]

On Sunday, April 28, Chancellor Giovani, acting on orders from Governor Viviani, instructed the lieutenant of the chancellery to conduct Tita under good escort to the borders of the state on the following day, starting at daybreak. Tita's request that he be allowed to board ship for La Spezia did not please Viviani, who demurred on the score that Tita might be drowned! Byron, who had received letters from Collini and Dawkins during the day expressing confidence that an order would come from Florence permitting the change in plan, learned of Viviani's refusal and sent Lega Zambelli to appeal to the governor's auditor, Pazienza. The appeal was denied on the ground that notice had already been given the Buon Governo that Tita's destination was Bologna. Moreover, during the evening letters arrived from the President of the Buon Governo and the Commissioner of the Santa Croce Quarter confirming the original arrangement. Byron, bitterly disappointed, informed Dawkins of the latest developments in a highly emotional letter:

Pisa. April 28th 1822.

Dear Sir,

Notwithstanding your two letters of this morning—for which I beg to add my acknowledgements—an order has arrived to transfer Tita to Florence.—This has rather surprized me because Collini's letter stated that he would be permitted to go to Spezia or elsewhere as he pleased—& yours apprized me that I should hear of any positive decision.—With regard to the rest—I must leave it to the Great Men of this great Nation to settle in their own way—having done my best to save the poor fellow from their persecution—for there has been neither justice nor honour in their proceedings towards him hitherto.— —I presume that his *beard* (a whim of his own by the way—which I neither approved nor disapproved of—allowing all about me to wear their faces as they like—so that they don't neglect their business) is as little likely to find favour at Florence as in Pisa—where the Auditor &c. actually pleaded the *fear* which he inspired to a City—with twenty thousand thieves for inhabitants—as the reason for his exile!—My wish was to have got him to Leghorn—or on board of my Schooner—as one of the Crew—or to Spezia for a Season—for they will probably maltreat him in the Austrian territory—because he was in *my* Service—for there has been some time a sufficient detestation between that tyranny and myself—and I say this without presumption—for there is *no* individual too humble nor too insignificant *not* to be obnoxious to it's Cowardice or it's Cruelty.—Of this I had sufficient proofs both during my residence in Lombardy and in Romagna—so that I do not err in stating what might seem ridiculous if spoken of *any other* Government.—Last year they for a long time refused to permit at Milan the contradiction of a foolish falsehood in their papers with regard to myself—alledging their "hatred of me as the reason"—and it was with difficulty that Mr. Hoppner obtained the counter-statement—although they admitted that they had spoken falsely.[83]—I mention all this nonsense—merely in proof that I concur with you in my apprehensions of the treatment that this poor devil may meet with in the Austrian states—especially as he was with me during the threatened troubles in Romagna—which ended when those patriots—the Neapolitans ran away.— — I shall be very anxious to hear one word of the result of Tita's presentation to the president of "*Good* Government"* the *first* Government of that kind mentioned in history.—— Believe me ever & faithfully

Yr obliged
& obedt Sert
Noel Byron [84]

P.S.

"*The party of* the Pisan Professors!". this is the first I have heard of them—I did not know that there were any professors except Rossini Taaffe's printer—whom I have heard him mention —What is their profession?—I wonder. Mr. Taaffe [85] is going to Egypt—"col' principe Turco."—

At daybreak on April 29 Tita left Pisa, escorted by troopers Domenico Baroni and Agostino Celosci, in a carriage arranged for by Zambelli. Count Pietro Gamba and the Gamba agent, Giacomo Batuzzi, had preceded him to Florence by the night coach and, with an order obtained by the Advocate Collini, they visited him next day in the Palazzo di Giustizia, recommending to his jailors that he be supplied with a bed and that he be well treated. Watchful eyes observed that they then returned to their inn and that they were visited later by Sebastiano Fusconi,[86] a physician from Ravenna, and Count Vincenzo Gamberini Battaglini, who stayed until very late at night.

There is no record of how well Tita's keepers treated him, but while he was in the Palazzo di Giustizia he was required to shave his great Asiatic beard. He made no objection, supposing that it was to be sent to his patron; but when told that this was not so, he wrapped it up carefully in a sheet of paper.

In a letter now lost Dawkins informed Byron of the fate of Tita's beard and then, evidently feeling that Byron was unconvinced of the malice of the professors and was disputing the point, must have supported his original statement, for Byron's next letter begins with the subject:

Pisa. May 1st 1822.

Dear Sir,

I by no means intended to "correct you"—& believe that you were perfectly right—I merely asserted my own ignorance of the

* A literal translation of *Buon Governo,* of course.

names of these Professors—and, my consequent innocence of any offence towards them.—With what has been done upon the subject of Tita—I have every reason to be more than satisfied as far as *you* are concerned, and I hope it will be a lesson to him to shave in future;—since the beard of Julian which offended the people of Antioch—I doubt if so much stir has been occasioned by the same quantity of hair, on the same place. However—it shall go hard—but I repay in one way or the other—these Pisan Μισόπωγαι.[87] —It is to be feared that I have appeared to you more than enough irritable on this occasion—but I beg you to attribute it to a concurrence of causes—rather than to this one in particular—and to forgive the infirmity which I neither pretend to deny nor excuse. — — I have not been insensible to the *generosity*—of your conduct throughout—which you will call only *justice*—but as the world goes—*Justice is* generosity—and of all others—the *generosity* least to be met with.— — Many thanks for the *book* which Count G[amba] brought safely—I will take all due care of it—till I have a private opportunity of restoring it.— — Believe me ever & truly

Y^r^ obliged
& sincere S^t^
Noel Byron [88]

The authorities at Florence agreed that Tita might change his destination and go to Lucca, and he was kept in the Palazzo di Giustizia over night only. On the following morning, under escort of a member of the police corps, one Silvestrio Vantaggioli, he was taken along the Pescia road in a carriage provided by Byron till he reached the frontier of the Grand Duchy of Lucca. From there he made his way to the Shelleys, who were then at the Casa Magni near Lerici. On May 3 Shelley wrote to Byron: "I ought to tell you Tita is arrived with Mrs.[89] Dawkins' passport, and has reassumed his marine life. He seems as happy as a bird just let loose from a cage." [90] Torelli says that Tita boarded the *Bolivar* as a member of the crew when it came to the Gulf of Spezia and was several times seen in the vicinity of Leghorn after Byron went into summer quarters at Montenero. His statement is supported by a sentence in a letter of May 16 from Shelley to Trelawny: "Tita is with me, and I suppose will go with you in the schooner to Leghorn."[91] But Byron, writing to Dawkins on June 26 (*infra*, p. 171), assured him that Tita was still at Spezia. There is thus a hiatus in the history of Tita until the following September, when he rejoined his master at the Casa Saluzzo at Genoa.

Hay, on his way to England, arrived at Geneva on May 1 and went at once to Hentsch's bank, expecting to have news of the judicial proceedings from Byron. Disappointed to find none, he wrote to Byron in part as follows:

> My anxiety & my cursed Liver complaint so worried me on the road that I was obliged to stop for three days at Suza & I am still very unwell but could I have heard that the two innocent prisoners had regained their liberty & that things were going on well I doubt not I should have felt considerable relief at all events on the score of anxiety if not on that of the Liver—I now entreat of your Lordship to write to me if it is only two lines to say in what train affairs are—& if you have seen Collini. . . .
>
> This letter I send under cover to Mr Webb for two reasons—one—that before this time you will most probably have removed from Pisa to your Summer residence & the other a more powerful one which is that I was assured from indisputable authority that all letters to or from your Lordship risk'd being opened & for this same reason I have to beg you will direct to me under cover to Danoot[92] at Brusselles. . . .
>
> . . . What has become of the False-Taaffe he had writen that he proposed passing the Summer at Florence if he goes there he will meet with but a cool reception. . . .[93]

Byron, in reply, excused himself for not writing on the score of the death of Allegra and the lack of news in the legal process, the only developments in which had been the banishment of Tita and the continued imprisonment of Maluccelli.[94] But in fact the legal process was dragging toward an end, although not even Dawkins seemed aware of the fact. Less than a week before the judgment was rendered he sent Byron an English newspaper containing an account of the affray and wrote pessimistically of the progress of the process.

17 May

My Lord

After one or two Reports extracted from French Journals which are too absurd to do you the slightest harm or to cause you one moment's uneasiness, the English Newspapers have inserted an account of the affray at Pisa nearly similar to the Deposition you sent to Mr Kinnaird, which I should think is perfectly satisfactory to Your Lordship. As you may not be in the habit of receiving the papers from England, I enclose the *Courier* containing it.

Collini asked me the other day to write to Your Lordship for a small sum sufficient to cover the expense of his journey to Pisa—I told him to do the dirty job for himself and do not think the better of him for having done it—He has never a farthing in his pocket, and is a most extravagant fellow—An intimate friend of his told me, when I was making enquiries on the subject by Your Lordship's desire, that his expenses would probably amount to about sixty sequins—I mention this to put you on your guard, and I hold myself bound to take the onus of checking him upon my own shoulders if he should become importunate. Nothing can be said against his claim to this first loan—

I wish I could say anything satisfactory respecting the trial—The Report is come to Florence where there is every inclination to put it by with what they call their dirty linen—We must not appear to be impatient; but after some further time has elapsed, I propose to call upon them officially in Your Lordship's name for a statement of the proceedings—before I do it, I shall talk the matter over with Collini, and I may possibly have occasion to write to you—Depend upon me however for giving you the least possible trouble—

Mr Taaffe has sent me his "Comment on the Divine Comedy," and I have obtained a promise from Leoni [95] to translate it.

I have the Honor to remain
Your Lordship's very faithful & humble Servant
E. J. Dawkins [96]

Dawkins, indeed, had received one of the earliest copies of the first volume of the *Comment*, which Taaffe had remained in Pisa to see through the press. Although the hot-headed Trelawny was gone, Taaffe seems to have kept out of Byron's way; but that Byron, in shaking hands with Taaffe on April 3, had forgiven him—almost entirely—is clear from Byron's reply to Dawkins:

Pisa. May 17th 1822.

Dear Sir,

I return you the paper with many thanks for that and for your letter.—It is the first English Newspaper (except Galignani's *Parisian* English) which I have seen for a long time—and I was lost in admiration of it's size and volume.—The Statement is near enough the truth to prevent any very erroneous impression—and is therefore satisfactory, as far as it goes.—Our friend Collini wrote to me for a hundred sequins—which I shall send him—as soon as I see my banker at Leghorn —where I am going tomorrow.—You are perhaps a little too hard on the premature demand of our Man of law—if you had had as much to do with law and lawyers as I have (which I hope you never will), you would perhaps be more inclined to marvel at his modesty—though to be sure—his pecuniary assault is somewhat of the quickest in point of time—as the process is not only not begun at Florence but perhaps never may —though it *ought*—or else *why* all this bother with Judges &c. both there and at Pisa—on the part of the Tuscan Government?—I am perfectly disposed to do or not to do what you think proper in the affair—and will give you as little further trouble as I can possibly help.—I am very glad that Leoni will undertake Mr. Taaffe's comment—which I think contains valuable matter— & information—and he is so anxious about it that I should be glad to hear of any success for his work—which has been one of time and expence.—My friends in England are a little scandalized at his *own* account of his *own* conduct in the row—and on his trying to swear himself out of it afterwards—but the Man is a good natured fellow—and now that any little irritation at his—what shall I call it?—say blunder—it is a decent word——is over——I could wish him and his Commentary to have fair play—and due favour.— — I beg leave to repeat myself ever & faithfully

Yr. *obliged fd.*
& Set.
Noel Byron [97]

Let us now go back in point of time to the examination of the members of the Pisan circle in the dragoon affair and the judgment of the court concluding the case. Cancelliere Lapini, who was sent from Florence to take the evidence, disliked the Pisans, expected a present from

Byron, and was more than civil to the English group.[98] Examination of one witness often required hours, and there were about seventy witnesses. Mary Shelley's description of the method of procedure is both amusing and sufficiently explanatory:

> The Cancelliere, a talkative buffoon of a Florentine, with "mille scuse per l'incomodo," asked, "Dove fu lei la sera del 24 Marzo? Andai a spasso in carrozza, fuori della Porta della Piaggia." [99] A little clerk, seated beside him, with a great pile of papers before him, now dipped his pen in his ink-horn, and looked expectant, while the Cancelliere, turning his eyes up to the ceiling, repeated, "Io fui a spasso," etc. This scene lasted two, four, six hours, as it happened.[100]

Lapini's plan seems to have been to reserve the testimony of the gentry until last. By the time he got to them, Hay, of course, had already left Pisa. Mary Shelley and Teresa Guiccioli, the first members of the Pisan circle to be examined, were examined, contrary to law, in their own residences on April 19.[101] Teresa is reported by Williams to have said that she could not swear, but she thought Mr. Taaffe had stabbed the dragoon.[102] Taaffe himself was examined on April 21, as was Byron.[103] The examination of Trelawny took place after dinner on April 22, Williams acting as interpreter.

Taaffe's testimony was remarkable in one respect: a long farrago of almost meaningless verbiage from which nothing emerges clearly, it represents a modification of the statement that he had given to Byron earlier. That the modification was deliberate and not accidental—the result perhaps of the pressure of Byron and Trelawny, as well as the advice of Dawkins and Collini—is proved by the following letter to Dawkins:

> Private
>
> Pisa, Monday, April 22, 1822
>
> My dear Sir
>
> Your advice is certainly good, and I thank you for it. I have already acted most fully in conformity with it. But it was never for

an instant in my *intention* to make any protest reflecting in any way on these Gentlemen. My letters to you as they were marked *private* were ever intended to remain so by me. I was irritated at being treated with less candid kindness than my own, and took the liberty of intrusting my complaints to you—but it was most distant from my intent to utter them *officially* to any one, much less to a court of justice. Even as to my proposed deposition which you read, although in *substance* I could not change it, I never intended to make any difficulty about giving it another *form.* I gave it that form because I judged it the best; but on Mr *Collini's* advice I restricted it yesterday when before the Court to a mere statement of the facts I witnessed without any reflections whatever. They afterwards questioned me at length to which I returned the necessary answers. In fine, my juridical deposition contains all and only the *facts* you before read in my own writing; and the cross examination upon it a great quantity of words, but in *substance of reflection* rather less than the proposed deposition perused by you contains. My evidence will in no way obstruct, but rather, as far as it goes, facilitate Mr Collini's cause; as he will himself tell you, I have no doubt. . . . What a quantity of time and paper wasted! My deposition containing so little matter occupies nine foglio pages. What will that of the others? What the entire trial? So many weeks since the affair and I believe I was the first (at least of the English) examined. Is a trial of importance ever ended in this country?

Now that my judicial deposition is made I would be glad every other paper of mine on the matter were in the fire. If Lord Bradford comes to Florence you in speaking with him would oblige me by representing to him from me—1st that if his name has been once mentioned in this affair, it is not my fault; for that after promising I would not name him, I would have had my head cut off before doing so. 2dly that now that he can hear the whole account much better from you, he would act with kindness to me and go upon surer ground in tearing to pieces mine. Mine was written in the kind motive of withstanding the idle rumours of assassination: and it is probably necessary to read it in that spirit, for it was penned in a hurry and while my own head was perhaps somewhat heated though I thought the heads of others far more so. At the least it is liable to the being termed an *ex-parte* statement; so that though it might answer the momentary purpose of contracting [*i.e., contradicting*] indecent reports, when nothing official was yet made out, it becomes useless now that the matter can be clearly ascertained from a public authority like you. . . .

I intended about this time to have asked you for a passport for Egypt—under the idea of making an excursion for a few months to Thebes, and at the same time of receiving your commands: but circumstances seem to intervene that will oblige me to defer doing so for another season. . . .

Your obt. & very faithful Servant
J. Taaffe Junr [104]

The judgment of the court, signed by Justices Nissi, Raffaelli, Andreucci, and Angeloni, was handed down on May 22. It was declared that there were no grounds for criminal proceedings against Falcieri (Tita), Giuseppe Strauss, Maluccelli, and Vincenzo Papi on the charge of wounding Sergeant-Major Masi, and the charge of bearing arms illegally was also dismissed against Tita. Tita, Maluccelli, and Strauss, as foreigners, however, were recommended to the attention of the Potesta Economica (*i.e.*, the police). Torelli, who believed that Byron had expended 3,000 scudi in bribery of witnesses to achieve this judgment, commented cynically that it only proved that the guinea is current in any country.

In view of the haste with which Tita had been hustled out of the Grand Duchy, it is surprising that the Buon Governo exhibited no eagerness to be rid of Strauss, who accompanied Byron to Montenero in May and was under the care of a Leghorn physician, or of Maluccelli, who remained in the *bargello* at Pisa. Not until June 30 did the order for their banishment come.

The assailant of Masi was never officially discovered. The Pisani and the spy Torelli were certain that it was Maluccelli; but they were wrong. The guilty man was Papi, the coachman. Trelawny named him to W. M. Rossetti as the assailant,[105] and Papi himself was willing to assume the doubtful honour. Years later Medwin encountered him at Sienna, a broken wretch with a wooden leg begging for the means of travelling to Rome. Medwin gave him something, and in further conversation he confessed that it was he who had wounded Masi.[106] If this is not enough, further testimony is at hand.

Tribolati, revising in 1891 an earlier account of the

affray, quotes excerpts from the unpublished memoirs of a gentlewoman friend of Byron's, herself a witness in the proceedings, whose name he was not at liberty to mention.[107] This, of course, could only be Teresa, and the Marchesa Origo has been good enough to verify for me that the excerpts are indeed from the unpublished *Vie de Lord Byron en Italie*. In the excerpts the coachman is named as the assailant, and the explanation is given that he escaped identification by altering the arrangement of his hair, shaving his beard, and changing his livery. Byron, hoping that the freeing of Papi would end the matter, kept his peace. I am indebted to the Marchesa Origo for additional excerpts from the *Vie* not quoted by Tribolati. According to Teresa, Byron felt that the coachman, because he had acted from loyalty rather than malice or personal interest, deserved pardon. As the investigation dragged on, however, Teresa did not share this feeling; she thought that Papi should be sent away in order to keep suspicion from falling upon the innocent.[108] Her account goes on to say that after Maluccelli was arrested, Byron did indeed send Papi away and caused the report to be spread about that he was the culprit; but by that time it was too late.[109] This is a most surprising statement. If Papi was sent away in order to advertise his guilt, how is it that there is no mention of the fact in the journals of Williams and Mary Shelley, the letters of Byron, the diary of Torelli, or Cancelliere Lapini's exhaustive summary of the investigatory proceedings? (And sent where? A short time later, as we shall see, he is living at Montenero with Byron and engaging in another altercation.) If this statement is surprising, her next is even more so—that Teresa and Mary named the guilty man to Lapini, relating the circumstances, and insisted strongly on Maluccelli's innocence.[110] Such a statement is not borne out by the testimony of Teresa and Mary or by Lapini's summary. Did Teresa—writing after the passage of long years—confuse fact with fancy? Did her memory telescope the two altercations in which Papi was involved? Or is she merely an untrustworthy witness? We can only guess. Of the main fact, however—that Papi was the man who struck Masi down—there can be no reasonable doubt.

As might be expected, it was the unfortunate dragoon who suffered the only permanent effects of the affair. When he had sufficiently recovered from his wound, he was removed to Florence and was subsequently dismissed from the service. Having a wife and several children, he was in actual want when the Grand Duke of Tuscany, who according to Masi[111] made him recount his story several times, came to his aid with a pension of fifty francs a month. In 1824 he set up in business in Pisa as a tobacconist and was still conducting his shop when Poujoulat interviewed him in 1838.

CHAPTER 8

The Summer Colonies

(a) The Shelleys at Villa Magni

TRELAWNY'S idle dream of a summer colony on the Gulf of Spezia, with Byron, the Shelleys, the Williamses, himself, and books, horses, and boats, was never to come true.[1] As for Shelley, long before the arrival of the season to leave Pisa, he had ceased to wish it to come true. His great admiration of Byron's poetic talents and accomplishments had never blinded him to his friend's personal shortcomings, and two events of the Pisan sojourn had made the continuing intimacy with Byron irksome to him. The first related to Allegra and Claire and the second to Leigh Hunt.

Shelley's disappointment at his failure to induce Byron to take Allegra out of the convent at Bagnacavallo and bring her to Pisa with him must have been very great. Claire had subsequently been full of wild schemes for kidnapping Allegra, and though Shelley dissuaded her from them as impracticable, his sympathies were nonetheless entirely with her.

> It is of vital importance both to me and to yourself, to Allegra even, that I should put a period to my intimacy with L[ord] B[yron] and that without *eclat* [he wrote to Claire]. No sentiments of honour or justice restrain him (as I strongly suspect) from the basest insinuations, and the only mode in which I could effectually silence him I am reluctant (even if I had proof) to employ during my father's life. But for your immediate feelings I would suddenly and irrevocably leave this country which he inhabits, nor ever enter it but as an enemy to determine our differences *without words.*[2]

And again: "I shall certainly take our [summer] house *far* from Lord Byron's, although it may be impossible suddenly to put an end to his detested intimacy." [3] We must remember that Shelley was addressing Byron's implacable enemy and that though he may have meant what he said at the moment of writing, because of the degree to which he entered into Claire's feelings, his words probably reflect an exaggeration of his day-to-day feelings.

Shelley's sympathies were no less engaged on behalf of Leigh Hunt. Had it been within his power, he would have relieved Hunt's devouring need fully, but it wasn't. Byron had no such charitable impulse. Had Hunt arrived within a reasonable time after Byron made his proposal about *The Liberal*, matters would almost certainly have been better, but in dealing with an unstable character such as Byron's, delay is often fatal. In the eleven months that elapsed between the invitation and the arrival of the Hunts, Byron had been listening to the jealous sniping of friends in England, had been assailed by his own doubts, and had lost his enthusiasm for the project. In the end it was not that he acted so unhandsomely by Hunt as that he did not quite act handsomely toward him.[4] And to Shelley, who had to act as intermediary, the lack of real generosity on Byron's part was apparent and revolting. Shelley's words to Hunt are almost an echo of those he had written to Claire: "Particular circumstances, or rather I should say, particular dispositions in Lord B's character, render the close and exclusive intimacy with him in which I find myself, intolerable to me. . . ." [5]

When Shelley and Williams had made their house-hunting expedition to the vicinity of Lerici in February, Shelley could not have been sorry to find that there was no house suitable for Byron. This being the case, the Shelleys invited Claire to come and stay with them during their *villeggiatura*. She arrived in Pisa on April 15, only to learn that the houses that Williams and Shelley thought they had arranged for were not available. Byron offered the interesting explanation that "it is in consequence of the late disturbances that the Piedmontaise Government object to S[helley]'s residing there."[6] Now the house-hunting had to be begun all over again, and on April 23 Williams, Jane, and Claire left on an unsuccessful search at Spezia. When during their absence news of the death of Allegra came to Shelley, he felt it imperative to remove Claire immediately from the vicinity of Byron. A single unfurnished house with three bedrooms was available near Spezia—the Villa Magni, located between Lerici and San Terenzo—and on April 26 Mary, Claire, and Trelawny left hurriedly to treat for it.

Williams, remaining behind with Shelley to supervise the loading of their furniture, underwent a brief examination in the dragoon affair and later in the day took leave of Byron.[7] Shelley and the Williams family, leaving Pisa late on the 27th, were at Lerici by noon the next day. On the day following, having arranged with the customs authorities about their furniture, they heard from Mary that she had taken the Villa Magni, but that there was no house for the Williamses, who, despite the inadequacy of the Shelleys' house, perforce became their guests. Claire, comprehending the situation, insisted upon returning to Florence, and Shelley was forced to break the news of Allegra's death to her.[8] "You may judge of what was her first burst of grief and despair," Mary wrote to Mrs. Gisborne; "however she reconciled herself to her fate sooner than we expected; and although, of course, until she form new ties, she will always grieve, yet she is now tranquil. . . ."[9]

From the beginning Mary was unhappy in her new abode. Besides its inadequacy and its state of disrepair, its isolation caused servant trouble and made for difficulties in obtaining needed supplies. Jane Williams, who with her family was allotted one room, shared in Mary's feelings. ". . . Jane is by no means acquiescent in the system of things, and she pines after her own house and saucepans to which no one can have a claim except herself," Shelley wrote to Claire, who after all could not be persuaded to remain and had departed on May 21.—"It is a pity that any one so pretty and amicable should be so selfish."[10]

Shelley and Williams, happy in one another's society and oblivious of the deficiencies of the ménage, settled down to await the delivery of Shelley's boat, the fatal bark that was to be their plaything during the summer. Trelawny had gone on to Genoa to see about the boats and to take charge of Byron's *Bolivar* when she was finished. In a letter to Byron, "written on board the Bolivar," Trelawny said: "On my arrival here I found the Don Juan (a name which every lady here particularly admires) ready for sea[.] She is a fine spanking boat, and sails like the devil, I shall send her to Shelley in a day or two. . . ."[11] On May 8 Williams heard from Trelawny that the boat was finished and would be delivered on the following day. So excited were the little colony that all eyes were strained toward the sea, hoping to see her come in. But they were disappointed; bad weather postponed her appearance until the 12th, when they saw "a strange sail coming round the point of Porto Venere which proved at length to be S[helley]'s boat."[12] After a closer look at her Williams wrote, "She does indeed excite my surprise and admiration."[13]

Shelley likewise was delighted. "She is a most beautiful boat, and so far surpasses both mine and Williams's expectations," he wrote to Captain Roberts, "that it was with some difficulty that we could persuade ourselves that you had not sent us the Bolivar by mistake."[14] She was indeed a beautiful boat—except for one flaw. Originally she was to have been built in partnership with Williams and Trelawny, who had suggested the name *Don Juan* for her. When Shelley took her over, he proposed renaming her the *Ariel*, but Byron, "in his contemptible vanity or for some other purpose,"[15] had Roberts paint the original name on the mainsail. All efforts to remove the offending letters were unavailing, and finally a piece of sail had to be removed and reefs put in. "I do not know what Lord Byron will say," Mary wrote acidly to Mrs. Gisborne, "but Lord and Poet as he is, he could not be allowed to make a coal barge of our boat."[16]

Children with a new toy could not have taken greater pleasure in it than Shelley and Williams took in the new boat, and, ironically, even Mary found her only moments of peace in lying with her head on Shelley's knee on board the little boat that was so soon to rob her of all happiness. Shortly after the boat's arrival Shelley and Williams made a trial run down to Porto Venere, with Mary and Jane aboard, and beat back in splendid time. "The boat sailed like a witch," recorded Williams proudly.[17]

To Shelley the indolent routine of writing a little, reading, sailing, and listening to Jane's simple melodies was like living in some dream world, removed from ugly realities. But occasional realities forced their way in, as when he received a letter from Lega Zambelli, enclosing one from Collini, written at Byron's instance. Phrased in legal Italian, both were unintelligible to Shelley, who wrote to Byron in reply:

Lerici, May 16, 1822—

My dear Lord B.——

I recieved this morning a letter from Lega, with one enclosed of Collini's relating, if I rightly understand them, to the prosecution of Masi.—I wish it to be understood that I *personally* have not the least desire to proceed against the poor devil; but if you think it might conduce to Antonio's enlargement or be in any other respect advantageous to you I am willing to act as you think best—Pray write to me precisely what you wish me to do on this subject, & how to proceed; for as to Lega's compositions, & that enclosed as they seem written under the supposition of my having a secretary at my elbow as learned in the law as himself, they are & probably will continue to be totally unintelligible to me.—[18]

It may well be that Byron's impotence to revenge himself on the Buon Governo for the banishment of Tita and the continued imprisonment of the other servant accounts for some of Byron's vindictiveness toward poor Masi, which with the passage of time showed no signs of weakening. His answer to Shelley's letter was as follows:

Pisa, May 20th 1822.

Dear Shelley,—

It is proper that you should prosecute on every account; but you need not apprehend that any punishment will be inflicted on the fellow, or expect any very splendid severity from the Tuscan Government to their own ragamuffin. After their obvious injustice in the case of Tita and Antonio, I really see no occasion for any delicacy with regard to the Serjeant—either on account of his own conduct or that of his Government. As he did *not* assault me, and as I gave him a card (believing him to be an officer) which with us bears a hostile Interpretation, *I* cannot prosecute him; but otherwise I would, I assure you, and shall be very much surprized if you decline to do so. Indeed it is absolutely necessary on account of Antonio and Tita. The accounts in England of the Squabble appear on the whole to have been tolerably fair, and without prejudice as far as I have heard or seen. . . . [19]

A little later, Shelley, who had heard from Hunt that he and his family were embarking for the third time, wrote to Byron informing him that the Hunts might be expected at Leghorn almost any day and asking Byron to have Dunn "or some other omniscient of that sort" intercept Hunt before he went on to Pisa and give him Shelley's address. "I shall sail over to pay both him and you a visit as soon as I hear of his arrival," he promised. Adverting to the dragoon affair once more in conclusion, he shows how fundamentally different his own views were from those of Byron:

What news of our process? I hear that Antonio is treated with more mildness & likely to be released—They say too that Masi is to be degraded & severely punished. This would be a pity, & I think you would do well, so soon as our points are gained to intercede for the poor devil—whom it w^d^ not be right to confound with his government, or rather with the popular prejudice of the Pisans to the suggestions of which the government conformed itself. [20]

Williams's journal reveals that he wrote twice to Taaffe during the residence at Villa Magni, once asking Taaffe to pay the postage and forward his mail. In June, upon the completion of the printing of the first volume of Taaffe's *Comment*, Shelley received a letter from Taaffe informing him that his copy was ready and asking where it should be sent. Shelley's response was as cordial as ever:

Lerici, June 11. 1822.

Dear Taaffe

On my return from a little voyage in this neighbourhood with Williams I am agreably surprised by the intelligence of the completion of the *Comment*, & that you have favoured me by the destination of the remainder of what was wanting to my copy, for me.—If you would be so obliging as to send it to M^rs^[21] Mason's or even to my own lodgings addressed to me, I shall recieve it safe. Pray let me know what arrangement you have made with Murray, & whether it is yet published.—I have not yet recieved any answer from Ollier to the proposition of last June, & it is probable that he puts off writing till the day of judgement when he expects to meet me in the lobby, & when I shall certainly oppose his passage to the dress boxes on the ground of this & several other malversations—

We are delighted with this place & pity those whom June detains in Pisa—What are your motions this year? Should they lead you towards Spezia—we should be most happy to give you the rude hospitality of these rocks—premising, that you must content yourself with a sincere welcome—*for little else will you find* [22]—& the esteem with which I am, Dear Taaffe

Your very sincere &c
P B Shelley [23]

On June 13 the long-expected *Bolivar*, with Roberts and Trelawny aboard, was sighted, and Shelley and Williams in the *Don Juan* received a six-gun salute. A race developed, but the *Don Juan* was no match for the *Bolivar* and was soon outdistanced. Roberts and Trelawny were guests at dinner that evening and remained in the vicinity until the 18th, when Trelawny took the *Bolivar* on to Leghorn, leaving Roberts behind to assist in refitting the *Don Juan*.[24] While visiting his friends, Trelawny had an opportunity to go out in the *Don Juan* and see how they handled her. Shelley, attempting to steer with a book in his hand, received orders from Williams, did everything wrong, and was properly blown up by him. "You will do no good with Shelley," warned Trelawny, "until you heave his books and papers overboard; shear the wisps of hair that hang over his eyes; and plunge his arms up to the elbows in a tar-bucket."[25] As they had only a boy to assist them, Trelawny recommended the addition of a Genoese sailor to the crew, but Williams indignantly spurned the suggestion.

Claire, surprisingly tranquil, arrived for a visit on June 7, and two days later Mary became "alarmingly unwell,"[26] threatened with a miscarriage, which occurred on the morning of the 16th. For seven hours she lay almost lifeless, kept from fainting by stimulants, and was at last restored by Shelley's bold action in ordering unsparing applications of ice while they awaited the coming of the doctor.[27]

Shelley wrote little at the Villa Magni.

> It is impossible to compose except under the strong excitement of an assurance of finding sympathy in what you write [he wrote without bitterness to John Gisborne]. . . . I do not go on with "Charles the First." I feel too little certainty of the future, and too little satisfaction with regard to the past, to undertake any subject seriously and deeply. I stand, as it were, upon a precipice, which I have ascended with great, and cannot descend without *greater*, peril, and I am content if the heaven above me is calm for the passing moment.[28]

The spell of La Spezia grew upon him and the fascination of the *Don Juan* held him tighter in its grip.

> I still inhabit this divine bay, reading Spanish dramas and sailing, and listening to the most enchanting music [he wrote to Horace Smith].—We have some friends on a visit to us, and my only regret is that the summer must ever pass, or that Mary has not the same predilection for this place that I have, which would induce me never to shift my quarters.[29]

Daily he and Williams were occupied in working on the boat or sailing in her. Williams's journal during these last days of his life contains little else. Hauling her out on the beach, they cleaned and greased her, added a billet head which Williams thought a great improvement because it made her two feet longer and gave the appearance of another two.[30] When on June 22 they launched her again, she floated three inches lighter than before, even with all her ballast in.[31] With the task of smartening her up with paint finished on the 25th, there was nothing left to do but enjoy her.

On June 20 came word that Hunt had arrived at Genoa. Only a relapse by Mary, induced by Shelley's harrowing sleep-walking experience on the preceding night, prevented Williams and Shelley, who had already prepared the boat, rigged the sails, and laid in provisions, from sailing to Genoa to meet him.[32] On the 28th Hunt sailed from Genoa to Leghorn,[33] and by July 1 Mary was well enough for Shelley and Williams to sail down to see him. Stretching across to Lerici, they picked up Roberts, and with a side wind arrived at Leghorn at 9.30 — a run of forty-five to fifty miles in seven and a half hours. Anchoring astern of the *Bolivar*, they borrowed cushions from her and slept aboard the *Don Juan* having arrived too late to be cleared by the health authorities.[34]

Next morning they heard that Byron was leaving Tuscany in consequence of the Gambas being exiled, and on reaching shore they met the Gambas just leaving the police office.[35] Williams, encountering Byron at Henry Dunn's, said goodbye for what was to be the last time, was introduced to Hunt, and paid a call on Mrs. Hunt.[36] He then remained in Leghorn while Shelley accompanied the Hunts to Pisa and established them in the apartment that Byron had furnished for them in the Palazzo Lanfranchi. Byron also returned to Pisa, and Shelley succeeded in working out an agreement on *The Liberal* between Hunt and Byron. He remained in Pisa until July 7, and Hunt says that the two had one delightful afternoon together, wandering about the town and visiting the Cathedral and other points of interest. On his last day in

Pisa Shelley called on Mrs. Mason, who had never seen him in such excellent health or such high spirits,[37] picked up the copy of Taaffe's *Comment* that awaited him there,[38] and then took the night post-chaise for Leghorn.

Williams, meanwhile, had cashed bills on July 3 for considerable sums of money—two for £50 each, one for £25, and still another for £35.[39] Shelley also had on his person the £50 which he had just borrowed from Byron.[40] After purchasing necessary provisions for the household at Villa Magni on the morning of July 8, they boarded the *Don Juan* at one o'clock. Trelawny, proposing to accompany them into the offing, was under weigh in the *Bolivar* when he was overtaken by the guard boat and forced to turn back because he had failed to obtain his port clearance papers. Casting anchor and furling his sails, he took up his glasses to watch the *Don Juan* slipping into the distance. Pointing to the southwest, his Genoese mate observed: "Look at those black lines and the dirty rags hanging on them out of the sky—they are a warning; look at the smoke on the water; the devil is brewing mischief." [41] Looking again, Trelawny saw the *Don Juan* disappearing into a sea-fog that enveloped her. His friends were never seen alive again.

(b) Byron at Montenero

On April 9 Byron had entered into an agreement to lease from a banker named Francesco Dupuy a furnished house, with stables, coach-house, and garden, at Montenero (near Leghorn) for the period from May 1 to October 31.[42] When May 1 came, however, his constitutional hatred of moving caused him to stay on at Pisa; ostensibly he was waiting for action from Collini at Florence, hopeless as that appeared to be. It was the 18th before he could bring himself to leave, accompanied of course by Teresa and the Gambas.

One of the consequences of Pietro Gamba's participation in the dragoon affair was that he and his father thereafter became *personae non gratae* in Tuscany. Writing to President Puccini on April 29, Governor Viviani said, with a touch of grim humour: "The air here is little salubrious to Count Gamba, and I shall limit the duration of their visitors' cards to the end of this affair unless I receive a different order from Your Excellency."[43] Pending a final decision about the Gambas, Viviani issued them visitors' cards good for ten days and renewable at the pleasure of the authorities. Byron, who had tried to shield Pietro Gamba in the dragoon affair and overestimated his success, was quick to conclude that the Tuscan government, like the Romagnese government, was hitting at him indirectly. Resentful at what he regarded as a miscarriage of justice—the exile of Tita, the continued imprisonment of Antonio, and the failure to punish Masi—he was glad at first to exchange his Pisan palazzo for the more retired Villa Dupuy, which Trelawny describes as a "new flimsy-built villa—not unlike the suburban verandahed cockney boxes on the Thames" and "ten times hotter than the old solid palace he had left, with its cool marble halls, and arched and lofty floors that defied the sun."[44] But he was still in Tuscany, and in exchanging Pisa for Montenero he had left none of his troubles behind. So distasteful was the suspense in waiting for decisions from Florence that, had it not been for his fear of the fiction that would be told when he had been driven out, he would gladly have left. In an almost chronic state of irritation he renewed his complaints to Dawkins:

(Monte Nero.) Livorno. June 7th 1822.

My dear Sir,

For my sins (I presume) & for your troubles I must intrude upon you again about this business of the Pisans &c.— — —
We are waiting here in a most unpleasant state of suspense—they refuse to give any answer or decision—and the family of the Gambas

are without any renewed papers or security of any kind—and all for *what?*—what on earth had *they* to do with the matter?—Is it because they are exiles and weak that they are to be persecuted or because they are friends of mine?—I know that *you* can do little for them—as they are not English subjects—but you may perhaps be able to obtain some information.—Of course their fate—must be mine—where they go—I accompany them.—Madame Guiccioli, who is ill, was ordered here by Vaccà for the benefit of Sea-bathing and we know not whether she will be permitted to remain. —Such conduct is indeed infamous—and can have but one object —viz—the persecuting *me* through *them*—that when they have driven us from their States—they may tell the Story in their own way.—*This* will I trust at least be prevented—and that you will obtain a *publication* of the conduct of the whole business.—Whatever personal vexation or inconvenience it may be to give up my houses &c.—& remove my furniture before the expiration of the period assigned for their occupation—I care little for leaving such a country—but I *do* care for the constructions to which (at this time) my departure may give rise. — — — —
The Courier [45] (they may exile him if they like) is in danger from his blow—as the enclosed note will certify.—All that I could wish to know is a *decision* of some kind—that I may know where to go —of course—what they decree about the Gambas is decisive with regard to myself.—Collini has had his 100 Sequins—and I hear no more of him.—I have taken the liberty—with *you*—to request the older Count Gamba to present this note—which has swelled into a letter—as he can explain anything you may think worth asking.— Believe me in all cases and in all places—with much esteem and obligation

ever y^rs^ faithfully
N. B. [46]

P.S. With regard to the fellow who has (I am *now* sorry to say) survived the consequences of his cowardly outrage—the other Gentlemen may prosecute—but it would be difficult for *me* to do so—as I was not one of his victims, except in the bad language which he has sufficiently paid for.—When I say that I am *sorry* that he has recovered—it is because I see many innocent persons suffering on account of such a miscreant.— — — —

Dawkins, who did not accept Byron's persecution theory, now for the first time betrayed some impatience on his own part while urging patience upon Byron:

"YOU MUST ALLOW ME TO DIFFER"

Florence 13 June 1822

My Lord

I received Your Lordship's letter last Saturday, and had an interview with Count Gamba on the following morning—He is so good as to say he will take charge of this—

The System of the Government here has become of late much more strict than it used to be in the treatment of Italian refugees, which I believe to be the case throughout Italy—It certainly exposes Count Gamba to some inconvenience by obliging him to come frequently to Florence, and by refusing to extend his personal security beyond the term of ten days; but I have advised him not to press, for the present, for an exception to their general rule—I may be wrong; but if he were my best friend I should hold the same opinion. I do not believe they wish to mark him, or to treat him with peculiar harshness; and I am convinced it is not their object to persecute Your Lordship through his family. Upon this point you must allow me to differ most decidedly from you altho' I shall appear presumptuous for so doing—On the importance of your remaining in Tuscany untill the whole business is cleared up and brought to a decision (which depends solely on Collini) and upon the construction to which your departure at this time would give rise, a former letter of mine will have shewn Your Lordship that we entirely agree—

I cannot induce Collini, who is regaling his friends in a Villa, to send me a statement of his last proceedings with the *buon Governo*; and I cannot close the business without it. He is as profligate as he is clever; and your 100 Sequins have enabled him to indulge his favorite propensity & to give his talent it's favorite direction.

I regret sincerely the annoyance that all these delays must cause to Your Lordship, and I perfectly understand the strong feelings called forth by the apparently uncertain situation of Count Gamba; but I hope and believe that a little time will put an end to both, and, in the mean while, I am not conscious of being to blame for either.

I hope you will excuse me My Lord the freedom of this letter, and not attribute it to want of that regard & respect with which I have—[47]

Hoppner, consulted through Byron's old friend Lord Clare, who came from Genoa to visit Byron, agreed with Byron that he, not the Gambas, was the real object of the Government's measures; but in his reply to Dawkins, Byron gracefully yielded the point, though without much show of conviction:

Villa Dupuy. June 16th 1822.

Dear Sir,

I have received your letter, & I fear that I have not made myself quite understood.—Believe me I never did nor could intend to throw the slightest shadow of blame upon you, for the evasions and apparent uncertainties of the T. Government in this affair.—Were I now or in future to do so—I should not only be *ungrateful* but *insolent*.—If I express myself strongly—on *their* apparent conduct—it is because I *feel* so—& because I never could—and I fear never *shall* be able to—measure my words and phrases as a wiser man would in similar circumstances.—But I am not quite Child enough to beat my Name—nor to confound for an instant your kindness—with their conduct.—I shall be very glad to find it as you state—and that the Gamba family at least will have fair play, for myself—it is a matter of much less importance—and I must bear it—as I have borne greater injuries.—My friend Lord Clare—who came over the other day from Genoa to see me [48]—states to me in a letter since his return (I had requested him to ask Mr. H[oppner] some questions as to the probability of their permitting the Gambas to remain in the Sardinian States—with me—in case of our quitting Tuscany) that Mr. H[oppner] agreed with Clare and myself in thinking that *I* (and not *they*) was the obnoxious object.—I am very glad to hear it—so that it secures *them*.—It is very presumptuous in me perhaps to conceive myself of importance enough to be obnoxious at all—but you know what human Nature is—and especially in Italy at present—where few persons who can read or write—are sufficiently insignificant to be beyond the dislike or Suspicion of the existing Governments, whether they be native or foreign.[49]—As to Collini—when he has drunk out—or otherwise expended his Sequins—I presume that he will proceed to earn them.—You seem almost to blame me for sending them—but what could I do? I never knew a lawyer that would move without them.—You say he is "profligate"—it is a great consolation to think that a Gentleman can continue so to so respectable a period of longevity.—I conceive that our friend must be between fifty and sixty—and he has a servant constantly by him at nights to change his linen—having apparently the same malady with the Canon Sedillo in Gil Blas.—It would not be unpleasant to know of what peculiar species his *present* profligacy may consist, that one might be aware of what may be reckoned upon in reserve at three score.—Will you do me the honour to believe me ever and truly

Yr. obliged
& faithl. St.

N. B.[50]

Dated two days later and written on a separate sheet of paper, the following postscript is obviously intended to accompany the preceding letter:

P.S.

The Elder Count Gamba is here—and will convey this letter.—Collini was at Pisa & was conversed with by Count Pietro—but of course nothing decisive could be ascertained from that "Light of the Council."—I enclose you an extract from an Austrian journal,[51] in which you will perceive how they have sunk all that made against the Serjeant—and added circumstances untrue.—The fellow had no blow from me—for I took him for an Officer—and expected of course a more satisfactory atonement.— — — I hear that Masi goes about Florence telling a story *different* even from his *own deposition*!—Let him make the best of it; he acted like a bully in the beginning; & with no great valour in the end—for when he was wounded—why did he not face about? he had strength enough to ride off at full gallop for a quarter of a mile—*after* he was hit—calling for help—in very distinct terms,—with the same effort he might have cut down a dozen.—But he seems to have expended his force in drawing on the unarmed and arrested party at the Gates.— — — — — —

I have every wish that the Investigation should be as full & fair as possible—without any favour to me. — — — — — — — — —

Meanwhile from Trelawny at Genoa came glowing praise of the *Bolivar*, which he described as "indeed perfection," borrowing Cassio's phrase for Desdemona. Two two-pound brass cannon, with Byron's coronet, were being cast for her at a cost of £25, he informed Byron, who in a grandiose moment had suggested four. Hoping to persuade Byron to take a long cruise in the boat, Trelawny had specified that the cabin should be commodious and comfortable and was trying to induce Roberts to spend the summer at Leghorn in order to take command on the cruise. Then in conclusion: "There has not been even a rumour at this place as to the Piesan row which reflected on you—although I am told Lord Bradford is not your *friend*. report says Mrs. Beauclerk certainly does not go to England but remains in Italy." [52]

The construction of the *Bolivar* had not escaped the

notice of the vigilant Buon Governo, which was alarmed by the reports which reached it. On May 30 President Puccini wrote to G. Falconcini, the Auditor of the Governor of Leghorn, that he had been informed that Byron was building a boat called the *Bolivar* at Genoa which was to be armed with cannon and used during Byron's *villeggiatura* at Montenero. "I would be grateful," he wrote, "if you would inform me if this is true and if you would communicate to me such facts about it as may have come to your attention." [53] Puccini was, in fact, better posted than Falconcini, who replied that although it had been known that Byron was building a boat at Genoa, it had not been known that it was to be called the *Bolivar* or that it was to be armed with cannon. "Perhaps," he added hopefully, "he only expects to place on the prow a piece of wood shaped like a cannon as is sometimes done by way of ornament." Governor Spannocchi had already been warned, Falconcini went on to say, that Byron would ask for a licence to keep the boat at the landing at Ardenza and was inclined to grant it if the sanitary laws were complied with. "I have informed him," wrote Falconcini, "that there are no stationary boats on this coast except some little boats belonging to the manors and that it would be dangerous to give this permission to Lord Byron, whose conduct and especially that of his servants has not been discreet or law-abiding in Pisa."

Puccini, whose rank and authority were superior to those of the Leghorn officials, decided to intervene. "This department," he wrote to Falconcini, "has written to the Lord Governor to refuse Lord Byron permission to keep his noted boat on the coast, acting from the information we already possessed and not from the confidential information in your letter." At the same time he wrote to Governor Spannocchi, repeating the information in his first letter to Falconcini and then concluding tactfully: "Although persuaded that Your Excellency in his wisdom would do so of his own accord, I should like to suggest that this is a case when the sanitary laws should be strictly adhered to and that the permission should be denied when it is requested."

Spannocchi at once fell in with Puccini's wishes. "I had already directed," he wrote, "that the permission should not be given without my express order, which would never be issued without a formal application which I would propose to communicate to and discuss with the Sanitary Commission. Now that Your Excellency has notified me of the intention of the Government in this matter, I shall be guided by it in my treatment of Milord if he really makes an application."

This would seem to have been the state of affairs when the *Bolivar* put in at Leghorn on June 18 or 19. To Byron the position taken by the authorities was but another example of their persecution of him, as he shortly wrote to Dawkins:

Montenero. June 26th 1822.

Dear Sir,

As a further specimen of the kindness and civility of the Tuscan authorities towards me—I am obliged to inform you that they refuse at Leghorn to accord permission to cruize in sight of the port in my little yacht—which arrived from Genoa last week.—They also refused to let me have a boat from the port (off the Sea-baths which are in *shallow* water—) to undress in when I go out to swim—which I prefer of course in deep water.—My Yacht which was allowed to cruize at Genoa without molestation & which cost me a considerable sum in building &c[54]—is thus rendered perfectly useless to me—& the expence entirely thrown away.—She is a little thing of about 22 tons—but a model to look at—& sails very fast.—She has nothing obnoxious about her that I know—unless her name ("the Bolivar") should be so—and all her papers are in regular order—& admitted to be so—& no one on board but the Crew.—Tita is still at Spezia. — — — — — — Thus matters stand with me at present—I only wait for a decision in the affair of the Serjeant to take steps for quitting a country from whose authorities I have experienced every petty vexation and insult—which they could devise—and without cause that I know of. I neither write nor speak of them—nor *to* them.—I merely state this to you—(for I have long given up any idea of obtaining any species of redress from the Government—) to show you the kind of disposition which their authorities uniformly evince in all which regards me.—

Believe me very truly
& faithfully
y^r^ obliged Servt
Noel Byron [55]

In the end Byron was forced to anchor the boat at Leghorn and was not allowed to embark and disembark passengers at will, disregarding the sanitary regulations. Although Dawkins must by now have realized the hopelessness of obtaining concessions for Byron, he nevertheless recommended that some relaxation of the strict regulations be made. The recommendation was refused, however, by President Puccini, who ruled that Byron must conform to the same regulations as applied to Tuscans. Torelli, who gleefully records this decision, thought it a part of a calculated plan to make Tuscany so unattractive to Byron that he would leave it of his own accord. In this respect at least he and Byron were of one mind.

We have already seen that Hunt, by his own account, sailed on June 28 for Leghorn, where he found Trelawny "standing with his knight-errant aspect, dark, handsome, and mustachio'd" in the *Bolivar*.[56] Going out to the Villa Dupuy, probably on the following day, to see Byron, Hunt found himself pitched into the midst of a comic opera incident. No clear account of what happened is possible. Two conflicting police reports were made, and the Marchesa Origo has recently added a third version, based upon Teresa's unpublished *Vie*. According to the more likely of the two police reports, Byron's cook and his coachman (Forestieri and Papi) suspected one of Teresa's servants of cheating them of a fair share of the perquisites and began a quarrel in which Pietro and Teresa intervened on behalf of their servant. Pietro received a slight knife wound under the right eye for his trouble, apparently from his sister's servant. Byron is reported to have shown himself on the terrace with pistols and to have put an end to the affair.

But according to the Marchesa Origo the trouble began when Papi, who had been sent to fetch water from the spring, suddenly balked and "began declaiming against the rich and the aristocracy, and speaking of equality and fraternity."[58] Other servants crowded about, talking loudly and shouting, and Pietro came out to issue sharp orders. Papi drew a knife with which he grazed Pietro's arm, whereupon both Pietro and Byron drew pistols.

There is something unsatisfactory in both of these accounts. In the police report it is Teresa's servant that wounds Pietro when he intervenes on behalf of the servant. Unless we are to assume that the wound was accidental, one can't help being sceptical. And as we have Hunt's testimony that Pietro's *arm* is in a sling, the wound under the right eye is a palpable error. In the Marchesa Origo's account Papi not only forgets the strong obligation he is under to one who has helped shield him in the Masi affray but spouts equalitarian sentiments that seem quite out of character for him.

At any rate, when Hunt arrived, Fletcher had gone for the police, and the house was in a state of siege: outside, Pietro's assailant (most likely Papi) stood guard, threatening to assault the first person who issued forth. Hunt, looking out the window, "met his eye glaring upward, like a tiger." When it came the hour for the customary afternoon ride, all crowded forward to be first to face the danger. The affair ended with unexpected ridiculousness: the knife-wielder threw himself upon a bench, extended his arms, and burst into tears, beseeching pardon and begging Byron to give him a kiss of forgiveness. Byron pardoned the man but dismissed him from his service and only suffered his hand to be kissed. Pietro, "a generous good-humoured fellow," thereupon shook the servant's hand with great good will. "The man was all penitence and wailing," concludes Hunt, "but he was obliged to quit. The police would have forced him, if he had not been dismissed."[59] Later on in the course of the drive, Byron and Hunt met Fletcher returning to the scene with a police officer.

The consequences of this second affray in which the police had to be called in have been—forgivably—misinterpreted by most of the biographers who have mentioned it at all. Torelli, Hunt, and Williams have all contributed to the misinterpretation by leaving the impression that it was the final straw with the Tuscan authorities and that it was responsible for the exile of the Gambas and therefore indirectly for Byron's own departure from Tuscany.[60] Yet the truth is that it had nothing to do with the expulsion of the Gambas, the banishment of any of Byron's or Gamba's servants (though Hunt is no doubt right in surmising that the assailant would have been banished had Byron not dismissed him), or Byron's departure from Tuscany. In fact the Government had already decided upon the exile of the Gambas and the banishment of Giuseppe Strauss and Antonio Maluccelli before it knew anything about this second affray.[61] That its decision was the outgrowth of the affair with the dragoon, though Byron's politics, his pistol-practice, and his inconvenient request to be allowed to embark and disembark passengers at will may well have entered into the matter, is proved by the following order, dated June 29, which went forth from the President of the Buon Governo to Auditor Pazienza at Pisa:

> You will have accompanied to the frontier, with orders of exile from the entire Grand Duchy on penalty of imprisonment for one year in the workhouse of Volterra if they do not obey, the well-known Antonio Maluccelli and Giuseppe Strauss, implicated in the known procedure concerning the affair of Sergeant Masi with whom your [communication] of the 29th of May [dealt].
>
> You will then inform Count Ruggero and Count Pietro Gamba

that their conduct, and particularly of the second [of these], in the above matter not having been satisfactory, their continued stay in the Grand Duchy cannot be tolerated; that in consequence they cannot obtain further extensions of their permits of residence, and that they must therefore get ready to depart together with all the members of their household,[62] that your Honour will determine, otherwise they will find themselves subjected to a formal order of exile. In case any of the individuals concerned in the present order should be in Leghorn, Your Honour will request subsidiarily execution by that Tribunal. You will at once communicate the import of the present order to the Governor and to me you will then give notice of execution.[63]

It was this communication which the Gambas had just received at the Leghorn tribunal on July 2 when Shelley and Williams encountered them. On the preceding day a letter had come to Byron from the Commissariat of Police at Leghorn courteously requesting him to send to the police tribunal without fail on the following morning at eight o'clock Counts Ruggero and Pietro Gamba and Giuseppe Strauss.[64] The Gambas were then given four days in which to leave Tuscany. As Byron proposed to accompany them, he now appealed directly to the Governor of Leghorn for an extension of time in which to order his affairs so that he might leave with them. The original letter has been lost, but the following is a translation of Torelli's Italian version:

Sir:

I write to you in English since I know you do us the honour of understanding our language. There has been issued by you an order of arrest and of exile for my courier and an intimation to the family of Count Gamba to leave Tuscany at the end of three days.[65] I am preparing to depart with them as I do not wish to stay any longer in a country where my friends are persecuted and where asylum is denied to the unfortunate. Since I have some affairs to arrange, I beg you to grant them a delay in order that I may depart with them.

[Noel Byron] [66]

Count Gamba at once presented himself to the Governor to petition for delay, but the Governor on the pretext of inconvenience refused to see him and referred him to the Auditor. Falconcini pointed out that the order had come from a superior authority and that he was therefore unable to modify it. He had, however, written to Florence in order that the Governor might answer Lord Byron's letter and would be glad to make known the reply as soon as it came.[67]

The arrival of Hunt and the necessity of getting something settled about *The Liberal* probably caused a change in Byron's half-formed plan to leave with the Gambas. At any rate when Shelley and the Hunts left Leghorn for Pisa on July 3, Byron and Teresa followed them. Torelli, observing Teresa's return disapprovingly, attributed it to "the imbecility of the Governor and the ambitious pusillanimity of the Auditor Pazienza," who permitted it. Now Byron said no more of leaving: "Instead, he was awaiting the arrival of a certain Smith, another English poet, with whom and another Englishman who prided himself upon being called an Atheist on his Passport, he had planned to write a journal on the governments of Italy, to be sent to London for printing in order to gain treasure."

Taaffe, who was about to leave for Florence and who properly felt some responsibility in the exile of the Gambas, called at once on Byron with a desperate proposal for saving them. Byron, who saw the proposal in its true comic aspect, had the good sense to reject it, as revealed in a letter carried by Taaffe to Dawkins, in which Byron's bitter feelings welled up and overflowed:

Pisa. July 4th 1822.

Dear Sir—

I regret to say that my anticipations were well founded.—The Gamba family received on Tuesday—an order to quit the Tuscan States in four days.—Of course this is virtually my own exile—for where they go—I am no less bound by honour than by feeling to follow.—I believe we shall try to obtain leave to remain at Lucca —if that fails—Genoa—and failing that—possibly America—for both Captain Chauncey of the American Squadron—(which returns in Sept.r) and M.r Bruen an American Merchant man at Leghorn offered me a passage in the handsomest manner—the latter sent to me to say that he would even send his vessel round to Genoa for us—if we chose to accept his offer.—With regard to the interpretation which will be put upon my departure at this time—I hope that you will do me the favour of letting the truth be known—as my own absence will deprive me of the power of doing so for myself—and I have little doubt that advantage will be taken of that circumstance. — —

This letter will be presented to you by M.r Taaffe—who is in considerable confusion at a measure to which his own heedlessness has a good deal contributed.—But—poor fellow—I suppose that he meant no harm.—He wanted the Countess Guiccioli to go to Florence and fling herself at the feet of the Grand Duchess—

"a supplicant to wait
While ladies interpose, and Slaves debate"

I can only say—that if she did any thing of the kind—I would never fling myself at *her* feet again.— — —

Collini's office has now become a Sinecure—and I wish him joy of it.—The inconvenience—and expence to me will be very considerable—as I have two houses, furniture—Wines, Dinner Services—linen,—books, my Schooner—and in short—a whole establishment for a family—to leave at a moment's warning—and this without knowing where the Gambas will be permitted to rest—and of course where I can rest also.— — — —

The whole thing—the manner in which it was announced—by the Commissary—&.c was done in the most insulting manner.—The Courier treated as if he were a delinquent—& sent away with Soldiers to take charge of him and lodged in the prison of Pisa—by way of Hostel.— — — —

I trust that this just Government is now content, my countrymen have been insulted and wounded by a rascal—and my Servants treated like Criminals though guiltless—while a noble and respectable family including a sick lady are ordered away like so many felons—without a shadow of justice, or even a *pretence* of *proof*.—With regard to yourself—I can only add that my obligations and feelings towards you are the same as if your exertions had been attended with Success.—I certainly did at one time think—that whether they considered the person who applied in our behalf—or the persons in whose behalf the application was made—we should at least have had a *fair* trial—as I afforded every facility for the investigation—as it is—I will *not* express my sentiments—at least for the present I cannot—as no words could be at all adequate to describe my Sense of the manner in which the whole has been conducted by these people who call themselves a Government.— [68]

The Gambas, who had remained at Montenero, were granted an extension of time until July 8, but with the departure of Byron and Teresa they had little use for it and were probably glad enough to exchange Leghorn for Lucca. According to Torelli they hoped to have the order of exile revoked "through connections at Florence" and return to Pisa. Their only hope, of course, was Dawkins, who, in response to Byron's letter of July 4, offered to do all in his power to obtain an asylum at Lucca for them. Byron's answer was addressed to Dawkins in care of Thompson's Hotel at San Marco, near Leghorn:

Pisa. July 6th. 1822.

Dear Sir,

Certainly—if any thing will be of use at Lucca, it is probable that a letter from you may have that effect.—I should be sorry to give you the personal trouble of a journey—on any account.—With regard to the Gambas I beg leave to observe that the Countess Guiccioli is *not* an exile, and her passport is or *was* given in the usual manner.—When She was separated from her husband in 1820—by the Pope's decree—it was enjoined by his Holiness that she was to reside with her father—or—otherwise to forfeit the alimony or *any* money (or whatever the word may be in the Roman or Romagnole Doctors' Commons) allotted to her from her husband's estates by the Papal order.—When her father and brother were exiled for political reasons—Count Guiccioli as was natural and conjugal applied to have her shut up in a Convent—on the plea that she was no longer residing with her family.—A minister of the Legation [69] gave me notice of this application and it's probable result in time for her to rejoin her relations in Tuscany—I could not then accompany her in person—as it would have [been] construed into an Elopement—but I joined her afterwards at Pisa.—If you can obtain permission for *them* or for *her* at least to reside within the Lucchese territory—it would be a great service—till I can make arrangements for the removal of my establishment—I shall go with them—but could then return here to settle my business.—

I do not even know upon what pretext She was ordered to quit Tuscany—or even if she really was so—since her name is not in

the letter—nor is she an exile—and is besides in very delicate health as Sr Vacca testified & can testify.— — — — — —
Believe me yrs very truly

& obliged

Noel Byron [70]

P.S.

Would you like to take a cruise in my little Schooner? it would console me for not being allowed to use it myself—if it could be of any pleasure to you while at Leghorn.— — — —

When the Gambas arrived in Lucca, Count Ruggero carried with him a letter from Dawkins to Marquis Mansi, Minister of Foreign Affairs. On behalf of Lord Byron it inquired whether the Government of Lucca would object to the Counts Gamba residing in its territory, depositing any caution it wished to impose.

I am able to add in support of the entreaties of my distinguished compatriot [continues the letter], that the Tuscan Government has officially declared that Lord Byron has never been suspected of having participated in the criminal part of the affair which made some noise in Pisa in the month of March past, and that I have a positive assurance from Count de Bombelles that he does not remember having pronounced the name of Count Gamba in his reports either to the Court of Austria or that of Tuscany. I have every reason to believe that the conduct of Count Gamba has been without reproach since he has lived in Tuscany. I am ignorant of the reasons which have removed him from it.[71]

The question was so important that Mansi referred it to the Grand Duchess for decision:

Confidential

9 July 1822

. . . I have no knowledge of the motives which have led the Governments of Rome and of Florence to exile from their states Count Gamba. All I know is that Lord Byron pays his court to Countess Guiccioli, daughter of Count Gamba, and that the aforesaid lord is as much celebrated for his poetic talents and literary culture as for his extravagance and his pernicious principles.[72]

On his arrival at Lucca Count Gamba had also presented himself to the President of the Buon Governo, with the request that he be permitted to reside in the Duchy. The President's report to the Grand Duchess lends weight to Byron's belief that he himself rather than the Gambas was the real object of attack by the various Italian states:

July 9, 1822

Yesterday Count Gamba of Ravenna arrived in Lucca with a son, and a daughter married to Count Guiccioli . . . Lord Baylon's [Byron's] lady-friend, and this morning they called upon me to request the privilege of domicile in the Duchy. They come from Tuscany where they have resided for some time in company with the aforementioned Lord Baylon, from which they have been expelled on account of a quarrel which took place resulting in the serious wounding of a certain Sergeant Masi, of which their respective servants have been accused of being the perpetrators, not without grave suspicion of connivance on the part of their masters; what has been the outcome of the trial I am not able to state; but I do know that the Tuscan Government has expelled them not so much because of the Gambas as for the aforementioned Mr. Baylon a most dangerous individual, not only on account of his fiery nature but also on account of his talents and his resources. He is going to arrive shortly, as he is following the above-mentioned Countess Guiccioli.

I have not [wished] to give any positive reply to the request for domicile without learning the sovereign will in the matter, but I would respectfully observe that in case it is desired to tolerate the Gambas, the same would not be possible in the case of Baylon for the reasons given; in case it is thought best to secure his expulsion without a direct measure, it would be advisable to follow the same course adopted by Tuscany, namely to order the above-mentioned Countess to choose another country for her residence. I shall await the most revered instructions of Your Royal Majesty in the case; in the meantime I have permitted the above-mentioned persons to remain in Lucca.[73]

Marquis Mansi supplemented his original letter to the Grand Duchess with a second letter on the following day, in which he stated that Count Gamba wished to remain in the duchy for a limited time only "since he hopes shortly to be permitted to return to Tuscany when some things have been cleared up which have been submitted to that government." He added that according to his information Count Gamba, Countess Guiccioli, and Lord Byron all had lived secluded lives in Pisa, where they were never seen in society. He concluded by informing the Grand Duchess that Mr. Dawkins was expected in Lucca during the following week and would be able to clarify any questions about Count Gamba's conduct that might be needful. And so the matter rested for the moment.

On July 11 Trelawny, searching for clues of Shelley and Williams, arrived in Pisa and communicated his fears to Byron. "When I told him," writes Trelawny, "his lip quivered, and his voice faltered as he questioned me." [74] Two days later Mary Shelley and Jane Williams came to the Palazzo Lanfranchi on what Miss Mayne calls "that most terrible quest in history" [75] and confronted a smiling Teresa with the dread question: "Where is he—Sapete alcuna cosa di Shelley?" [76] It was midnight, but they pressed on to Leghorn, hoping that Trelawny or Captain Roberts could tell them something of their husbands. They were taken to the wrong inn, and it was six o'clock before they found Roberts at the Globe Inn. Roberts, like Trelawny, had watched the *Don Juan* with his glasses until she disappeared into the fog, and a single look at his face seemed to confirm their worst fears. Only the forlorn hope that the boat had been driven over to Corsica remained. Saved from their despair by even so little, they resolved to return to Lerici. By nine o'clock they were on the way.

As soon as they were gone, Roberts wrote to Byron, asking permission to use the *Bolivar* in searching along the coast. The following prompt reply came from Byron:

Pisa. July 14th 1822.

My dear Sir,

Your opinion has taken from me the slender hope to which I still clung.—I need hardly say that the Bolivar is quite at your disposition as she would have been on a less melancholy occasion—and that I am always

Yr. obliged
& faithful friend
& Servant
Noel Byron [77]

To Capt. Roberts R.N.
Leghorn

Byron himself joined in the search, which lasted until the second of the two bodies (Shelley's) was washed ashore on the 18th.[78] Then on the following day Trelawny, after establishing the identity beyond doubt, left for the Villa Magni with the terrible news. Going upstairs unannounced, he entered the room where the two women were.

I neither spoke, nor did they question me. Mrs. Shelley's large grey eyes were fixed on my face. I turned away. Unable to bear this horrid silence, with a convulsive effort she exclaimed—

"Is there no hope?"

I did not answer, but left the room, and sent the servant with the children to them.[79]

Byron, at Pisa, was imperfectly acquainted with the situation at the Villa Magni and apparently thought that Trelawny had not told them the full story, as is revealed by the following letter to Captain Roberts:

Pisa. July 21st. 1822

Dear Sir,

I have just received your letter.—The account seems to tally with all that we had heard before.—Trelawney is expected in Pisa this evening with the ladies—who are not aware of the extent of their calamity—and still cling to some slight hopes.—Shelley's body has been completely identified by a book in his pocket—which was found by the Health-Officers upon him,—in his Jacket.—That of Williams is supposed to be the one found near the Serchio—(where we went in search on Thursday).—You have done well to heave down "the Bolivar."—Do you know where Mr. Wentworth is? or could you find out? and do me the favour to write him a line to say that I should not be indisposed to treat with him?[80]—Believe me ever

& truly yrs.
N.B.[81]

In accordance with the quarantine regulations the bodies of the two men were buried with quicklime in the sand where they had washed ashore. Cremation was necessary before they could be moved, and as it was Mary's wish that Shelley should be buried in the Protestant Cemetery at Rome beside their son William, Dawkins was helpful in obtaining the necessary permissions and in smoothing away all obstacles.

Despite Byron's disclaimer, that friendship was a commodity in which his genius was wanting, the shock of Shelley's and Williams's deaths was very great to him.[82] During the days when the two were missing and their tragic end was all but certain, the fortunes of the Gambas must have seemed of minor importance indeed by comparison. But the business of the world was not to halt because an eccentric English poet and his friend were missing, and Dawkins, passing through Pisa at this time, sent Byron a letter which he had received from the Marquis Mansi in reply to his letter of July 7. "Up to this time," Mansi had written in part, "I have not received any answer from Her Majesty and consequently I am ignorant what her intentions are on this subject. Perhaps knowing that you intend paying a visit here, she is resolved to make a decision after having received some further clarification, but this is only a simple supposition of my own." [83] Byron's reply, accompanying the return of Mansi's letter, was addressed to Dawkins "Alle 3 Donzelle," the inn at Pisa: [84]

July 16th 1822.

Dear Sir,

Excuse the wet condition of your Marchese's letter—I received it in a bath—and have scrambled out of the water to acknowledge your note.—I shall feel greatly obliged if you will do what you can for the Gambas—or rather us all—at Lucca. Did you receive a letter I sent you by Mr Trelawny of Count Pietro's—stating that they were afraid of *me* and my turbulence!!—& not of the Gamba's at Lucca; I enclose you a letter received from Mr Hill *

* English minister at Genoa.

yesterday—which I will thank you to return—excuse haste—I am dripping like a Triton—& believe me ever & faith.lly

Yrs

N. B.[85]

A few days later when Dawkins came to Lucca, he was informed that the Gambas could not be permitted to reside in the duchy except on a day-to-day basis. Byron's last letter to Dawkins was written in response to a letter containing the bad news:

Pisa. July 19th 1822.

Dear Sir,

Your letter would be as satisfactory as it is kind—if the Lucchese Government had given papers of Security even for a few months to the Gambas.—In the present state of uncertainty—it would be useless for me to take a villa out of which we might be all turned tomorrow as we have been here—and have the whole contract to pay nevertheless.—As it is we are exactly where we were—in a continual state of doubt and indecision,—but I am not the less obliged to you for having done all that could be done in the circumstances.—Believe me ever

& truly yrs.

Noel Byron [86]

P.S. I had no intention of residing in the City—nor indeed *would* do so if they would make me a present of it.—I wished to have obtained a quiet Country residence if possible not very far from the Sea.— — —

So it was hopeless even with "connections at Florence" and had to be given up. The Gambas, drifting on to Genoa, settled down to wait until it should suit Byron's pleasure to bring Teresa and join them.

CHAPTER 9

The End of the Pisan Circle

THE news of the death of Shelley and Williams reached Taaffe in Florence on July 20 as a dreadful and garbled rumour that Shelley and Mary had been drowned. Since the peace settlement of April 3 Byron had acted kindly enough toward Taaffe, but he had not bothered, during the days of awful uncertainty when Shelley and Williams were missing, to answer two letters that he had received from Taaffe. Taaffe's hesitation at addressing a third letter to Byron was overcome by his grave concern over the fate of the Shelleys and his hope that Byron would be able to contradict the story.

Florence
Saturday July 20 1822

My dear Lord Byron

This moment have I heard the most frigh[t]ful report with regard to M^r^ and Mrs Shelley—that they have been lost at sea. The details related are horribly particular: but it is these that make me hope the whole an invention (I have heard so many untruths lately!) for they say that the proof of the tidings being true is that a young female was found on the shore much disfigured but still recognised as Mrs Shelley and that this happened many *days ago.* Now Mrs Shelley was not in Leghorn at all but with Mrs Williams at Spezzia when I left Pisa. It was only Shelley himself and Williams (of whom no one says anything) that were in Leghorn. There would have been hardly time for them to have returned to Spezzia; and for Shelley & Mrs Shelley to have come back to Leghorn and be drowned—*returning back again from Leghorn several days ago.* In fine I believe this to be a malicious invention or at least what I hate an ill-timed improper practical jest: but still I cannot rest till I am assured it is so. I certainly would not trouble your Lordship, did I know who else to write to. But it requires so many days to have an answer from Spezzia itself; that I hope *that* and the horrid nature of the report will excuse me for requesting you will in some way or other have me informed of the truth of the matter by return of post. I wrote to you twice lately, once by Mr Dawkins and in the course of this week by post. As this latter contained the representation of M. de Monbel [1] the Austrian Minister (and indeed being therefore almost official) I am very sollicitous to know that it reached your Lordships hands safely.

I have the honor to be
Yours truly
J. Taaffe Junr [2]

At Spa, Captain Hay chanced to pick up a copy of the *Courier* and found there an account of Shelley's death:

My only hope of its being untrue [he wrote to Byron] is the horrible way in which the rascally Editor of the Courier has mentioned it—The paragraph is too infamous to transcribe & as you do not take in that paper I hope the cold blooded report may never meet your eye—I am so compleatly confounded & hurt by the brutal manner in which the Courier has indulged itself that every thing else is driven out of my head for the time or I would ask you what Collini has done in the Police affair I have never recieved the Power of Attorney you mentioned in your last letter & it will not I hope be necessary now to send it as I flatter myself I shall be in Italy again before the end of November should things not turn out worse than their present appearance gives me reason to expect. . . .[3]

Medwin, on his way from Naples to Genoa, claims to have been exposed to the same squall that took the lives of his two friends. At the Hotel de l'Europe he heard a rumour that an English schooner had been lost and two Englishmen aboard had been drowned. With no thought that the two might be Shelley and Williams he wrote to them at the Villa Magni and went on to Geneva, where presently a letter from Mary brought him post-haste back over the Alps too late for the cremation ceremonies.[4]

Trelawny, who from the first had assumed the multiple burden of directing the searchers, patrolling the coastline, and keeping alive a spark of hope in the hearts of Mary Shelley and Jane Williams while any hope remained, now undertook the arrangements for the cremation of his friends' bodies. On August 13 he took aboard the *Bolivar* an iron furnace, two wooden boxes, and spices such as Shelley's beloved Greeks used on their funeral pyres, and sailed to the point where Williams's body was buried in the sand.[5] The next day seems to have been occupied for the most part with obtaining the necessary official sanctions and making various preparations. Byron, who had promised to meet Trelawny that day, failed to come, and Trelawny sent him a note by one of the soldiers on duty to see that the sanitary laws were not violated. Early the next morning the following answer came from Byron:

Pisa. August 14th 1822.

Dear T—

Hunt and I propose being with you tomorrow by about noon—I do not know the distance between the two places of V[iareggio] and S[erchio]—& therefore you had better let a man be at the former where we shall stop first.—I delayed to-day on account of the post which however brought me no news

Yrs ever

N. B.[6]

On August 15 the body of Williams was cremated, followed by that of Shelley the next day. The story of the funeral rites for Shelley—the throwing of salt and frankincense into the furnace and the pouring of oil and wine over his body—of Byron stripping and swimming out to the *Bolivar* to conceal his emotions, and of Hunt sitting moodily in the carriage is too well known for repetition here. Following the collection of Shelley's ashes, which were put aboard the *Bolivar*, Byron and Hunt returned to Pisa in their carriage. "There is thus another man gone, about whom the world was ill-naturedly, and ignorantly, and brutally mistaken," Byron wrote to Moore. "It will, perhaps, do him justice *now*, when he can be no better for it." [7]

The days that followed were for Byron days of brooding, of working on *Don Juan*,[8] and of fretting over his money affairs. On August 15 he wrote to Kinnaird:

> I have just received a long letter from you—which however does not mention nor even allude to what I have written to you upon *twenty times* at least—viz—my half year's remittance from the funds which has *never arrived here* nor at *Leghorn.*—I need hardly repeat the extreme anxiety as well as inconvenience which this unaccountable delay has occasioned—now still increased by your *silence* upon the subject.[9]—Do pray—let me know what I am to think of this—has the money been sent? has it miscarried—or what has occurred? [10]

Five days later, when the remittance still had not arrived, he wrote again to Kinnaird, petulantly:

> I must still continue as in duty bound to bore you by every post till my remittance from the funds arrives—*which it has not yet done.*—I have been very unwell and all my skin *peeled off in blisters* besides some fever—owing to swimming three hours in the sea at Via reggio [11]—in the heat of the Sun.—But all this has been increased by the vexation of this unaccountable delay.—I receive at length a long letter from you about business—but not *one* word of my money!—so that I do not know whether it has been sent or not!—This is really most irritating and hardly excuseable.—Every thing seems to go wrong—and instead of gaining by this pretended accession of property *—you actually withhold my *own*—so that I am anything but a winner.— [12]

He was mollified by the arrival of the remittance a day or so later, which he wrote on August 24 to acknowledge:

> I am pacified—& soothed by the arrival of "fee" though tardy—but do not send your notes on the tour of Europe another time—it is making them too *Circular*—by nature as well as by name.[13]

But the amount did not seem right to him; it was too small: "I will have my own fee entire." There was more about the Noel business, and then: "I have also quite three nearly four Cantos of D.J. ready—now I wish to

* The Noel property.

consult you—supposing them at par as compositions—what ought they to produce us in the present state of publicating."

He strove desperately to understand all the details of his financial affairs, but he had never given himself to finance and it was too late to begin. "I do not understand how Lady Noel who died in *January*," he wrote plaintively—"can be entitled to rents beyond *Lady Day*—and I never heard of payment of rents except at Lady-day & Michaelmas.—Do you mean to tell me that *I* should be entitled to the *next* half year's rent if Lady B. was to be translated at present?"[14] He thoroughly distrusted Lady Byron's trustee, Dr. Lushington, and wrote a strong condemnation of him. And a final complaint: ". . . You must own that the whole of this Noel affair has been but a series of vexations from beginning till now.—"[15]

A part of his irritation sprang certainly from the Hunts—the commitment to Hunt that he grew daily more to regret, the vulgarity of Mrs. Hunt, the boisterousness and depredations of their children.[16] There was not much consolation in regarding Hunt as an unfortunate legacy that Shelley had left him. Moore and others had warned him against the *Liberal* enterprise,[17] and he felt it necessary to justify the money that he had lent or given Hunt: "I could not help assisting Hunt—who is a good man—and is left taken all aback by Shelley's demise."[18]

With all his irritations he was making progress on *Don Juan*. On September 7 he sent Cantos six and seven to Kinnaird. Three days later he wrote:

> I now transmit you the 8th and 9th—and request a line of acknowledgement—and also your opinion—I have no objection to listen to any suggestion of omissions *here* & *there*—but I *wont* be dictated to by *John Murray Esqe*—remember—let me hear from you.—Address to me—Genoa—Villa Saluzzi—where I mean to pass the winter—and don't forget to let me hear from you—[19]

His accumulated suspicions of Murray now concentrated themselves into a fear that Murray would persuade

Kinnaird to accept less than the real value of the works in Kinnaird's hands.

> As to what regards Murray [he wrote darkly on September 12] —that great man ought to be narrowly watched—*don't* you be talked over by the fellow.—He will prate of piracy. . . . In short —Doug.—the longer I live—the more I perceive that money (*honestly* come by) is the Philosopher's Stone—and therefore do thou be my man of trust & fidelity—and look after this same— my avarice—or cupidity—is *not* selfish—for my *table* don't cost four shillings a day—and except horses and helping all kinds of patriots —(I have long given up *costly* harlotry) I have no violent expences —but I want to get a sum together to go amongst the Greeks or Americans—and do some good—my great expense this year has been a Schooner which cost me a thousand pounds or better—[20]

But in spite of this sizeable investment he took a violent distaste to sailing: since the death of Shelley and Williams he had not made a single voyage in the *Bolivar*.[21]

Though the desire to get a sum together to go among the Greeks or Americans was not the full explanation of Byron's avarice, the desire to change scene was genuine enough. He had almost exhausted Italy as a place of residence, and his love for Teresa no longer sufficed as a main object in life. Moreover he was haunted by a fear of declining popularity in England and felt the need to make some dramatic move that would re-establish him in the public favour. Back in Ravenna days he had thought of taking Allegra and going to a new country; he had continued to talk vaguely about it at Pisa. First it was a province in Chile or Peru—"of course with a gold or silver mine to pay usance for my monies," he had remarked archly to Trelawny;[22] then it was Mexico and a copper mine; at still another time America; and finally even Van Diemen's Land.[23] To Trelawny it seemed that there was a beginning but no middle or end to his enterprises. But, says Trelawny, "the under-current of his mind was always drifting towards the East. . . . His thoughts veered round to his early love, the Isles of Greece, and the revolution in that country. . . ."[24]

Hobhouse, arriving for a visit on September 15, remained till September 21.

> [He] told me [said Hobhouse] that the Pisans disliked him because he would not associate with them and the professors of the University, and because he would not go to a ball given last Christmas. . . . It seems Madame Guiccioli and her father and brother lived together in a house apart until the Gambas went to prepare Lord Byron's house at Genoa. This is Italian morality.[25]

Byron was glad to see Hobhouse, but Hobhouse's departure left him depressed. To Kinnaird he wrote dejectedly: "Hobhouse went this morning—these glimpses of old friends for a moment are sad remembrances. . . . Write to me at *Genoa*—where I am going directly." And then in a suspicious moment he added: "Don't you be cajoled by [Lady Byron's] banking with you but remember yrs. ever, N.B."[26] Writing to Hobhouse, then at Florence, on September 26, Byron sent greetings to Collini, and announced: "We are all packaging, to set off at *daybreak* to-morrow morning, a preliminary which by no means agrees with my dormitory habitudes."[27]

The hubbub, din, and confusion occasioned by the move were frightful, says Trelawny. "If the Casa Lanfranchi had been on fire at midnight it could not have been worse, nor I more pleased at escaping from it, as I did, under the plea of getting the flotilla ready at Leghorn."[28] Mary Shelley had gone on ahead and had made arrangements for Byron and the Gambas to live at the Casa Saluzzo, at Albaro, near Genoa, while she and the Hunts established themselves not far away at the Casa Negrito.

"All that were now left of our Pisan circle established themselves at Albaro—Byron, Leigh Hunt, and Mrs. Shelley," writes Trelawny. "I took up my quarters in the city of palaces. The fine spirit that had animated and held us together was gone! Left to our own devices, we degenerated apace. Shelley's solidity had checked Byron's flippancy, and induced him occasionally to act justly, and talk seriously; now he seemed more sordid and selfish than ever."[29] Byron's sordidness and selfishness took the form of miserliness: it was Trelawny who had to supply the money for Mary Shelley's travelling expenses to England after Byron had reneged. Perhaps Trelawny was too severe on Byron; but he is accurate beyond doubt in his observation that it was Shelley, not Byron, who held the little circle together and without whom it disintegrated quickly. The wounding of Sergeant-Major Masi, which was directly responsible for the banishment of the Gambas and thus ensured Byron's departure from Pisa, would in the end have proved a damaging blow to the Pisan circle; but had Shelley and Williams not lost their lives on July 8, there might nevertheless have continued to be a Pisan circle—somewhat dimmed in lustre without its brightest member, it is true—but still a Pisan circle comprised of the Shelleys, the Williamses, Trelawny, Taaffe (prudently avoiding Trelawny), and perhaps the intermittent Medwin. But it could not exist without Shelley. Although Byron did not leave Pisa until the end of September,[30] the real end of the Pisan circle occurred on July 8—the day of Shelley's death.

CHAPTER 10

After Pisa

For Byron, Genoa was merely an interlude. He was to live there until the following July; he was to write there the 11th–16th cantos of *Don Juan;* he was to meet there Lady Blessington and provide her with the materials for her valuable *Conversations with Lord Byron.* He was tiring of Italy, tiring of Teresa, tiring of inaction, but he lacked the initiative to break away. Trelawny, who had been trying to get him out of Italy, gave up in despair and left him. In the following June a message from Byron caught up with Trelawny at Rome: "You must have heard that I am going to Greece. Why do you not come to me? . . . Pray come, for I am at last determined to go to Greece; it is the only place I was ever contented in."[1] Trelawny, knowing Byron, ignored the summons until Byron wrote that he had chartered a vessel; then Trelawny hastened to Genoa. On July 16, with Pietro Gamba, Tita, Fletcher, a physician, and a bevy of servants, they set sail. For Byron it was to be the last journey—a journey that was to redeem all that was mean or weak in his character and to lift him for ever to his proper place with the immortals.

Trelawny, separating from Byron in Greece, joined the faction of Odysseus, whose young sister Tersitza he married. He arrived at Missolonghi four days after Byron's death on April 19, 1824, and was taken immediately upstairs by Fletcher to the room where Byron's embalmed body lay. Remaining in Greece till 1827, he was shot by traitors and lay prostrated in a cave on Parnassus for two or three months, barely escaping with his life. "Death thought me his own—he seized me by the body and limbs—but relented ere his icy paw had clutched my heart," as he put it.[2]

In 1828 he was briefly in England before going to Florence, where his daughter by Tersitza lived with him and where he was friendly with Landor. Rebuffed by Mary Shelley, to whom he applied for assistance in writing a life of Shelley, he wrote instead the first instalment of his own life, which was published in 1831 as *Adventures of a Younger Son*. The following year he brought his daughter to England before setting off for America, where he travelled for about a year and a half. Between 1835 and 1845 he lived mostly in London and was the cause of a divorce in 1841 between Sir Harry Dent Goring and Lady Goring, whom he subsequently married.

From 1847 to 1858 he was farming at Usk, on the Welsh border, where he wrote *Recollections of the Last Days of Shelley and Byron* (1858). More and more his thoughts had been turning back to the halcyon days at Pisa. "He wrote his *Recollections* as though he had been absent from the Casa Magni thirty-six minutes rather than years, an old man conversing with the long dead in some land of eternal youth," comments Massingham.[3]

His marriage broke up in 1858 as the result of his introduction of a second female member into the household. Browning, who encountered him some years later, was not attracted to him: " 'The Trelawnys,' " he wrote to Isa Blagden in 1867, "are problematical to me,—he has so many wives and daughters,—the last he married, I fancied had been the Baronet's wife, whose divorce he caused. . . . He lives with a niece,—I suppose she is *that*, but won't swear. . . ." [4]

In 1878 appeared his *Records of Shelley, Byron, and the Author*. Details of the last years of his life are scanty, but it is known that he lived on in London and later at Sompting, a village near Worthing, with undiminished vigour of body and mind until the time of his death on August 13, 1881. He was buried, as he had earlier arranged, beside Shelley in the Protestant Cemetery at Rome.

Medwin, who remained in Pisa only a few days, made a pilgrimage to the Villa Magni on his way to Genoa and eventually Paris.[5] In December, Byron heard that he was to be married and wrote him a letter of congratulations, but the report turned out to be premature. He had not given up his literary aspirations and was working on a "dramatic legend" entitled *Ahasuerus*, on the subject of the Wandering Jew. In a letter of April 22, 1823,[6] he asked permission to dedicate it to Byron. "In one of the characters under the name of Julian," he wrote, "I have attempted to give a sketch of our poor friend Shelley & this may perhaps prove some claim to your sanctioning my dedication." The permission was given, though Byron warned that his own popularity was not such as to recommend the work of another to the public, and the poem appeared in 1823.

Circumstances having deferred Medwin's marriage another twelve months, he solicited Byron's assistance in obtaining employment. A place on the staff of a Spanish duke of the Constitutional party had to be refused because he could not get leave from the Horse Guards to accept it. He now had thoughts of joining the Greek cause, to which the same obstacles did not apply. Would Byron help with advice or introductions? Of his own poem, he volunteered the information that he had written twice to Murray, proposing publication, "but with an insolence common to that Autocrat (and which were he a Gentleman would require chastisement) I received no reply." Byron wrote a letter to Hobhouse informing him of Medwin's desire to help the Greek cause, but apparently nothing ever came of it.

In 1824, when Byron died, Medwin was in Switzerland;

later in the year he published his *Journal of the Conversations of Lord Byron in 1821 and 1822*, which excited both interest and controversy, provoking Hobhouse to write a pamphlet contradicting many of Medwin's statements. In 1825 occurred the marriage that Byron had prematurely congratulated him on—to Anne, Baroness Hamilton of Sweden, by whom he had two daughters; but falling into debt, he deserted her and led an unsettled life thereafter.[7] Continuing his literary work, he wrote a memoir of Shelley in 1833 that was afterwards expanded into a biography. Trelawny, encountering him years later, says that he had lost none of his enthusiasm for Shelley. The appearance of the memoir, however, induced Trelawny to write to John Murray: "... Medwin is a mesureless & unprincipled liar. . . ." [8] After twenty years spent in retirement at Heidelberg, he returned to Horsham, where he died on August 2, 1869.

Mary Shelley remained in Genoa—trying to piece together the shattered fragments of her life, copying Byron's *Don Juan*, trying to smooth away the difficulties between Byron and Hunt—until her departure for England in July, 1823. Loving Italy now and hating England, she was motivated entirely by her son's interests. In the following year she and Jane Williams, who had preceded her to England, saw from their windows Byron's funeral procession as it wound slowly up Highgate Hill, on the way to Nottingham, and knew "that in the passing before their eyes of the mortal remains of Byron there had gone, too, the last symbol of the life they had lived so fully in the companionship that Trelawny had called the 'Pisa Circle.' " [9] Sir Timothy Shelley would do nothing for her, but he made Percy Florence a small allowance which was increased parsimoniously as the boy grew older. An edition of Shelley's *Posthumous Poems* which Mary published in 1824 had to be suppressed to prevent the loss of this allowance.

In slightly easier circumstances after 1831, she sent her son to Harrow, hoping that they would teach him conformity—which Shelley had spent his life rebelling against. Her novels, *The Last Man* (1826) and *Lodore* (1835), were both successful; and though she lived much in the past, collecting her husband's works and letters, the present was not completely barren of interest. In 1844 her son inherited the baronetcy, which added to her material comfort. If happiness was never again to be her lot, at least she found serenity in the years before her death in 1851.

Jane Williams soon found a devoted admirer in Shelley's early friend Thomas Jefferson Hogg. It was a bitter disillusionment to Mary to discover that Jane did not reciprocate her affection in equal measure and was spreading stories about Shelley and Mary and the life at Pisa and Villa Magni which wounded Mary deeply. In 1827 Jane joined her fortunes with Hogg's without benefit of clergy and bore him one child, which Mary, despite her hurt, stood godmother to.

For a time after Byron's departure for Greece, Teresa lived with a former teacher at Bologna, her father being at Ferrara. Her allowance from her husband had been stopped by the Pope in July, 1822, because of her living in the same house with Byron, and she was entirely dependent upon friends. From Cephalonia Byron wrote to her: "You may be sure that the moment I can join you again, will be as welcome to me as at any period of our recollection,"[10] but in her heart she must have known it was not true. From Missolonghi few letters came. A petition of September 26, 1823, filed on her behalf by Annibale Ginnasi,[11] a distant connection, for the restoration of her alimony in the original amount was vigorously contested by Count Guiccioli, but the Pope ruled in her favour in the following April. Between 1825 and 1831 her father served six years of a twenty-year sentence in the fortress at Ferrara, after an attempt, in which he had no part, to kill Cardinal Rivarola. His last years were spent on his estate at Filetto, where he died in 1846.[12]

In 1826, "hoping that time and experience might have produced some change in [Count Guiccioli's] character,"[13] Teresa returned to her husband at Venice. Crafty old Guiccioli, writing to Taglioni on June 25, said: "[My wife] is coming here in status of separation, with the mutual project of negotiating to see whether a reunion can be arranged which would ensure a stable peace between us. In these circumstances I propose beforehand . . . to have a brief private document drawn up as by mutual consent between us."[14] It provided (1) that the alimony should be suspended during the reunion, (2) that since in 1820 Teresa "did in fact withdraw . . . in superabundance the entire moveable effects settled in the ante-nuptial settlements," she might take only her personal clothing in the event of another separation, and (3) the 1,000 scudi unpaid remainder of her dowry should remain unpaid, but in case of another separation the interest upon it should be paid to Teresa.

The reunion was not a success: after five months they separated permanently, and the Count was ordered to pay Teresa 150 scudi a month.[15] She went to live at Ferrara and then at Rome, where in 1828 she saw John Taaffe, with whom for a little while she talked of the old, happy days in Pisa.[16]

In company with her brother Vincenzo she visited England in 1832–33. There she met Byron's half-sister Augusta Leigh and some of his friends—John Murray, Henry Drury (Byron's tutor at Harrow), and Dr. John Pigot, among others. She also made a pilgrimage to Newstead Abbey, bringing away a red rose, a branch from a beech tree on which Byron's and Augusta's names were carved, and an acorn from an oak.[17] She made two more visits to England, in 1834–35—when she dined with

Trelawny and saw Mary Shelley several times—and in 1839.

Count Guiccioli having died in 1840, she married the wealthy Marquis Hilaire de Boissy in 1847 and presided over a fashionable salon at Paris in which the portrait of Byron was hung prominently. The Marquis is said to have introduced her with pride as "Madame la Marquise de Boissy, ma femme, ci-devant maîtresse de Lord Byron."[18] Upon his death in 1866 she returned to Italy; she lived mostly in her villa at Settimello, near Florence, where she died in March, 1873.

Her brother Pietro, who had discreetly followed Byron's body to England in another vessel, to avoid unpleasant gossip, helped Hobhouse wind up Byron's affairs and then returned to Greece, where he became a Colonel in the army.[19] In 1827 he contracted typhoid fever and died on the isthmus of Metana. He was buried in the fortress of Diamantopoulous, subsequently destroyed, and no trace remains of his grave.[20]

Taaffe spent the autumn and winter of 1823 at Florence. Lady Hardy, widow of Nelson's captain, writing to Byron[21] on February 13, inquired whether Byron was to be in Genoa at the end of March, as she was considering a visit there.

> I therefore *beg* you to write to me three lines just to say if you will be there still as I heard Mr. Taaffe tell M$^{\underline{de}}$ D'Albany the other night you were going to travel again towards Greece. I did not like that Mr. Taaffe much so I w$^{\underline{d}}$ not gratify him by asking him when you were to go on as if I thought he could know anything about you.—Perhaps I am wrong as I very often am in my hasty judgements but He is such a *Pat* that his voice before I looked at him put me against Him.[22]

What Byron said about Taaffe in reply may be guessed from this further comment of Lady Hardy's in a subsequent letter: "I am so pleased that my *instinct* made me dislike Mr. Taaffe before I knew his *dirty cowardly* conduct: but how few Men there are that are really proof in time of need. It makes one cross with ones Species."[23]

Upon his return from Florence, Taaffe worked on his translation of Dante for a time before abandoning it. He alone of the little circle was now left in Pisa. During the next two years he wrote a number of long poems, all doomed to be unpublished. One of them, *Alphonso and Isabel or The Last Eighteen Hours of Cadiz*, was inspired by his friend Madame Regny; another, *Belgrade*, was a tribute to Nicholas, sixth Viscount Taaffe. During the summer of 1824 he lived on the shore of Lake Como and was visited usually once a week by the Fortises and his daughter—but without the child's knowing that he was her father.

In 1825 he travelled a good deal about the continent, visiting the Austrian branch of his family and securing the promise of their interest for his son. With the departure of Madame Regny from Pisa in 1826 the town lost its sole remaining attraction for him, and he determined to leave. The death of his parents in 1825 having removed any obstacle to his children's living with him, his son was now with him. Sea bathing was recommended for the boy, and after consulting Vaccà, Taaffe selected Fano as a place to spend some months.

He and his son found an apartment in the unoccupied Palazzo Gabuccini, the Marchese and the Marchesa being absent; and upon their return in the spring of 1827, he persuaded them to allow him to continue living there. When the Marchesa went to Venice for the following winter, Taaffe and his son accompanied her. They lodged in the Palazzo Mocenigo, where Byron had once lived, and at the Countess Benzoni's they were shown the sofa on which Byron sat beside Teresa on that first evening when he was introduced to her. Two of Taaffe's sisters came out from Ireland to join him upon his return to Fano, and he attempted to claim his daughter but was prevailed upon by the Fortises to leave her with them on an extended visit. The Gabuccinis and the Taaffes wintered together at Rome and Naples in 1827-28, and it was at this time that Taaffe encountered Teresa. In his autobiography he devotes several pages to a condemnation of Lady Byron and a justification of Teresa.

At the proper age his son was placed first in the Lyceum at Venice and later in the Ingenieurs Accademie at Vienna. At intervals Taaffe's daughter came to stay with him or to travel with him, but always after a time she went back to the Fortises at Milan. In 1834 the Marchese Gabuccini contracted a fever and died. Such intimate members of the family had Taaffe and his son become that the Marchesa promised Taaffe, in the event of her death before him, to make his son her heir. It is not then very surprising that in 1836 she was married to Taaffe, with whom, though she was many years younger than he, she seems to have lived happily.

During the two or three years preceding his marriage and for several years after, Taaffe was working on the poem that was to be his masterpiece—*Adelais*. The subject, Richard Cœur de Lion and the Crusades, was originally suggested by Madame de Staël, and Taaffe had made a beginning on the poem as early as 1821. Byron, shortly after his arrival in Pisa, heard of it and asked to be allowed to read it, but Taaffe always turned the conversation to something else. The poem appears not to have been completed until 1841, when Taaffe had it printed at his own cost. More than his less ambitious poems it shows the futility of his continued labour in a field of endeavour in which he lacked the gift; subsequently he burned all but five copies.

Following his marriage, Taaffe brought his bride on a visit to Ireland and England, where he received permission to appear at a king's levee in the uniform of the Order of St. John of Jerusalem, of which he was a Commander. His interest in this order may have been partly a matter of family pride, several of the members being commanders in it. In 1848 Taaffe was in Malta, and his wastebooks of the time suggest that the idea of writing a history of the Order of St. John of Jerusalem (or Knights of Malta) may have occurred to him while there or else that the visit was made for the purpose of collecting material. The interval between 1848 and 1852, when his history was published in four volumes by Hope, was principally occupied with its composition. As might be expected it did not pay expenses.

From 1856 to 1862 he was compiling an Arabic Grammar, which was not completed before the death of his wife on April 19, 1860, to whose memory he dedicated it. It was copied for him by his devoted son,[24] by that time an army officer of many years' experience, who had scarcely finished his task when Taaffe died at Fano on August 28, 1862, and was buried in the same sepulchre with his wife. It had been fifty years before that he had set out on his travels, which were expected to last only a few years, until the affair with Mrs. Colebrooke had blown over. Fortune had decreed otherwise: for fifty years he had been an exile from his native country, but so deep lay his affection for it that he willed that his right hand should be cut off and sent back to Ireland for burial. It lies buried today at his beloved Smarmore.

BYRON, SHELLEY

AND THEIR PISAN CIRCLE

Appendix A

ELEGY
ON THE DEATH OF
HIS ROYAL HIGHNESS PRINCE CLEMENT
DUKE OF SAXONY, etc., etc.

By John Taaffe, Esq.

I

Woe! Woe! Woe!
At dead of night—a winter night—
Death bestrode the blast,
And conscious Arno's high-swoln river
Swelled wildlier as he past;
On black and heavy vans he took his flight.
Roll, thunders, roll! Ye lightnings quiver!
Woe! Woe! The storms he with him drew
O'er land, o'er billow;
And as he flew,
Anon, anon
The Monarch started from his throne,
The Peasant from his pillow.

II

Woe! Woe! Woe!
Within the Palace gate,
Within the hall of state,
Where Goths and Moors of yore
The Spanish sceptre bore,
Amid his Council at the witching hour
The King prolonged debate.

III

But in a room beyond that Council (now
Wan with a watch so long)
Was seen a lovely Queen reclining,
Young, lovely,—Ah! how young!
Thought seemed to sit upon her stately brow
Collected half, and half repining;
While o'er her couch, her fairy form,
Her snowy arm her pale cheek raising,
And her long, loose, un-jewelled hair,
Lay light and shade distinct and warm,
Shed by the taper near her blazing;
So that she seemed of marble fair,
But for her sweet eyes' holy gazing,
Which had abashed a fiend—
The fiend of that same stormy night,
Who rode on hail, and wind.
Then came a breath of odour streaming,
A swell of music softly thrilling
And that fair, lonely chamber filling;—
While slow descends the air along,
Robed in a flood of silver light,
A form celestial brightly beaming,—
Too bright for mortal song.

IV

Starting with rapture from her ivory couch,
Her arms of snow she thrice flung wide—
And thrice within her vain embrace
Found air, and nought beside.
"Sister, no more—as even my looks avouch—
"I am no more of mortal race;
"With human change of foul and fair,
"With men deluded or deluding
"My spirit ethereal strives no more.
"One moment hath sufficed to bear
"This essence—time and space eluding—
"From distant Arno's shore;
"Where some on me must long be brooding.
"With them I have left my dust,
"Alas! a fleeting trust!

"I knew 't was dust—yet, ere the wind
"Had wafted me away,
"I cast a tender look behind—
"I could not scorn that lifeless clay:
"Poor, faithful partner! fresh it lay,
"Age had not dimmed its flower;
"And though it will fade till all must loathe it,
"We know that glory yet shall clothe it.
"Yea! on that medium of our love
"Thy doating eyes again shall pour;
"And I, its soul, already soar
"To be thy guard above.

V

"Lo! the first journey of my soul is to thee—
"Since death has set me free,
"Since fleet, aspiring, burning, gushing
"I have snapt my links of earth
"And go through ether flushing—
"To *thee*, for though ye all are dearest,
"All fair and young,
"Yet thou art a younger one,
"And where thou steerest
"Clouds are hung;
"Nor placid seems the course thou hast to run.
"I have died as Kings should die—humanity (*)
"Valour and honor should be their's from birth.
"Still, still be thine
"These virtues of our Line!
"And, though no gaze can go
"Within the veil that wraps futurity,
"It is enough to know
"That my sweet sister (whatso'er await her)
"Shall ne'er belie
"Her lineage high.
"A little sooner, later,
"(When met in dear communion)
"This parting shall but seem a bell
"That tolled for our eternal union.
"Who best my name would cherish
"Should let vain sorrow perish:

(*) *H.R.H. is said to have caught his death by visiting one of his sick menial servants. If so, it is a specimen of the characteristic humanity of his family.*

"He whom ye loved and love so well
    "Precedes you to the skies
"To spread your couch in Paradise:
"He goes to act a glorious part
"Where all are kings, and all are loyal
"To One great Monarch: he retires
    "To join our mighty sires:
    "The Power who made us royal
    "Ordains a royal heart."

VI

She spoke not, sunk not—o'er her mien
A deep, meek, wondrous calm was spread;
    Who viewed had said—
If her high spirit ere repined,
    'T is now resigned;
Whate'er her doom, she 'll still be seen
    A SAXON QUEEN.

TO THE BARONNESS OF STAEL

Believe me, lady, if remain
    My voice unheard, mid many a song,
Tis that I know no lively strain;
    Nor other strain than sorrow, long.

T'would mar the tones, were I to sing
    Of virgin-beauty and above
What roses in Elysium spring
    For Hymen's wreath by Cupid wove.

So mourning too is this:—is this
    That bids Adieu to thine and thee!
Yet to have been where thou in bliss
    Hast been is soothing much to me.

When in the verdant isle of mine,
    Or Albion, where thy name is dear,
I muse upon some page of thine,
    That wakes for injured love a tear,

Or lofty science of the mind
Unfolds, or faction's veil day
When other far than wave or wind
Assailed in vain thine onward way,

Or ardent fancy bids thee view
The sun, and that mysterious land,
Where once the purpled lillies knew
Of pest and famine's meagre hand,—

I'll turn from even that brilliant theme
And in remembrance love to bear
Me back to Arno's Mountain-stream
And think I meet thy spirit there.

JOHN TAAFFE

Pisa Feby. 22. 1816.

Appendix B

TAAFFE'S DEPOSITION

Io sottoscrivente giuro che essendo stato à cavallo insieme col Principe Turco, Mehemet Effendi, e trovando il mio cavallo troppo riscaldato lasciai il Principe entrare solo in Città, ed io andava passeggiando tranquillissimamente quando incontrai Milord con quattro altri Signori e seguito da un servitore. Dopo pochi passi fatti insieme (giacchè io avevo voltato nell' incontrargli) un Dragone passò fra me ed il fosso in gran carriera: onde il mio cavallo (è sempre molto vivo ma allora più che mai vivo per causa delle galoppate fatte col Principe Turco) fece un salto subitaneo; onde io commosso voltaia Milord dicendo "Avete mai veduto una cosa simile?" Il Dragone non mi toccò. Le mie parole furono perchè il salto del mio cavallo mi turbò. Io non posso giurare, nè conviene giudicare delle intenzioni d' altrui: ma bensì giuro che la mia pretta idea fu che Milord aveva semplicemente l'intenzione di far vieppiù saltare il mio cavallo (uno suo solito scherzo con me) quando dando una spronata partì di galoppo seguito, (o preceduto, o accompagnato giacchè a questo io non badai) dai quattro Signori ed anche dal Servitore. Io allora non pensava ad altro che a ritenere il mio cavallo, ed a tranquillizarlo. Ma tanto saltò che senza buttarmi per terra mandò per terra il mio capello. Onde io sorridendo voltai ad una di due donne che passavano lagnandosi dei cavalli che galoppavano per la strada—"Vedete, buona donna, io almeno ritengo il mio cavallo ed è per amor di voi, sicchè vi prego di darmi il mio capello." Essa me lo diede, ma tutto coperto di polvere: onde io mi fermai un istante per ripulirlo temendo che Milord dicesse che io fossi caduto. Allora partii trottando via verso la porta. Alla voltata della strada essendo arrivato in vista della porta vidi vicinissimi ad essa il dragone attorniato dai Signori. Mi parevano essere in rissa ma soltanto di parole per un istante e mi sembrò vedere Milord offrire al Dragone qualche cosa che pareva un biglietto; e Milord immediatemente entrò in città con due o tre altri. Mentre cosi faceva il Dragone stese la mano alla guardia gridando "*fermategli tutti*," e quasi nel medm̃o momento sguainò la sua sciabola e cominciò a ferire furiosamente a dritta e a sinistra contro i tre Signori che cercavano di seguire per la porta Milord e gli altri già passati. Tutto questo passò rapidissimamente: giacchè quantunque io era già bastante vicino quando il dragone gridò "*fermategli tutti*" per sentirlo, e che non fermai il mio cavallo (almeno non credo di così aver fatto) nientedimeno quando entrai per la porta il Dragone già rimetteva la sua sciabola nel fodero. Io non vidi altra mano alzarsi che la sua, egli mi parve d'aver tutto il torto e di aver menato la sua Sciabola con ogni sforzo, solamente non dando più ferite a quei Signori per che erano troppo vicini a lui. Io non aveva niente in mano—assolutamente niente. Nondimeno (il dragone essendo in atto di remettere la Sciabola nel fodero e tutti quei Signori essendo partiti) io m'accostai a lui è prendendolo per il braccio gli dissi "Non avete vergogna di tirar la sciabola contro gente inerme?" e credendo riconoscerlo aggiunsi, "mi pare di avervi veduto altra volta, e di avervi conosciuto per un galant'uomo, etc." Egli non mi fece nulla. Ma due di quei Signori ritornando si voltò contro loro con delle minaccie furiose e quasi sguainando la sciabola: giacche non posso giurare se la sguainò intieramente o no. Poi diede una spronata e partì. Anche quei Signori io non vidi più: e voltando il mio cavallo tornai dentro la porta per dire alla guardia di badar bene di fare il rapporto giusto giacche vi erano tanti testimoni. In fatti c'era una folla di gente alla porta. Io giuro di non aver veduto più di quanto ho rapportato quì.

In quanto alle parole citate:—quelle dette da me a Milord sono tradotte dall' Inglese e giuro che sono *esatte precisamente* essendo esse una esclamazione mis solita; per quelle dette alla donna ed al dragone sono *esatte in sostanza*, giacchè per le precise parole litterali io non posso giurare.

Nota. Quando dico sopra ch'era un modo solito di Milord di scherzare con me, etc. non voglio dire ch'egli era solito di far saltare il mio cavallo ma bensì di riddersi dei salti che il mio cavallo spesso faceva e delle conseguenze (come di entrare nel fosso) che sono successe alla volta.

Pisa il 28 Marzo 1822.

TRANSLATION

I the undersigned swear that having been riding horseback with the Turkish Prince, Mehemet Effendi, & finding my horse too heated, I let the Prince enter the city alone, and I was riding along very quietly when I encountered Milord with four other gentlemen & followed by a servant. After having taken a few steps together (since I had turned around upon the encounter) a Dragoon passed between me and the ditch at the edge of the road going at full speed: so that my horse (which is always very lively but at that time livelier than ever because of the galloping done with the Turkish Prince) made a sudden jump; whereupon I, agitated, turned to Milord, saying, "Have you ever seen the like of that?" The Dragoon did not touch me. I made the remark because the jumping of my horse startled me. I can not swear nor is it fitting to judge of the intentions of others: but I do swear that my definite impression was that Milord had simply the intention of making my horse jump some more (his customary jest with me) when, spurring my horse, he departed at a gallop, followed (or preceding or accompanied, because I did not note this detail) by the four gentlemen and also the servant. At the time I thought only of restraining my horse and of quieting him. But he jumped about so much that without throwing me, he made my hat fall to the ground. Thereupon I smiling turned to one of two women who were passing complaining of the horses which were galloping through the street: "As you see, good woman, I at least restrain my horse and it is out of consideration for you; therefore I pray you to give me my hat." She gave it to me, but all covered with dust: therefore I paused an instant in order to dust it off, fearing that Milord would say that I had fallen. Then I left trotting toward the gate. At the turning of the road, having arrived in sight of the gate, I saw very near to it the dragoon surrounded by the Gentlemen. They seemed to me to be in an argument but only in words for an instant & it appeared to me that I saw Milord offer the Dragoon something that appeared to be a card; and Milord immediately entered the city with two or three others. As he did so, the Dragoon stretched out his hand toward the guard, crying out, "Arrest them all," and almost at the same moment he drew his sabre & commenced to strike furiously to the right & left against the three Gentlemen who were endeavouring to follow through the gate Milord and the others who had already passed. All this happened very rapidly: since, though I was already close enough to hear him when the dragoon shouted, "Arrest them all" to the guard, and though I had not stopped my horse (at least I do not believe that I did so), nevertheless when I entered through the gate the Dragoon was already replacing his sabre in its sheath. I did not see another hand raised except his, (and) he alone seemed to me to be in the wrong and to have brandished his sword with full force, not doing the Gentlemen more hurt only because they were too close to him. I had nothing in my hand—absolutely nothing. Nevertheless (the dragoon being in the act of returning the sabre to its sheath and all the Gentlemen having gone) I accosted him, and taking him by the arm, said to him, "Aren't you ashamed to draw your sabre against unarmed gentlemen," and thinking I recognized him, I added, "It seems to me that I have seen you before & have known you for a man of honour, etc." He did nothing to me. But two of the Gentlemen returning, he turned against them with furious threats and almost drawing his sabre: for I cannot swear whether he drew it entirely or not. Then he spurred on and left. Also I did not see those Gentlemen further: and turning my horse I returned within the gate to say to the guard to take care to make an accurate report since there were many witnesses. In fact there was a big crowd at the gate. I swear that I did not see more than I have reported here.

In regard to the words cited: those by me to Milord have been translated from English and I swear that they are *exactly correct*, they being a customary exclamation of mine; as to those said to the woman & to the dragoon they are *exact in substance*, since I cannot swear to the precise words.

Note : When I say above that it was the custom of Milord to jest with me etc. I do not mean to say that it was his custom to cause my horse to jump but rather to laugh at the jumps which my horse often made, and at the consequences (such as getting into the ditch) which sometimes resulted.

Pisa, March 28, 1822.

Appendix C

TAAFFE'S *Comment on Dante*

IN consenting to offer Taaffe's *Comment* for sale in England, Murray was merely obliging Byron. His judgment must have been against the book, in which he had no real interest, though he dutifully advertised it. The entire cost of publication was borne by Taaffe, who sent 400 copies to Murray to be sold on whatever terms he chose to offer. Murray seems not to have kept Taaffe posted on the fate of the book, and Taaffe complains that directions for the distribution of specially-bound gift copies were neglected and that some of the copies were misplaced. A year passed during which he was kept in ignorance of the public reception of the book; then in response to increasingly strong demands for information, he received a statement for over £50 due Murray.[1] Although Taaffe felt that he had been treated inconsiderately, his desire that Byron's publisher should be his publisher was so great that more than a dozen years later he sent Murray sample verses of his poem *Adelais* and asked whether Murray would be interested in it.

The stages in Taaffe's disappointment over his *Comment* may be traced in the following correspondence with John Murray:

Letter 1

Pisa Jany. 23. 1822.

Sir

This note will be accompanied by an introduction from Lord Byron—who allows me the honour of calling him my friend Lord Byron; and by the sheets of part of a volume which will, I hope, be entirely finished printing as soon as the return of this post from London. After the encouraging opinions I have had from those whose right to pronounce a judgment is incontestible, I flatter myself the work has that merit which will make it succeed. It is the only book on the same subject in English and consequently is without a rival. For though there is a M.S. translation of Dante to which it occasionally refers; yet I have suppressed it for the present, perhaps for ever (after having had a few pages printed) in order to avoid any rivality. As I have consulted a great variety of M.S. I have certainly much historical detail occasionally, which is not to be found in even any printed Italian work—much less in any Italian commentary on Dante. There are also various political and theological views and some explications, which would prevent the book's having an exact rival even in Italian—since there is no Italian work precisely giving the same matter. Mine will be the first comment in any language that endeavours to confront the Pagan & Christian religions as treated by Dante & to explain him by a reference to his two great Pedagogues Aquina & Origen. Mine will also be the first to speak of his Hebrew & Arabic knowledge—and so explain clearly some verses that hitherto passed for Gibberish. This latter matter has indeed been treated of in an Italian pamphlet: but never in any comment on Dante, nor ever in English, french, or any other European tongue that I know of.—I could not avoid saying thus much, in order to give you some idea of my intentions. How I am likely to fulfil them, I dare say Lord Byron himself will give his opinion; and the accompanying sheets will speak for themselves. But in looking over them pray observe—that many introductory remarks are to be made in the Preface, and that Mr. Carey's mistakes in the two first Cantos must be pointed out there; for my translation was not suppressed until after the printing of the two first Comments had begun; and then having that translation of my own to refer to it was my intention to have said nothing of his. But now it is requisite to point out what seem to me to be his occasional mis-interpretations. That I have begun to do, as you may see, in a few instances in the third comment, and will continue to do: and as to those that are wanting in the two first they shall be noticed in the Preface. I must also remark that the part most likely to interest in this volume will be, none of what I send you, but the fifth Comment: and moreover that if any critical eye discover a gross blunder in page 151 it is an error of the press, in consequence of which that page shall be printed over again. This volume (and I should say each succeeding one) will contain about 500 pages and three, perhaps four, drawings. It will cost me in printing about £80 sterling, and there are 400 copies and the copy right for sale. Whether the whole, or what portion of that expence you may think proper to refund to me on delivering those copies into the hands of your correspondent in Leghorn to have them shipped off, or what share of any subsequent profits I may pretend to, I really stipulate nothing. I leave it to yourself, Sir; if the work is successful we shall become well acquainted, for it will comprize several volumes —at least if, besides the work's being successful, its Author lives. I hope, Sir, his Lordships recommendation and the frankness of this my offer may induce you to become thus the literary partner of

Your ob[t] hu[me] Servant

J. Taaffe Jun[r]

The edition shall be ready for embarcation as soon as I get your answer, so that if you please you may announce it as speedily to be published. Before the end of March it may be in London.

Letter 2

Pisa March 6th 1822.

Sir,

I[n] consequence of a communication from my Lord Byron (who as he was friendly enough to make me acquainted with you and interest himself for my book, is pleased not to discontinue such marks of friendship) I have sent the printer a title page with your name—the delay about which title page is infact the reason why the volume was not already on the high seas some weeks ago. It consists of 499 pages of text; which with preface, title pages and drawings amount in all to 546 pages. I hope you will find the style in which it is got up (I mean as to printing) not discreditable. The expence from first to last will not be less than £100 for the printing; but rather some trifle more—for I have not as yet paid all the accounts. I repeat, I candidly leave the whole to your own consideration without myself attempting to stipulate any thing: and give me leave to add, I do so from my conviction that it is a great piece of good fortune to have the honor of having you for my publisher on any terms. I see the book cannot fail to be flatteringly introduced into the world being your property and after that on the long run it must continue to stand on its own merits or fall. I shall then by the very first vessel from Leghorn which will sail in about a week send you the four hundred copies making them as well as the copy-right of the volume your sole or our joint property in whatever way you please. I have been *half*-promised two or three reviews of it—particularly in the Edinburgh and Quarterly —by Gentlemen whose opinion sways your literature: but as these were given, so they were received by me as *half* promises; which, however glad I should be to find them realized, I have no right to claim. I hope however you yourself can have me reviewed in the Quarterly, either for good or for bad. According as those reviews may point out, and as you can inform me of the public opinion, I can much modify the future volumes of the work; if it obtains enough of attention to engage me to continue it—either by encreasing the historical annecdotes or the speculative parts, or diminishing or encreasing the parts explanatory of the Italian text. On embarking the copies I shall of course forward the bill of lading by the post to you as well as also one copy. One of my sisters who, being in London, had my permission to ask you to let her see the portion of the book which Lord Byron sent you, writes to me that you thought it was all about the allegorical part of Dante: but permit me to assure you, you will find the very principle on which it is composed to be quite the contrary—although indeed the nature of those three first Cantos might have naturally led to that misapprehension. You will find that shaking off all exploded allegories, or at least those that according to the taste of our day *deserve* to be exploded, I endeavor to give my reader, instead of them, as much plain reasoning and historical narratives as I can. I think it scarcely possible that some of those narratives become not popular; and certainly they are quite new. The title page is this A Comment on the Divine Comedy of Dante Alighieri—By . . . . —Vol. 1. —Nous avons bien plus de poètes que de juges et interpretes de poesie. Montaigne—London—John Murray: Albemarle-Street 1822. And at the back of the little title, what they call here the 'eye' (occhio) is, Italy: printed with the types of Didot. I notice this that if it be proper to advertize its publication regularly before its arrival you may. I flatter myself that our acquaintance, thus begun under his Lordships auspices, may prove mutually agreeable: and have the honor,

Sir, of subscribing myself
Your ob^{t} hu^{e} Servant
J. Taaffe Junr

My address is
John Taaffe Esqre
Pisa
Italy: and I give it to you, that, without adding superfluously to the trouble which his Lordship has already had the kindness to take on my account, you may be able to favour me with your letter *directly in my own person*

Letter 3

Pisa
Novbr 21st, 1822

Sir

When I tell you that I dispatched the 400 copies of my *Comment* to you above six months ago & that I have not as yet received any account of their arrival, you will surely rather wonder at my long patience (which I do myself) than be surprised at my now at last writing to you. The fact is I fear the said copies may have been seized & confiscated by the fishes. To be sure I dont know what they could well make of them—food, no; & I don't choose to imagine any thing viler. The kind of food I would desire my book were found to be is such as the tenants of the ocean do not probably much indulge in—I mean mental food. But in truth I am without any intelligence of its having reached your hands. Perhaps Lord B— knows, but I have not seen him this long time for I was first absent from this town myself, and he is now removed to Genoa. A lady has told me that he informed her my *Comments were arrived in London*, but that he said that in a hurried manner so that at best I have only some slight grounds to hope they are for she might very well have mistaken or forgotten his words. He might on the contrary have only asked if they had arrived in London? If they have then, let me assure you that your letter to me to say so has been lost. I have never received it. For I wont do you the injustice to suppose you could have neglected informing me of the book's arrival if it had arrived. Another thing—even if you had, you could not at least have failed to forward the copies that bore addresses according to their addresses, and yet I have not received a single word of acknowledgment from any one of the persons in question. If it were only my own family, I am sure they would have written to thank me for the book the instant they had received it. On the whole then I know not what to conclude. Pray *by return of post* have the goodness to inform me whether it be really *many* a *fathom deeply drowned* or not. As to the pecuniary affairs of this volume (as I have before said) I confide them implicitly to you. But before I go on towards a second, I must receive some encouragement. I wait for this with impatience; the more so that it will be necessary for me to take a quick but expensive journey out of Italy to visit & verify certain objects, before I can furnish a second volume. I now see that this work will extend to *seven volumes* in all. If this *first* merit any success, I can confidently affirm that the second will be found less undeserving of it. The flattering letters

I have had from various persons in this country, & the handsome manner in which some of the Italian Reviews have spoken of it, make me hope. You however are my true organ on the subject. I beg of you then to let me hear from you as soon as possible—and have the

honor of being
Sir
Your ob Serv[t]
J. Taaffe Jun[r]

Letter 4

Pisa Feby. 18. 1823

Sir

Not having as yet received either any answer from you to any of [my] letters; nor even from any one of my friends in England, the least tidings with regard to my book; except indeed a complaint of their not having received it; I must take the liberty of telling you I am much surprised as well as disconcerted at it. How many months have gone by since you must have received it (except it have gone to the bottom of the sea which may have been the case for any information I have got to the contrary) I cannot exactly tell: but above seven or eight months surely. I am incapable of expressing myself over-harshly; but am at the same time unaccustomed to be treated slightingly; and at all events I cannot say less than that I am entirely at a loss to account for your apparent neglect: so that I am willing to ascribe your silence to some strange mistake or stoppage in the post office or even to something unfortunate in the voyage of the book itself—rather than imagine for an instant that it is to be attributed to sheer inattention. As a Gentleman treating with a Gentleman I would have a right to put you in mind of the courtesy which Gentlemen owe each other mutually: and speaking to you as a man of business, I would have to remind you both of the irregularity of not writing to acknowledge the receipt of those parcels of which I sent you the bills of lading, if they have been received; as well as of the superior regard which I may have some reason to think is due to me for having placed such entire confidence in your character for liberality & honor as to send you the entire edition without any kind of stipulation but trusting implicitly to yourself. But I rather express my opinion that there is some excuse for your silence of which I am not aware; and of which indeed I can form no notion. I confine myself then to adding that at least as fast as the post can convey an answer to this present letter, I look confidently to receiving one. I am informed it is true that you have had & perhaps still have some misunderstanding with him who first had the goodness to introduce me to this correspondence with you; but I am far above entertaining any suspicion of your intending anything hostile to me in consequence. His Lordship certainly intended an act of kindness to me at the time; but whatever be his relations with you at present (of which I have no knowledge except from mere rumour; not having been in his vicinity for a great many months, indeed never since his departure for Genoa) I am most clear from having merited unkindness from you. I repeat then Sir that I am willing to believe your *apparent* neglect has not been *real* or *intentional*; but that there is something in the matter inexplicable to me, and that as a Gentleman & a man of business I request you may favour me with an explication without delay. I have many things ready; and could indeed prepare a second volume without loss of time: but cannot advance until I know something of the first. This *Comment on Dante* will consist of 7 volumes and if the first has any success at all, I have no difficulty in assuring you that the others must have more from their more interesting historical details.

I have the honor to be
Sir
Your obt. hue. Servant
J. Taaffe Junr

Letter 5

Pisa feby. 25th. 1823 [2]

Sir

I wrote to you on the 18th. But having since had a letter from one of my sisters informing me that none of my friends had as yet received one of the Copies of my *Comment*, I cannot refrain from taking my pen up again and sending you this note by a relative who will deliver it into your own hand. Since some strange & to me inexplicable inaccuracy in the post is the only excuse I can imagine for your silence, I adopt this mode of securing the reception by you of this. Whatever cause of complaint you may have or think you have against Lord B—you can possibly have none against me. I reject the suspicion therefore that your conduct towards me is influenced by your pique against him. I reject every suspicion as at least as unworthy of me to entertain as of you to be attacked with. I have been informed that you received the cases of books a great many months ago; otherwise I should conclude they were lost on the voyage. The bills of lading I forwarded to you by the post. It is hard to think that that letter (as well as the cases too) was lost. Had I even heard from you that you had *not* received the cases, I could have complained to the Leghorn Merchants who gave me the bills of lading of which I possess *duplicates.* Sir Walter Scott too wrote to me sometime ago that he had not received my book then; & since he added that as soon as he read it he would write to me again, I conclude *he* has not received it any more than my other friends. But without useless dirges over the past disaster, let me apply myself to the future remedy; & beg of you to attend to my volume—to recollect the entire confidence I have placed in your honor—that I sent you the book printed without making one single stipulation—that my continuing the work is hindered by your not giving me any information with regard to that first volume—that not the expence of copying alone but very considerable ones (of the purchase of books & of at least one journey before giving the finishing hand to the second volume & of two voyages before finishing the third volume) are necessary—that such expences I cannot be supposed prepared to incur, until I have some reason to be assured of public support—and infine that I have lost nearly a year already and that every hour will be a loss of time until I receive a satisfactory answer from you of the volume I have sent you. I can form my opinions only from the letters I have received & the sentiments I have heard; and these have been without one single exception most flattering to me. When I say *I have no other ground for forming* an opinion of the book, I speak *with regard to England.* For in this Country two reviews of it have appeared (one in the *Anthologia* of Florence & the other in the *Memoirs of the Royal Academy of Lucca*) both of which load me with encomium. There has been indeed (*I am told for I have not myself seen the work*) some favourable notice of it taken in the *Liberal*; but to what extent I am uninformed. Infine I again intreat you to attend to the publication of the volume; & if you have not already answered my letter of the 18th to do so immediately on receipt of this. If you act by me with some degree of kindness, you shall find me as willing to confide in your sense of honor & liberality as I have been already.

I have the honor Sir
of being Your Obnt. Serv[t]
J. Taaffe, Jun[r]

N.B. I am always ready to make allowances for your press of business, and, by my silence so long, have already made them: in return you will have the goodness, in future, to make fair allowances for me.

Letter 6

Sir,

Your letter of March 18th which I this moment receive really astonishes me—I mean not with regard to the sale or rather *non-sale* of my book, but to the preremptory manner with which you request me to remit to you *immediately* the balance in your favour on the state of our account, although you yourself were so far from acknowledging *immediately* & regularly your receipt of the parcels that you now only write to me after a lapse of months with an apparent declaration that those boxes were wanting in their contents. Had you informed me of this at once & indicated exactly what deficiency was in the real contents as contrasted with the note of the alleged contents I could have taken the necessary steps. Did you even clearly indicate it to me now & inform me of what should be done to obtain redress, I would do it instantly: for I can *possitively swear (& so can others) to the state of all the parcels when delivered into their hands* who *wrote the regular bills of lading which I transmitted to you.* As to the larger paper, it is a mistake; except with regard to one single copy which was on a little larger. But besides the 400 copies for you, Sir, there were 8 others most distinctly marked—1st by each having attached to it one or more little poetic compositions, some printed on white & some on coloured paper—& 2dly by having each one a direction to one of the following persons—Mrs Taaffe, Miss Mary Taaffe, Miss Julia Taaffe, Mrs Catharine McDonnell, Robert Taaffe Esqre, George Taaffe Esqre, William Grainger Esqre, Sir Walter Scott.[3]—I dare to say that these copies are in your warehouse still unattended to & unnoticed. I must most urgently desire you will have them sought out & remitted. *On my oath* therefore Sir your account of the contents of the boxes on arriving does not agree with their contents when leaving this. Since moreover this was not notified to me by any letter at the time, I think I have every reason in the world to believe that the error is not with the people of the ship but with your own people who through negligence or otherwise have mislaid those copies. In one of my former letters I also requested of you to present one or two copies for me to other persons—particularly to Il Sig. Ugo Foscalo & to Mr Hobhouse[4]: neither of which Gentlemen have certainly had them, I presume, or I should have heard from them. I must repeat that you have acted with no courtesy towards me. Strict justice I have however a right to require. Give me leave to affirm that it ought to assure me of other treatment. To ask anything *immediate* from me is far from being of a piece with the *dilatoriness* I have experienced from you.

Still, Sir, I must not forget both that you have me much in your power by being in possession of the entire edition of my book, & that I have often wished to have you for my bookseller whenever I became an Author. Both considerations engage me instead of ending this letter with any expression of resentment to intreat you to have those copies looked for and transmitted as directed. Even so doing might increase the sale. It is hard for me to believe that the book will not eventually—*if put forward by you*—have some tolerable sale; it would be to make me deem too many persons, who have spoken & written to me about it, grossly deceived. However as to the continuing of the work, I will certainly not continue to print it unless when you encourage me to do so. I am writing & will have finished in about six weeks a little poem. It will be of about 1400 verses. Is it at all likely it may suit you? Of course this cannot be quite answered without seeing the M.S.—But since it is a production which may acquire part of whatever success it may obtain from present politics I ask you the question in order that, if you at once decline it, even before seeing it, I may not lose time by sending it to you, but apply to another channel directly. To this therefore if your answer is to be in the *affirmative*, pray reply *immediately* & I will send you the M.S. for perusal; so that if upon that perusal, you like it, you may put it to press at once. Your silence I shall receive as a *negative*.

Your ob. hu^e^ Servant
J. Taaffe, Junr

Pisa April 2. 1823.

Letter 7

Dear Sir

I thank you very much. I send you what you may do with exactly what you please—the only Canto of my poem [5] I have with me. Nothing can be understood of a morsel thus taken from the middle, it is true: neither beginning nor end, but rather belonging to the beginning, it is likely to be the most insipid of the whole, & no fair sample. No matter, I have no other. The poem is to be in 10 Cantos & I have the eight first sketched out. This is my principal occupation; but besides I shall be happy to undertake whatever you think I am capable of. It is superfluous to add supposing it to agree with my own views & opinions—as I fully explained to your son. My compliments to Mrs Murray & the Misses Murray. I have the honor to be

Your's truly
J. Taaffe

1835.

NOTES

CHAPTER 1

1 According to Pelleschi, Claire Clairmont's singing master (*The Complete Works of Percy Bysshe Shelley*, ed. Roger Ingpen and Walter E. Peck for the Julian Editions, London, 1926–29, X, 140 fn.).

2 Mary Shelley to Maria Gisborne, November 29, 1819 (Jones, *The Letters of Mary W. Shelley*, Norman, 1944, I, 87).

3 André Vaccà Berlinghieri (1772–1826) was at this time in charge of the school of surgery at the University of Pisa. He had studied in Paris, where he had participated in the storming of the Bastille, and later in London. To science and patriotism, he added a love of literature, and when Madame de Staël was in Pisa in 1816, he was a frequenter of her salon. Vaccà was recommended to the Shelleys by Mrs. Mason (see pp. 4ff.), and Medwin (*Life of Percy Bysshe Shelley*, ed. H. Buxton Forman, London, 1913, pp. 266–67) says that though Vaccà's great practice and poor health—he was tubercular—left little time for social visits, he "was also Shelley's particular friend."

4 Mrs. Gisborne, then Mrs. Reveley, had taken Mary Godwin into her own home at the time of Mary Wollstonecraft's death. Upon the death of Mr. Reveley two years later, Godwin had proposed to Mrs. Reveley and been refused by her. She married, instead, John Gisborne, an unsuccessful merchant who retired with her and her son, Henry Reveley, to live at Leghorn on the remainder of his property (White, *Shelley*, New York, 1940, II, 15–16).

5 Shelley to Thomas Medwin, January 17, 1820 (*Julian*, X, 140).

6 Shelley to John Gisborne, January 25, 1820 (*Julian*, X, 142).

7 Angeli, *Shelley and His Friends in Italy* (London, 1911), p. 19.

8 Mary Shelley to Marianne Hunt, June 29, 1819 (Jones, I, 74).

9 Shelley to Thomas Love Peacock, June [20 or 21 ?], 1819 (*Julian*, X, 57).

10 Forman, in a note in Medwin's *Life of Shelley* (p. 240), says that upon the death of the Earl [see Peerage] Mountcashell, the union between "Mr. and Mrs. Mason" was regularized. In 1821–22 they lived at Casa Silva in the Via Mala Gonella, on the south side of the Arno.

11 Shelley to Thomas Love Peacock, June 5, 1818 (*Julian*, IX, 309).

12 Mary Shelley to Leigh and Marianne Hunt, May 13, 1818 (Jones, I, 50).

13 Hunt, *Autobiography* (London, 1850), III, 25–26.

14 *Ibid.*, II, 51.

15 Mary Shelley to Marianne Hunt, February 24, 1820 (Jones, I, 95).

16 Shelley to Leigh Hunt, April 5, 1820 (*Julian*, X, 154).

17 White, II, 180.

18 See his letter of August 16, 1821, to Mary (*Julian*, X, 315).

19 Shelley to Leigh Hunt, April 5, 1820 (*Julian*, X, 154).

20 Shelley to Thomas Love Peacock, February 15, 1821 (*Julian*, X, 235).

21 Dowden, *The Life of Percy Bysshe Shelley* (London, 1886), II, 279, says that two hundred and fifty copies in small quarto were struck off in August, 1819, by a Leghorn printer, probably Masi, and sent to England to be sold by Ollier.

22 Mary Shelley to P. B. Shelley, December 5, 1816 (Jones, I, 14).

23 White, II, 188.

24 Shelley to Thomas Love Peacock, May 16, 1820 (*Julian*, X, 170).

25 White, II, 183.

26 Shelley to John and Maria Gisborne [June or July, 1820], (*Julian*, X, 184).

27 Mary Shelley to Maria Gisborne, June 18, 1820 (Jones, I, 108).

28 Shelley to John and Maria Gisborne, June 30, 1820 (*Julian*, X, 180).

29 *The Poetical Works of Percy Bysshe Shelley*, ed. Mrs. Shelley (London, 1839), IV, 50.

30 In England Mrs. Gisborne told Godwin that the story of Claire's liaison with Byron was little known but added that it "might be rendered more public through the villainy of P. . . ." (unpublished journal of Maria Gisborne, from a photostatic copy kindly lent by the Duke University Library).

31 Shelley to Thomas Medwin, January 17, 1820 (*Julian*, X, 141). In *Julian and Maddalo*, Shelley thus apostrophizes Italy: "Thou Paradise of Exiles, Italy!"

32 Shelley to Thomas Medwin, April 16, 1820 (*Julian*, X, 158).

33 Shelley to Claire Clairmont, October 29, 1820 (*Julian*, X, 214).

34 *Julian*, X, 156, fn.

35 Shelley to Thomas Medwin, April 16, 1820 (*Julian*, X, 156).

36 Shelley to Claire Clairmont, October 29, 1820 (*Julian*, X, 214), and November, 1820 (*Julian*, X, 226).

37 Mary Shelley to Claire Clairmont, January 14, 1821 (Jones, I, 129–30). Yet years later (1829) Trelawny, in writing to Mary of Medwin, said: "You used to like him and laud him and thought me rash and violent in asserting him to be a coward, a liar, and a scoundrel—nevertheless he has proved himself all these" (Grylls, *Mary Shelley*, London, 1938, p. 218).

38 Mary Shelley to Marianne Hunt, February 24, 1820 (Jones, I, 96).

39 Jones, *Mary Shelley's Journal* (Norman, 1947), November 12, 1820, p. 140.

40 Medwin also says that Pacchiani's professorship was a sinecure and that he only mounted the *cathedra* once during the years of his supposed service. He told Medwin that he lost his office, not by the neglect of his duties, but by an irresistible *bon mot*: halted by the night watch and asked for identification, he is supposed to have replied, "I am a public man, in a public street, with a public woman" (Medwin, *Life of Shelley*, pp. 274–75). He died at Florence on March 31, 1835, in poverty, waited on by a woman of the streets. (This and other facts not derived from Medwin are drawn from Enrica Viviani della Robbia, *Vita di una Donna*, Firenze, 1936.)

41 Medwin, *Life of Shelley*, p. 275. Shelley had never heard Coleridge talk and was not speaking from first-hand knowledge.

42 Mary Shelley to Leigh Hunt, December 3, 1820 (Jones, I, 117).

43 Claire Clairmont's journal for December 11 and 14, and Mary Shelley to Maria Gisborne, *c*. December 15, 1820 (Jones, I, 121).

44 Jones, *Mary Shelley's Journal*, p. 142.

45 Mary Shelley to Claire Clairmont, January [14], 1821 (Jones, I, 128).

46 Mary Shelley to Maria Gisborne, *c*. February 12, 1821 (Jones, I, 134).

47 Mary Shelley to Leigh Hunt, December 3, 1820 (Jones, I, 118).

48 White, II, 255.

49 Mary Shelley to Maria Gisborne, March 7, 1822 (Jones, I, 161).

CHAPTER 2

1 At the Restoration, Theobald Taaffe was rewarded for great sacrifices and services in the Stuart cause with the title of Earl of Carlingford. Nicholas, second earl, was killed at the Boyne and was succeeded by his brother Francis,

who chose, because of Jacobite sympathies and the harsh legal code affecting Catholics, to enter the Austrian service. He became a Count of the Holy Roman Empire and during thirty years in the imperial service served as lieutenant general of horse, Marshal, and Counsellor of the state and cabinet. He was succeeded by his nephew Theobald, with whom the title became extinct. Nicholas, sixth Viscount Taaffe, also entered Austrian service, became a Count of the Holy Roman Empire, and distinguished himself under the name of Count Taaffe during the war with the Turks in 1738. He is said to have behaved with great bravery at Belgrade. His younger son Francis was likewise a Count of the Empire, a distinction held by other Taaffes also. It is not strange, then, that John Taaffe, Jr., should have had the title gratuitously bestowed upon him; but it was a title which he never claimed and by which he was never addressed by his English friends in Pisa. The titled branch of his family goes back to William Taaffe (d. February 9, 1626), while the Smarmore branch descends from Peter Taaffe of Pepperstown, County Louth, brother of William.

2 This is probably an overestimate. Taaffe's brother George, who supplanted John Taaffe, Jr., as heir, inherited no more than £5,000 per year, and the estate in 1883 (Bateman, *The Great Landowners of Gt. Britain and Ireland*, London, 1883) was estimated at £3,569 per year. But Taaffe's twelve sisters had £3,000 each, and the four sons who arrived at manhood were brought up expensively.

3 Mrs. Belinda Edwards Colebrooke, widow of Colonel George Colebrooke of Crawford Douglass, lived in Northumberland Street, Edinburgh, in 1810–11. According to the testimony of Sarah Stride, a servant, Taaffe and Mrs. Colebrooke were married at the beginning of 1811, almost certainly by simple declaration in the presence of witnesses. But a legal opinion of David Lynch in the Smarmore papers states that Mrs. Colebrooke had previously contracted a marriage with one Henry Butler by a declaration of the relationship of husband and wife in the presence of witnesses. About 1818 Mrs. Colebrooke commenced an action of divorce against Taaffe, who, she charged, had confined her in a madhouse as insane, separated her from her family, denied her admittance to her own house, and with the assistance of his servant carried from her house books, pictures, and other articles of value belonging to her. The action for divorce, she complained, was at first met by "paltry subterfuge" and later by a charge of bigamy. The charge of bigamy was apparently contained in proceedings for an act of nullity instituted by Taaffe or on Taaffe's behalf before the Lords Commissaries in 1820. This petition was not granted, for, in a legal opinion dated 1825, Nicholas Ball stated that since no divorce had taken place, Taaffe was responsible for the debts of Mrs. Colebrooke, whose wealth must have been illusory. Smarmore papers reveal that even in 1847, long after the death of Mrs. Colebrooke, Taaffe was in fear of a lawsuit and perhaps even of imprisonment. With reference to this affair, Taaffe wrote to his brother in 1847, "That I was a vain wild headstrong fool—the dupe of my own extravagant sensations is the worst that a man of the world would say of me."

4 Artemisia Castellini, daughter of an Italian father but Spanish by birth, married a Frenchman who later became financial adviser to Otto of Bavaria upon his accession to the Greek throne. The portrait of Taaffe which Madame Regny painted is now in possession of his great granddaughter, Mrs. Cesira More O'Ferrall. A portrait of Byron, painted after Shelley's death and intended to be a part of a picture of the cremation of Shelley, seems to have been lost.

5 In one of them (now in the Berg Collection of the New York Public Library) she thanked him for a copy of *Padilla*, which she praised for its imagination but found imitative of Lord Byron.

6 In his *Autobiography* Taaffe asserts that his wife was from an Irish family "fully as respectable as Taaffe." I have tried unsuccessfully to find some connection between Taaffe's wife and Mrs. Beauclerk (see below, note), who was a half-sister of the Irish patriot Lord Edward Fitzgerald.

7 The agreement was that Taaffe should pay 1,000 francs a year pension and that during her infancy and up to a certain point in her life Mr. and Mrs. Fortis were to be considered her real parents. The danger in such an agreement did not present itself at the time, but years later when Taaffe attempted to claim his daughter he was met with pleas and evasions and broken promises.

8 Mrs. Beauclerk, born Emily Ogilvie, was a daughter of the Duchess of Leinster by her second marriage and a half-sister of the Irish patriot Lord Edward Fitzgerald. Medwin says that she was a neighbour of Shelley's family in Sussex (*The Life of Percy Bysshe Shelley*, pp. 367–68). She was the mother of seven daughters who, in Byron's phrase, had to waltz for their livelihood, and on one occasion Trelawny escorted Mary Shelley to a ball at her house in Pisa.

9 From a copy of the original letter, dated December 25, 1820, in the possession of Mrs. More O'Ferrall.

10 Mary Shelley knew Mrs. Thomas well enough to request her to execute several commissions for her in 1823. In return she sent Mrs. Thomas copies of the *Liberal* and a copy of *Frankenstein* (now in the Morgan Library) "from her friend—the Author Mary Shelley." On the half-title, Mrs. Thomas wrote: "My acquaintance with this very interesting person—arose from her being introduced to me under circumstances of so melancholy a nature (which attended her widowhood)—that it was impossible to refuse the aid asked of me—I gave her all I could and passed many delightful hours with her at Albaro—She left Genoa in a few months for England. I called on her in London in 1824 but as my friends disliked her Circle of Friends—and Mrs. Shelley was then no longer in a Foreign Country helpless, pennylesse, and broken hearted—I never returned again to her, but I preserve this Booke and her Autograph Notes [for a second edition] to me—as at some future day they will be Literary Curiosities" (Jones, *The Letters of Mary W. Shelley*, I, 213–14 fn.).

11 From a copy of the original letter in the possession of Mrs. More O'Ferrall.

12 This is a questionable reading; it may be either *invites* (as in the *Julian* ed.) or *indites*. The doubtful consonant is not clearly the one or the other: it is not open enough for a *v* nor tall enough for a *d*. But many of Shelley's *d's* aren't. In spite of the repetition in meaning, I incline slightly towards *indites*.

13 From the original letter in The University of Texas Library. It is printed by both the Julian editors and Jones as a part of a letter by Mary dated Spring, 1821, in the *Julian* edition (X, 260–64) and May 11, 1821, by Jones. Although Professor Jones's date is correct for Mary's letter (see his argument in *The Letters of Mary W. Shelley*, I, 139–40), he has recently pointed out to me that Shelley's letter has been incorrectly joined to the wrong letter by Mary, the real conclusion of which is Shelley's letter printed in the *Julian* ed., X, 355–56.

14 See Appendix A.

15 Mary Shelley to Maria Gisborne, March 7, 1822 (Jones, I, 161).

CHAPTER 3

1 Medwin, *The Life of Percy Bysshe Shelley*, p. 267. The phrase "from Chalons" does not appear in the 1847 edition.

2 Mary Shelley to Claire Clairmont, January [14], 1821 (Jones, I, 129–30).

3 Garnett, Introduction to *The Journal of Edward Ellerker Williams* (London, 1902), p. 3.

4 Trelawny, *Recollections of the Last Days of Shelley and Byron* (London, 1858), p. 10.

5 *Ibid.*

6 *The Journal of Edward Ellerker Williams*, p. 16.

7 From the original letter in The University of Texas Library. It appears in the *Julian* ed. (X, 264) as a part of the letter incorrectly joined to Mary's letter of May 11, 1821.

8 Shelley to John Gisborne, June 18, 1822 (*Julian*, X, 403).

9 Shelley to Claire Clairmont, June 22, 1821 (postmark), *Julian*, X, 279.

10 *The Journal of Edward Ellerker Williams*, p. 16.

11 Taaffe, *Autobiography*.

12 The MS. of Acts II, IV, and V, according to Professor White (*Shelley*, II, 612), is in the Bodleian Library and reveals many corrections in Shelley's hand.

13 Medwin, *Journal of the Conversations of Lord Byron . . . at Pisa in the Years* 1821 *and* 1822 (London, 1824), p. 18.

14 The details of this adventure are taken from Dowden, II, 399–400, and White, II, 286–87.

15 Mary Shelley to Claire Clairmont, April 2, 1821 (Jones, I, 136).

16 From the original letter in The University of Texas Library. It appears in the *Julian* edition (X, 263–64) with editorial corrections. Here, and throughout, I have adopted the practice of printing original documents exactly as they were written except for occasional bracketed insertions for the sake of clarity.

17 Shelley to Claire Clairmont, June 8, 1821 (*Julian*, X, 273).

18 A doubtful reading which is not clearly anything. *Noon* is, I think, more likely than the *Julian* reading *a.m.* (X, 268).

19 From the original letter in The University of Texas Library. It appears in the *Julian* edition (X, 268–69).

20 *Julian: tempo molto*, a meaningless phrase. Mary's orthography is unmistakable (*matto*=*mad*). The reference is probably to the heat, no doubt responsible for Taaffe's fatigue, mentioned in Shelley's letter.

21 From the original letter in The University of Texas Library. It appears in the *Julian* edition (X, 269) and Jones (I, 144). Jones's text is taken from the *Julian* edition, with which it is identical.

22 The Gisbornes, who were about to return to England to live.

23 *Julian*, Jones: *Requy*.

24 Shelley to Claire Clairmont, June 8, 1821 (*Julian*, X, 273).

25 Bryan Waller Procter, who wrote under the name Barry Cornwall.

26 Shelley to Charles Ollier, June 16, 1821 (*Julian*, X, 276).

27 Shelley to Ollier [? July, 1821], (*Julian*, X, 286).

28 Shelley to Byron, July 16, 1821 (*Julian*, X, 284).

29 Shelley to John and Maria Gisborne [June 5, 1821], (*Julian*, X, 270).

30 This and other cancelled passages in the Preface were published by Garnett, in *Relics of Shelley*, 1862. In the Oxford Press *Complete Poetical Works of Percy Bysshe Shelley* they comprise a double-column page.

31 Giovanni Rosini, professor at the university and bitter enemy of Pacchiani, was the author of the *Monacca di Monza*. Byron (p. 145) speaks of him as Taaffe's printer.

32 Mary Shelley's journal for July 6, 1821 (Jones, 157), contains the following entry: "Shelley calls on Count Nazawly."

33 From Mary Shelley's journal: "Tuesday, June 19. . . . Mr. Taaffe and Granger call." "Tuesday, June 26.—Mr. Taaffe and Granger dine with us."

34 From the original letter in The University of Texas Library. It appears in the *Julian* edition (X, 281–82) with minor variations.

35 The paper on which it is written is identical with that of Mary's and Shelley's notes of June 5 and of Shelley's letter of July 4.

36 *Julian: am easily conscious;* MS.: *can easily concieve.*

37 I am unable to identify this ode with any poem of Taaffe's of this period. If I am wrong in believing the letter to have been written from the Baths of Pisa, the ode might be the one written on the occasion of the death of the Saxon Prince.

38 From the original letter in The University of Texas Library. It appears in the *Julian* edition (X, 400).

39 *Valperga: or Castruccio, Prince of Lucca,* Mary's second novel, was published in three volumes in 1823 by G. and W. B. Whittaker.

40 Mary Shelley to Maria Gisborne, June 30, 1821 (Jones, I, 145).

41 Grylls, *Claire Clairmont* (London, 1939), p. 133.

42 Prothero, *The Works of Lord Byron: Letters and Journals,* London, 1898–1901 (hereinafter abbreviated *L. and J.*), V, 269.

43 Shelley to Byron, July 16, 1821 (*Julian,* X, 284).

44 White, II, 306.

CHAPTER 4

1 Iris Origo, *The Last Attachment* (New York, 1949).

2 *Ibid.*, pp. 263–64.

3 Byron to John Murray, July 30, 1821 (*L. and J.*, V, 330). The two tragedies were *Sardanapalus* and *The Two Foscari.*

4 Byron to R. B. Hoppner, July 23, 1821 (*L. and J.*, V, 327).

5 Byron to Thomas Moore, June 22, 1821 (*L. and J.*, V, 311).

6 Byron to R. B. Hoppner, July 23, 1821 (*L. and J.*, V, 327).

7 The idea appears to have originated with Moore in 1812, but Byron was not interested then. References to the project occur in Byron's letters to Moore of December 25, 1820 (*L. and J.*, V, 143–45), January 2, 1821 (*L. and J.*, V, 215), June 22, 1821 (*L. and J.*, V, 309), and August 2, 1821 (*L. and J.*, V, 336).

8 Byron to Thomas Moore, August 2, 1821 (*L. and J.*, V, 336).

9 Shelley to Thomas Love Peacock, August 10 (?), 1821 (*Julian,* X, 306).

10 Shelley to Mary Shelley, August 10, 1821 (*Julian,* X, 305).

11 Shelley to Mary Shelley [August 10, 1821] (*Julian,* X, 303).

12 Shelley to Mary Shelley [August 15, 1821] (*Julian,* X, 312).

13 *Ibid.*, p. 315.

14 *Ibid.*, p. 311.

15 Shelley to Mary Shelley, August 15, 1821 (*Julian,* X, 311).

16 Shelley to Leigh Hunt, August 26, 1821 (*Julian,* X, 318).

17 See footnote 21.

18 Shelley to Byron [September (?), 1821] (*Julian,* X, 320–21).

19 Byron to Shelley, September 8, 1821 (from the original letter in the Pierpont Morgan Library).

20 Shelley to Byron, September 14, 1821 (*Julian,* X, 321–23). The Hoppners had accepted Paolo's story as true and had passed it on to Byron (*supra,* pp. 9–10).

21 In an almost illegible letter written by Giovanni Paoli, a Leghorn official, to the Buon Governo at Florence, when the Gambas and Byron moved to Montenero in the following May, it is stated that Teresa's visitor's card for Tuscany was dated August 4 and those of Count Gamba and Pietro July 21. On August 18 all were given permission to go to Pisa.

22 Tribolati, *Saggi critici e biografici* (Pisa, 1891), p. 233.

23 Mary Shelley to Maria Gisborne, November 30, 1821 (Jones, I, 150).

24 Torelli, *Arcana politicae anticarbonariae* (unpublished diary in the State Archives at Florence).

25 Published together in August, without the name of the author or publisher (*L. and J.*, V, 351, fn.).

26 Smiles, *A Publisher and His Friends, Memoir and Correspondence of John Murray* (London, 1891), I, 413.

27 Byron to John Murray, August 31, 1821 (*L. and J.*, V, 352).

28 Byron to John Murray, September 10, 1821 (*L. and J.*, V, 360).

29 An error for "last year."

30 An allusion, says Prothero (*L. and J.*, V, 185 fn.), to Pope's *Memoirs of P. P. Clerk of this Parish*, supposedly written in ridicule of Burnet's *History of my own Times*.

31 Byron to Thomas Moore, September 19, 1821 (*L. and J.*, V, 364–65).

32 Douglas James William Kinnaird (1788–1830), fifth son of the seventh Baron Kinnaird, had been educated at Eton and Cambridge. A partner in Ransom and Morland's bank and a member of the management committee of the Drury Lane Theatre, he was Byron's banker and business adviser after Byron left England in 1816.

33 Southey's *A Vision of Judgment*, eulogizing George III, had appeared earlier in the year.

34 Byron to Kinnaird, November 16, 1821 (from the original letter in the possession of Sir John Murray).

35 Moore, *Life, Letters, and Journals of Lord Byron* (London, 1838), pp. 538–39.

36 Shelley to Byron, October 21, 1821 (*Julian*, X, 330).

37 *Ibid*., p. 331.

38 *Ibid*. To Mr. Gisborne (October 22, 1821, *Julian*, X, 332–33) Shelley wrote in a different tone: "La Guiccioli his cara sposa who attends him impatiently, is a very pretty sentimental, innocent superficial Italian, who has sacrifized an immense fortune to live [*with* deleted] for Lord Byron; and who, if I know anything of my friend, of her, and of human nature will hereafter have plenty of leisure and opportunity to repent her rashness."

39 John Fitzgibbon, second Earl of Clare. "My School friendships," wrote Byron (*Detached Thoughts, L. and J.*, V, 455), "were with *me passions* (for I was always violent), but I do not know that there is one which has endured (to be sure, some have been cut short by death) till now. That with Lord Clare began one of the earliest and lasted longest, being only interrupted by distance, that I know of. I never hear the word '*Clare*' without a beating of the heart even *now*, and I write it with the feelings of 1803–4–5 ad infinitum."

40 From *Detached Thoughts* (*L. and J.*, V, 463).

41 *Recollections of the Table-Talk of Samuel Rogers* (ed. Alexander Dyce), London, 1887, p. 237.

42 White, II, 333.

43 The last stanza was composed after his arrival in Pisa.

44 From the unpublished portion of Williams's journal.

45 Byron to John Murray, November 3, 1821 (*L. and J.*, V, 469).

46 Byron to Hobhouse, October 12, 1821 (*Lord Byron's Correspondence*, ed. John Murray, London, 1922, II, 202–03): "As to the printers' errors,—Oons! what do you think of '*Adriatic* side of the Bosphorus,'—of '*praise*' for '*pair*'—'*precarious*' for '*precocious*,' and '*case*' for '*chase*.' Mr. Murray has received a trimmer, I promise you, not without cause."

47 *Marino Faliero*, dedicated to Kinnaird.

48 Identified in *Lord Byron's Correspondence* as Sir Ralph Milbanke, Lady Byron's father.

49 I have not been able to identify this person.

50 Byron to Douglas Kinnaird, November 4, 1821 (from the original letter in the Pierpont Morgan Library).

51 I am unable to find confirmation in Smiles's *Memoir of John Murray* of such a large loss. In November, 1820, Murray had paid Captain Parry 1,000 guineas for his *Journal of the Late Voyage for the Discovery of a North-West Passage*, only to have the work anticipated by the publication of another narrative on the same subject. Earlier he had published John McLeod's *Voyage of H.M.S. Alceste to the Island of Loochoo*, but I find no evidence of a heavy loss in it. Losses had been sustained in the publication of Belzoni's *Narrative of the Operations and Recent Discoveries within the Pyramids, Temples, Tombs, and Excavations in Egypt and Nubia*, of which only 1,000 copies were printed after Murray had invested £2,163 in the work; in the purchase of the copyrights of Crabbe's poetry; and in the failure of the *Guardian* newspaper, of which Murray was part-owner. Except for the *Guardian*, however, the losses would appear to have been spread over several years and not have belonged to the year 1820 alone. Though full details are lacking, I can see nothing like £28,000 all told.

52 Byron to Douglas Kinnaird, November 15, 1821 (from the original letter in the possession of Sir John Murray).

53 Mrs. Angeli (p. 234) says that Byron was mistaken in thinking the Lanfranchi a feudal palace, which she calls a sixteenth-century building.

54 Byron to John Murray, December 4, 1821 (*L. and J.*, V, 486–87).

55 Mary Shelley to Maria Gisborne, November 30, 1821 (Jones, I, 150).

56 The Williamses left Pugnano for Pisa before they could get possession of their apartment. On November 4 Williams writes in his journal: "Despatch the remainder of our things, and quit Pugnano, on a visit to S., at Pisa." On November 10 the Williamses are "busily employed in furnishing our House," and on November 30 they are purchasing plate, furniture, and the like. It is not clear just when they left the Shelleys and moved into their own apartment.

57 Mary's and Williams's journals record most of this activity, but the unpublished portions of Williams's journal add considerably to our knowledge of it. For example: (Nov. 11) "The Countess G. calls and Jane & Mary accompany her in her ride." (Nov. 13) ". . . After dinner call on Lord B. . . . The Countess & her brother call." (Nov. 15) "Taaffe calls." (Nov. 16) "The Countess calls." Again: (Dec. 17) "Din'd with Lord B—met there Shelley, Taaffe, and Medwin." (Dec. 21) "Taaffe called in the evening." (Dec. 25) "Dined with Lord Byron, met the same party as before." (Dec. 29) "S. breakfasts with us." (Dec. 30) "Dined with Mary and walk in the evening with S. . . ." (Dec. 31) "Mary and S. dine here." (Jan. 1) "Called on Dr. Nott and afterwards on Lord B—with whom & S. I played at billiards—Walked with Jane to the Garden in the evening and saw them shoot. Mary—S—and Tom [Medwin] dined with us."

58 From the MS. of Williams's journal The passage appears in Garnett's edition (pp. 23–24) with some inaccuracies.

59 An expression used by one of the characters in Scott's *The Antiquary*.

60 Mary Shelley to Marianne Hunt, March 5, 1822 (Jones, I, 158).

61 Torelli, *Arcana politicae anticarbonariae*. The shoe was on the other foot when Byron sent Lega Zambelli to Governor Viviani to ask permission to fire his pistols in the garden at a target. The Governor replied that it was not only against the laws of the country but that he had also refused others a similar permission.

62 Medwin, *Conversations*, pp. 21–22.

63 Shelley to Claire Clairmont, December 11, 1821 (*Julian*, X, 338).
64 *Angeli*, p. 246.
65 *Ibid.*, p. 247.
66 Medwin, *Conversations*, p. 19.
67 *Ibid.*, p. 20.
68 Shelley to Horace Smith, January 25, 1822 (*Julian*, X, 347).
69 Shelley to T. L. Peacock, January 11 [?], 1822 (*Julian*, X, 342).
70 Shelley to Mary Shelley [August 10, 1821] (*Julian*, X, 303–04).
71 Shelley to Claire Clairmont, December 11, 1821 (*Julian*, X, 338).
72 Shelley to Horace Smith, May, 1822 (*Julian*, X, 392).
73 Mary Shelley to Maria Gisborne, November 30, 1821 (Jones, I, 150).
74 Byron to Thomas Moore, November 16, 1821 (*L. and J.*, V, 475–77).
75 Mary Shelley to Maria Gisborne, March 7, 1822 (Jones, I, 161).
76 Countess Guiccioli, *My Recollections of Lord Byron and Those of Eye-Witnesses of His Life* (London, 1869), II, 287.
77 See chapter VI.
78 *Autobiography*.
79 *Ibid.*
80 Shelley to John Gisborne, October 22, 1821 (*Julian*, X, 333).
81 Shelley to Thomas Love Peacock [January 11 (?), 1822] (*Julian*, X, 342).
82 *The Journal of Edward Ellerker Williams*, p. 26.
83 From the unpublished portion of Williams's journal.
84 Mary Shelley to Mrs. Gisborne [December 20, 1821] (Jones, I, 153).

CHAPTER 5

1 Frederick North, fifth Earl of Guilford (1766–1827), was the third and youngest son of George III's prime minister. An enthusiastic philhellene, he was received into the Greek church at Corfu in 1791. He acted as Secretary to the Viceroy of Corsica from 1795 to 1796 and as Governor of Ceylon from 1798 to 1805 (*L. and J.*, 101–02, fn.). The Shelleys had met him in 1819, when he had called on them in Rome (Mary Shelley's journal for March 10). Byron, who seems to have known him only slightly, speaks of him disparagingly elsewhere as "the present Ld Guilford, who was the charlatan Frederic North" (*L. and J.*, IV, 141), and again as "the most illustrious humbug of his age and country" (*L. and J.*, IV, 182).
2 Medwin, *The Life of Shelley*, pp. 364–65.
3 Mary Shelley's journal for December 12 reads: ". . . Walk with the Williams'. While we are with them Shelley hears a rumour of a man to be burnt at Lucca. Calls on Lord Byron with Medwin." But the unpublished portion of Williams's journal shows clearly that Williams heard the rumour from Shelley at the Tre Palazzi. The impression left by Williams is that he attended neither meeting at the Palazzo Lanfranchi and that he derived all his information about the proposed action from Shelley.
4 Medwin, *op. cit.*, p. 365.
5 Unpublished portion of Williams's journal.
6 Byron to Thomas Moore, December 12, 1821 (*L. and J.*, V, 493–94).
7 Byron to Shelley, December 12, 1821 (*L. and J.*, V, 495).
8 From the original letter in The University of Texas Library.
9 *Autobiography*.
10 An error for Thursday, as is proved by Mary Shelley's and Williams's journals and by Byron's letters to Shelley and Taaffe.
11 *L. and J.*, V, 496.

12 See pp. 63, 64.

13 Byron to Thomas Moore, December 13, 1821 (*L. and J.*, 494–95).

14 Williams was responsible for the story that the offender was a priest; none of the other contemporary chroniclers refer to him as such, and on the face of it the story does not seem very likely.

15 From the original letter in The University of Texas Library. It is printed in the *Julian* edition, X, 339, and *L. and J.*, V, 496.

16 *L. and J.*, Moore: *Mephistofilus.*

17 From the original note in The University of Texas Library. It is printed in *L. and J.*, V, 495–96.

18 Medwin, *The Life of Shelley*, p. 367.

19 *Autobiography.*

20 Unpublished portion of Williams's journal.

21 *Ibid.*

22 Medwin, *The Life of Shelley*, p. 375.

23 Unpublished portion of Williams's journal.

24 *Ibid.*

25 *Ibid.*

26 The serpent is a symbol for Shelley (*supra*, p. 81).

27 Shelley to John Gisborne, October 22, 1821 (*Julian*, X, 333).

28 See Appendix C.

29 Byron to John Murray, January 22, 1822 (*L. and J.*, VI, 7).

30 Byron to John Murray, March 6, 1822 (*L. and J.*, VI, 37).

31 Byron to John Murray, March 15, 1822 (*L. and J.*, VI, 41).

32 Byron to Thomas Moore, March 8, 1822 (*L. and J.*, VI, 39–40).

33 See Appendix C.

34 An octavo volume, the *Comment* ran to 499 pp. and sold for 18 shillings. As the volume covers only eight of Dante's ninety-nine books, the extent of the projected work can be seen. It was reviewed in the *Monthly Review* (CII, 225–42) for November, 1823, the reviewer pronouncing Taaffe deficient in imagination and poetic qualities but conceding his industry and learning. Carey in the *London Magazine* for March and April, 1823, handled it severely. Hunt, in the first issue of the *Liberal*, referred to it complimentarily in his "Letters from Abroad" (p. 111).

35 *Autobiography.*

36 Medwin (*The Life of Shelley*, p. 361) reports several items of gossip about Dr. Nott—that as sub-preceptor to Princess Charlotte he attempted to promote a bishopric for himself but that over-anxiety and coquetry with his royal pupil lost him his sub-preceptorship and that from his successful evasion of several matrimonial entanglements he had earned the nickname of *Slip-knot.* Byron, punning on his name, said that he read one of the commandments affirmatively, "Thou shalt, Nott! bear false witness against thy neighbour."

37 Unpublished portion of Williams's journal.

38 Mary Shelley to Mrs. Gisborne, March 7, 1822 (Jones, I, 160).

39 Mary Shelley's journal for March 3: "A note to, and a visit from Dr. Nott. Go to Church" (Jones, 173). For April 10: "Call on Miss Nott" (Jones, 177).

40 From the letter to Mrs. Gisborne, cited above.

41 Mary Shelley to J. C. Hobhouse, November 10, 1824 (from the original letter in the possession of Sir John Murray).

42 Trelawny, *Recollections*, pp. 19–20.

43 *Ibid.*, p. 20.

44 Trelawny, *Recollections*, pp. 20–21.

45 *Ibid.*, pp. 24–25.

46 *Ibid.*, p. 26.

47 *Ibid.*, pp. 27–28.

48 By all accounts Byron had no taste in horses. "He used to keep several horses (ten or twelve) but not one that I saw even passably well looking," observes Taaffe. "About the pedigree of horses he seemed to care nothing, which might spring from his being conscious that his own horses were not worth the enquiry. His aristocratical predilections did not extend to his stud" (*Autobiography*).

49 Trelawny, *Recollections*, p. 28. Taaffe relates that he once saw two Royal ladies walking to and fro under Byron's window after his refusal to appear at their court, in hopes of catching a glimpse of him as he entered his carriage. Byron thwarted them by holding a handkerchief to his face, stepping quickly into the carriage and drawing the curtains (*Autobiography*).

50 Trelawny, *Recollections*, p. 29.

51 Quoted from Angeli, p. 239.

52 Unpublished portion of Williams's journal.

53 Captain Daniel Roberts, R.N., a friend of Trelawny's.

54 Trelawny, *Recollections*, p. 16.

55 *The Journal of Edward Ellerker Williams*, p. 35.

56 Trelawny to Captain Roberts, February 5, 1822 (Forman, *Letters of Edward John Trelawny*, Oxford, 1910, p. 2).

57 Trelawny, *Recollections*, p. 89.

58 *Ibid.*, p. 91.

59 Trelawny to Captain Roberts, February 7, 1822 (from the original letter in the possession of Mr. Carl H. Pforzheimer).

60 Origo, p. 298.

61 Massingham, *The Friend of Shelley: A Memoir of Edward John Trelawny* (New York, 1930), p. 45.

62 The first sight of an original letter or page of manuscript of Trelawny's, with its childish spelling, bad grammar, and ignorance of punctuation, usually comes with a shock even though one thinks he is prepared for it. And yet the man had a remarkable feeling for felicitous and colourful language.

63 Trelawny, *Recollections*, p. 37.

64 Nicolson, *Byron, The Last Journey* (London, 1924), p. 97.

65 From the original MS. in the possession of Sir John Murray.

66 Trelawny, *Recollections*, p. 53.

67 Mary Shelley's journal for February 9 (Jones, p. 168): "Taaffe and T. Medwin call. I retire with E. Trelawny, who amuses me as usual by the endless variety of his adventures and conversation."

68 *Mary Shelley's Journal* (January 19, 1822), Jones, p. 165.

69 Byron to John Murray, January 23, 1822 (*L. and J.*, VI, 8).

70 Byron to John Murray, October 4, 1821 (*L. and J.*, V, 386). (In defence of Murray it should be said that he was right in being afraid to publish *The Vision*; its publication by John Hunt resulted in a £100 fine.)

71 From the original letter in the possession of Sir John Murray.

72 Byron to Kinnaird, February 6, 1822 (*L. and J.*, VI, 9).

73 Shelley, quite independently of Byron, had the same distrust of the funds and, according to White (II, 163), "was tireless in urging [Mr. Gisborne] to withdraw his money from [them] as quickly as possible."

74 Byron to Kinnaird, August 7, 1821 (from the original letter in the possession of Sir John Murray).

75 From the original letter in the possession of Sir John Murray.

76 Byron to Kinnaird, August 16, 1821 (from the original letter in the possession of Sir John Murray).

77 Byron to Kinnaird, October 9, 1821 (from the original letter in the possession of Sir John Murray).

78 Byron to Kinnaird, November 16, 1821 (from the original letter in the possession of Sir John Murray).

79 Byron to Kinnaird, January 18, 1822 (from the original letter in the possession of Sir John Murray).

80 Byron to Kinnaird, December 4, 1821 (from the original letter in the possession of Sir John Murray).

81 Byron to Kinnaird, February 17, 1822 (*Lord Byron's Correspondence*, II, 212).

82 The heavy underscoring appears in the original letter, which is in the possession of Sir John Murray.

83 Byron to Kinnaird, February 20, 1822 (from the original letter in the possession of Sir John Murray).

84 Byron to Kinnaird, undated (from the original letter in the possession of Sir John Murray).

85 Byron to John Hanson, February 17, 1822 (from the original letter in the possession of Sir John Murray).

86 John Hanson to Byron, March, 1822 (from the original letter in the possession of Sir John Murray).

87 John Hanson to Byron, March 7, 1822 (from the original letter in the possession of Sir John Murray).

88 Canto I, CCXVI.

89 Kinnaird to Byron, March 19, 1819 (from the original letter in the possession of Sir John Murray).

90 Byron to Hobhouse, June 8, 1820 (from the original letter in the possession of Sir John Murray).

91 Byron to Kinnaird, November 16, 1821 (from the original letter in the possession of Sir John Murray).

92 Byron to Kinnaird, December 18, 1821 (from the original letter in the possession of Sir John Murray).

93 Byron to Kinnaird, February 23, 1822 (from the original letter in the possession of Sir John Murray). In *L. and J.* (VI, 9–13) parts of the letter appear in garbled form under date of February 6. Prothero, who did not see the original letter but was following Moore, rightly suspected that several letters had been incorrectly printed as one letter under this date. In *Lord Byron's Correspondence* (II, 216–17), where the letter appears under the correct date, the first two sentences in the passage above have been omitted without indication, and the next sentence is made to read, "My only extra expense . . . is a loan to Leigh Hunt of two hundred and fifty pounds' worth of furniture I have bought for him. . . ."

94 Southey's letter to the Editor of *The Courier* appears in *The Life and Correspondence of Robert Southey* (ed. Charles Cuthbert Southey), London, 1850, V, 349–54, as well as *L. and J.*, VI, 389–92.

95 A brother of Maria Edgeworth, the novelist.

96 Medwin, *Conversations*, pp. 147–48.

97 From the original letter in the Pierpont Morgan Library.

98 *The Journal of Edward Ellerker Williams*, p. 40.

99 In Garnett's edition of Williams's journal this incident is credited to "S. and T." in spite of the first person plural pronoun in the passage. The transcriber of the journal has consistently misread Williams's capital *S's* and *T's*.

100 Unpublished portion of Williams's journal.

101 *The Journal of Edward Ellerker Williams*, p. 36.

102 Kill.

103 An estate near Leghorn, well known for its shooting.

104 From a copy of the original letter made by the late Nelson Gay. (By permission of the Keats-Shelley Memorial in Rome.)

105 Moore, Mayne, Dowden, and White do not identify him; Jones (*The Letters of Mary W. Shelley*, I, 162) says that "Captain Hay has been no further identified than as a Maremma hunter and friend of Byron." Quennell (*Byron: A Self Portrait*, London, 1950, p. 487, fn.) merely calls him "an acquaintance both of Byron and Shelley." Hay, it may be remarked in passing, is both the *Captain Hay* and the *Mr. Hay* of the index to *Letters and Journals*.

106 Medwin, *Conversations*, p. 54.

107 Hay to Byron, December 22, 1811 (from the original letter in the possession of Sir John Murray).

108 Martin-Bladen-Edward Hawke (1777–1839), second son of the second Baron Hawke of Towton. Prothero (III, 160) confuses him with his older brother Edward, who succeeded to the title in 1805.

109 Scrope Berdmore Davies (1783–1852) whom Byron knew at Cambridge and with whom he became intimate later in London.

110 Hay to Byron, January 18, 1815 (from the original letter in the possession of Sir John Murray).

111 Hay to Byron, January 23, 1815 (from the original letter in the possession of Sir John Murray).

112 Moore and Prothero both give the name of Mary Duff's husband as Robert Cockburn, a wine-merchant of Edinburgh and later London. In *The Annals of Banff* (Aberdeen, 1841), I, 229, and *The House of Gordon* (Aberdeen, 1903), I, 131, it is also given as *Cockburn*. Though Hay plainly writes the name *Colbourne*, the likelihood is that he confused two similar names.

113 This part of the letter should read: "But I never forgot her, and never can.—If it is no impropriety in a 'married man,' who may very possibly never see her again, and if he did, we are both out of harm's way, you would oblige me by presenting her with my best respects and all good wishes." The letter has obviously been repunctuated by Prothero, who has wrongly divided the two sentences. Byron's habitual use of the dash to represent all degrees of stops makes such a mistake easily possible. Hay certainly read the two sentences as I do.

114 Byron to Hay, January 26, 1815 (*L. and J.*, III, 173–74).

115 Hay to Byron, January 31, 1815 (from the original letter in the possession of Sir John Murray).

116 Medwin, *Conversations*, p. 61.

CHAPTER 6

1 I adopt this spelling of the courier's name on the authority of the Marchesa Iris Origo. In the numerous Italian court records that I have examined it usually appears as Strunss, although Collini (Byron's lawyer) writes it *Strausi* or *Strunsi*. Ross, followed by Prothero, spells it *Strauso*. The man's Swiss-German origin makes *Strauss* more likely than any of the other forms.

2 In *The Last Attachment* Marchesa Iris Origo gives the servant's name as Maluchielli, and perhaps her spelling should be accepted as deriving from Teresa. But, having seen it spelled *Maluccelli* or *Malucelli* scores of times in the court records (including legal papers drawn up by the literate Collini), I am retaining the more usual form. As Maluccelli was unable to write his own name, his deposition, signed with his mark, is of no help.

3 "There goes a Gentleman," said Byron to Taaffe one day, seeing Mehemet Effendi ride by. "You see the Gentleman in his very looks, which is often the case with Turks" (Taaffe's *Autobiography*). Mehemet Effendi was a Georgian by birth but Turkish by upbringing. An accomplished linguist, he became a minister to the Viceroy of Egypt. Medwin (*Conversations*, p. 232) tells us that Byron also admired Mehemet Effendi's horse. "Their [the Turks'] cavalry falls very little short of ours, and is better mounted—their horses better managed," said Byron. "Look, for instance, at the Arab the Turkish Prince here rides!—"

4 This account is a synthesis of the various depositions of the principals of the affair, the testimony of some seventy witnesses who were subsequently examined, the official court summary, and the *Autobiography of John Taaffe, Jr.*

5 Masi, who told his story to Poujoulat in 1838, declares that he touched one of the gentlemen in passing (Poujoulat, *Toscane et Rome*, Paris, 1840; quoted from *L. and J.*, VI, 410). In the deposition subsequently signed by all of the party except Taaffe, it is stated that the rider jostled Taaffe; but Taaffe declared that the man did not touch him but that the "wind of his sudden rush was by no means courteous."

6 Although the witnesses Giuseppe Bini and Angelo Lapacci testified that Masi gave his name, it was apparently not understood by the Englishmen.

7 From the original document in the Keats-Shelley Memorial in Rome. (By permission of the Trustees.)

8 Taaffe, *Autobiography*.

9 So, at least, he wrote in later years in his *Autobiography*.

10 This is Byron's testimony.

11 Forestieri is identified by Marchesa Origo (p. 317) as a spy in the employ of Count Guiccioli.

12 From the manuscript of Williams's journal. The passage appears in Garnett's edition, p. 43.

13 From the manuscript of Williams's journal. The passage appears in Garnett's edition, pp. 43–44.

14 In the highly romanticized—and inaccurate—account of the affair in Barboni (*Geni e capi ameni dell' ottocento.—Ricerche e ricordi intimi*, ed. R. Bemporad & Figlio, Firenze, 1911, p. 167) Byron was unable to sleep a wink during the night.

CHAPTER 7

1 From a copy of the original letter made by Nelson Gay. (By permission of the Keats-Shelley Memorial in Rome.)

2 From the original letter in The University of Texas Library.

3 According to Masi's story as related to Poujoulat, "The next day Lord Byron sends to me his surgeon and 100 gold louis, sending also word that he deplored this misfortune and that he did not know the murderer. I did not wish to see the English surgeon, and I returned to Lord Byron his gold; I replied to him that I did not need his aid, that my pay sufficed me; that, if I did not die of the wound, I was going to demand justice of him, and that if I died, others would charge themselves with avenging me. Lord Byron did not know, he said, who it was who had pierced my side; he did not know him, perhaps, but it was nonetheless a man of his house" (*L. and J.*, VI, 411–12).

4 From the original manuscript of Williams's journal. The passage appears in Garnett's edition (p. 44), where the initials *S.* and *T.* have been incorrectly transcribed as *T.* and *I.*

5 *The Journal of Edward Ellerker Williams*, pp. 48–49.

6 *Ibid.*

7 *The Journal of Edward Ellerker Williams*, p. 45.

8 From a copy of the original letter made by Nelson Gay. (By permission of the Keats-Shelley Memorial in Rome.)

9 From the manuscript of Williams's journal. The passage appears on pp. 45–46 of Garnett's edition, where the initial *S* is consistently misread as *T*.

10 From the original note in The University of Texas Library.

11 From the manuscript of Williams's journal. In Garnett (p. 47) *S's* is incorrectly transcribed *T's*.

12 At the top of Sir John Murray's copy of Crawford's deposition is this note in Byron's hand: "Translated Copy of the deposition of Dr. James Crawford, M.D.—The original was sent to the Marquis Viviani, Governor of Pisa—and the other English Copy to the English Minister Mr Dawkins—now resident in Florence." In the margin appears this further note: "Note: I mistook the Sergeant Major for an *Officer* the whole time as he was well dressed & mounted—I was quite ignorant at the moment of what had occurred during the arrest at the Gates of the City. Noel Byron." And at the end: "Note* To give the hand (in some parts of the Continent) is a pledge either of hostility or otherwise according to circumstances. The reader of this must judge for himself in the present instance."

In the State Archives at Florence are copies of both the English and Italian versions of the deposition. Sir John Murray's copy is in Italian.

13 Vincenzo di Giuseppe Antonio Papi, a native of Macerata, who had been in Byron's service in Ravenna. Aged 34 at the time of the affray, he says of himself that he had always been a coachman. He is described as of medium height, with blue eyes, an aquiline nose, and a chestnut beard without moustaches of any sort. He was a family man, with a wife and several children who lived with him in the Palazzo Lanfranchi.

Leigh Hunt gives the following information about him: "He was a good-tempered fellow, and an affectionate husband and father; yet he had the reputation of having offered his master to knock a man on the head. . . . This servant his Lordship had exalted into something wonderfully attached to him, though he used to fight hard with the man on some points" (*Lord Byron and Some of His Contemporaries*, London, 1828, p. 69). Medwin (*Conversations*, p. 177) helps to explain the attachment: "Lord Byron was the best of masters, and was perfectly adored by his servants. His kindness was extended even to their children. He liked them to have their families with them: and I remember one day, as we were entering the hall after our ride, meeting a little boy, of three or four years old, of the coachman's whom he took up in his arms and presented with a ten-Paul piece."

14 Hay, writing on April 11 to Byron from Florence, requests Byron to reply in care of the "Chargé d'Affaires but omit Excellenzy as he says he has no right to that title" (from the original letter in the possession of Sir John Murray).

15 From the original manuscript in the possession of Sir John Murray. Byron always addressed Goethe as Baron, Trelawny goes on to say, though he knew Goethe had no claim to the title.

16 From a copy in the State Archives at Florence. It omits a paragraph reflecting on Italian testimony (see p. 127).

17 This statement, which sounds out of character for Taaffe, is mentioned by no one else.

18 Mary Shelley to Mrs. Gisborne, April 6, 1822 (Jones, I, 163).

19 Shelley to Claire Clairmont, [postmarked] April 2, 1822 (*Julian*, X, 368).

20 *The Journal of Edward Ellerker Williams*, p. 48.

21 From a copy of the original note made by Mrs. More O'Ferrall.

22 At least three copies of Taaffe's statement, written in Italian in his own beautiful hand, are extant. Kinnaird's copy is now in the possession of Sir John Murray; the copy sent to Dawkins is now in The University of Texas Library; and the copy sent by Byron to Sir Walter Scott, who later passed it on to Thomas Moore, is now in the possession of the Rosenbach Company. On Sir Walter Scott's copy Byron wrote a note blaming the whole affair on Taaffe and attributing his desire to escape blame to a fear of the Pisans.

As Taaffe's statement turned out to be such a controversial document, I have reproduced it in Appendix B from The University of Texas manuscript. It differs from the Kinnaird copy only in verbal changes.

23 The reference I take to be to Taaffe's statement and a note accompanying it.

24 From the original note in The University of Texas Library.

25 The facts are these. Towards the end of 1819 Taaffe engaged a mason named Ranieri Pettini to do some repair work on his residence, the Casa Mostardi. When Pettini asked for payment, Taaffe referred him to Michele Vallini, agent for the Mostardi family, who, however, did not pay him. Pettini persisted, and Vallini at last told him flatly that he never expected to pay him and suggested that if Taaffe would reread his lease he would find it clearly provided that all expense of improvement and repair should be borne by the tenant—unless the lease was a forged document [*una scritta falsa*].

This aspersion, duly repeated to Taaffe, greatly excited him. Arming himself with two pistols, he went at once with Pettini to Vallini's house and confronted him with the insult. When Vallini made no denial, Taaffe heatedly said that anyone who suggested that he was capable of falsifying a document was a vile person. Taaffe later deposed that Vallini thereupon threw himself upon him and pulled him through the room, assisted by Pettini. Managing to free an arm with difficulty, Taaffe pulled out a pistol, forced Vallini to release him, and, backing into a corner of the room, declared that he would defend his person against any violence. Vallini, however, slipped away into another room and got a gun, which from a position behind a door he pointed at Taaffe in spite of the efforts of one or more women to hinder him. They were apparently successful, for Vallini disappeared, and Taaffe seized the opportunity to leave quietly "without having the air of fleeing." (Vallini tells the story differently. He says that from the moment of Taaffe's arrival he attempted to calm him; but when Taaffe called him vile, he threatened to throw Taaffe out of the window. Taaffe then drew a pistol, which Vallini and Pettini prevented him from using by pinioning his arms and thrusting him out the door.)

Pettini, leaving with Taaffe, begged in vain that the matter should be forgotten. Taaffe went immediately to the police office, where he wrote out a report of what had happened and left the disputed lease. Chancellor Giovani, after weighing the evidence—Pettini, the only witness, sided with Vallini—concluded that Taaffe was at fault and that he should be given three days in which to apologize to Vallini or should be punished with five days of arrest in his own house. The case was reviewed by Auditor Pazienza, who agreed to the justice of the Chancellor's decision but recommended that, to avoid further trouble, the apology be dispensed with and Taaffe be confined to his own house for three days. The decision was also approved by Puccini, the President of the Buon Governo. Taaffe, however, appealed to Lord Burghersh, minister plenipotentiary at Florence, who sent the minister Fossombroni a copy of Taaffe's letter and requested him to look into the affair. Fossombroni promised to do so. Whether Taaffe ever received the punishment is not clear; several weeks later the case was still pending.

26 Prince Clement had died in January, and Taaffe's *Elegy*, printed with the types of Didot, had appeared not long thereafter.

27 Orlando, 2nd Baron and 1st Earl of Bradford (1762–1825).

28 A reference to Trelawny.

29 From the original letter in The University of Texas Library.

30 From a copy of the original letter preserved by Dawkins, now in The University of Texas Library.

31 From a copy of the original letter preserved by Dawkins, now in The University of Texas Library.

32 From the original document in the Keats-Shelley Memorial in Rome. (By permission of the Trustees.)

33 From a copy of the original note made by Mrs. More O'Ferrall.

34 Byron sent this note and a letter of April 11 from Mrs. Beauclerk on the state of opinion at Florence to Kinnaird. It is now in the possession of Sir John Murray, by whose kind permission it is used.

35 See p. 108 and note 3, ch. 7.

36 Antonio Maluccelli, a native of Forlì, near Ravenna, is described as tall in stature, with dark skin and hair and a goatee under his lower lip. Teresa kept her carriage in Byron's stables and used his horses and coachman. When her carriage went out, Maluccelli rode behind it, but when Byron's carriage went out, Tita rode behind it.

37 *The Journal of Edward Ellerker Williams*, p. 50.

38 From the manuscript of Williams's journal.

39 Mary Shelley to Leigh Hunt [April 10, 1822], (Jones, I, 166).

40 How much the affair was on Byron's mind and how much he was concerned about the reports of it which reached England is revealed by his correspondence. The following letters (all published) contain accounts of it or allusions to it: March 28 to Kinnaird; March 31 to Murray; April 2 to Kinnaird(?); April 11 to Hobhouse; April 13 to Murray; April 18 to Murray; May 1 to Murray; May 2 to Kinnaird; May 4 to Sir Walter Scott (with copies of all the documents); May 17 to Moore. In addition to these, several unpublished letters to Kinnaird in the possession of Sir John Murray, who has kindly permitted me to make excerpts from them, are concerned with it. On April 9 Byron wrote to Kinnaird: "By Thursday's post I addressed to you a packet containing various documents upon an affair which occurred here not long ago.—At your leisure acknowledge the same and believe me. . . ." Four days later he wrote again: "I sent you last week packets of an affair that occurred here—of which you will have heard enough by this time—I enclose you three more letters on the subject—they will enable you to judge still further for yourself.—" (Two of the letters were the formal note from Taaffe—see pp. 120–21—and a letter from Mrs. Beauclerk—*supra*, note 34 and *infra*, note 51. The third I have not been able to identify.) Still another note (of May 3) reads: "I expected a line of acknowledgement for some documents sent on the 4th of April—relative to a quarrel with a dragoon—&c.—all of which you have I trust safely received—and will employ—if necessary—to contradict any false statements—for it is now a long time—since a word of truth has been allowed to appear in the journals on *any* subject—literary or personal—in which I am concerned.—Duplicates of the same were also afterwards forwarded to Mr. Hobhouse.—"

41 See p. 120.

42 From the original note in The University of Texas Library.

43 From the original letter in the possession of Sir John Murray.

44 Medwin (*Conversations*, p. 242) quotes the *Courier Français* as follows: "A superior officer went to Lord Byron a few days ago. A very warm altercation, the reason of which was unknown, occurred between this officer and the English poet. The threats of the officer became so violent, that Lord Byron's servant ran to protect his master. A struggle ensued, in which the officer was struck with a poniard by the servant, and died instantly. The servant fled."

45 From the original letter in the possession of Sir John Murray.

46 See pp. 115–16.

47 From the original letter in The University of Texas Library.

48 See pp. 113–14.

49 From an unsigned copy or first draft preserved by Dawkins, in The University of Texas Library.

50 From the original letter in The University of Texas Library.

51 Taaffe's suspicions of Mrs. Beauclerk were in part, at least, justified. In the letter of April 11 to Byron she said, ". . . Beware how you ever trust the bad head tho good heart of your Irish friend——" Her intervention in the dispute between Taaffe and Trelawny and Byron seems to have cost her any pretensions she may have had to the friendship of Byron, for in a letter post-marked April 17 she wrote to Byron: "I set off towards England the first week in May. You probably will never hear of me more while I shall find wherever I go that you annimate & occupy the minds of everyone—let me however reflect with pride & pleasure on the transient moment you seemed inclined Dear Lord Byron to think of me favorably & allow me shortly to forget that ill nature & calumny deprived me of your friendship yet permit me to sign myself always Your sincere & obliged E. Beauclerk. Pray remember me to M[r] Trelawny" (from the original letters in the possession of Sir John Murray).

52 Taaffe to E. J. Dawkins, April 3, 1822 (from the original letter in The University of Texas Library).

53 From the original manuscript of Williams's journal. Williams wrote: "Lord B. willing to give his hand to Taaffe as usual—all right again——" Garnett incorrectly ends the sentence with *Taaffe* and begins the new sentence with *as usual.*

54 From the original letter in The University of Texas Library.

55 Wife of Lord Burghersh, British minister plenipotentiary at Florence.

56 The Comtesse d'Albany, wife of Charles Edward Stuart (the Young Pretender), whom she left in 1780. She then lived with Alfieri, the Italian poet and dramatist, at Rome, Paris, and (after the outbreak of the French Revolution) at Florence. After the death of Alfieri in 1803 she attached herself to François Fabre, a French painter, and presided over a *salon* to which all the intellectuals and artists were invited. Taaffe probably met her through Madame Regny.

57 From the original letter in the possession of Sir John Murray.

58 From the original letter in The University of Texas Library.

59 Postman or messenger.

60 Byron's valet.

61 From a copy of the original letter made by Nelson Gay. (By permission of the trustees of the Keats-Shelley Memorial.)

62 Illegible word transcribed as *substancely.*

63 From the original note in The University of Texas Library.

64 Hay's letter to Byron is missing.

65 From a copy of the original letter preserved by Dawkins, in The University of Texas Library.

66 He told Medwin (*Conversations*, p. 40) that the Rochdale suit had cost him £14,000.

67 From the original letter in The University of Texas Library.

68 Collini arrived in Pisa on April 20 and went to the Tre Donzelle to lodge, having declined Byron's offer of an apartment at the Palazzo Lanfranchi.

69 From the original letter in the possession of Sir John Murray.

70 From the original letter in The University of Texas Library.

71 Taaffe. See p. 121.

72 From the original letter in the possession of Sir John Murray.

73 Mary Shelley to Mrs. Gisborne, June 2, 1822 (*Shelley and Mary*, II, 808). It appears in Jones (I, 169) with minor variations.

74 From the original letter in The University of Texas Library.

75 Collini at Florence applied to the Buon Governo on April 24 for a safe conduct for Tita. On the same day Governor Viviani wrote to the President of the Buon Governo requesting that any safe conduct which would allow Tita liberty in Pisa be refused.

76 In his testimony Tita gave his age as twenty-four.

77 Colloquial for *police*.

78 From the original letter in The University of Texas Library.

79 No other letter of Byron's dated April 26 is to be found in the Byron-Dawkins correspondence.

80 From the original letter in The University of Texas Library.

81 This letter is missing from the correspondence.

82 From a first draft, containing many alterations and cancellations, in The University of Texas Library.

83 An allusion to a misstatement in a Milan newspaper that Byron had brought forward his *Marino Faliero* on the stage and that it had been hissed.

84 From the original letter in The University of Texas Library.

85 See pp. 151–52.

86 This is the same person mentioned by Marchesa Origo (p. 509, note 32) as Sebastiano Foscari. All I can say is that the orthography of the Florentine court records is quite clear.

87 *I.e.*, haters of beards. (Byron has used the wrong ending.)

88 From the original letter in The University of Texas Library.

89 Unquestionably an error in transcription for "Mr."

90 Shelley to Byron, May 3, 1822 (*Julian*, X, 385).

91 Shelley to Trelawny, May 16, 1822 (*Julian*, X, 390).

92 Bankers at Brussels.

93 From the original letter in the possession of Sir John Murray.

94 This letter, printed in *L. and J.*, VI, 62–63, is in The University of Texas Library.

95 Michele Leoni, translator of Byron's *Lament of Tasso* and Canto IV of *Childe Harold's Pilgrimage*.

96 From the original letter in the possession of Sir John Murray.

97 From the original letter in The University of Texas Library.

98 Mary Shelley to Mrs. Gisborne, June 2, 1822 (Jones, I, 168).

99 "Where were you the evening of March 24? I went for a drive in the carriage, outside the Piagge gate."

100 Mary Shelley to Mrs. Gisborne, June 2, 1822 (Jones, I, 168–69).

101 Mary's journal, with the entry for April 19, "An examination at the house of T. Guiccioli," leaves the impression that her own examination was at Teresa's house. But Lapini inserts this preamble into her testimony: "A notice was given by Mr. Percy Shelley of an indisposition of Madame his wife, requesting, that she might be examined at her own dwelling; so for that reason I questioned the undersigned at the house of habitation of the said Sir Shelley,

situated on the Lung' Arno, where was introduced to me the lady Mary, wife of Mr. Percy Shelley. . . ." Torelli comments that examination in their own houses is a privilege enjoyed by English lords.

102 I do not find this statement in the official testimony.

103 Prothero (*L. and J.*, VI, 408–09) says that Byron's examination, originally scheduled for April 24, was postponed until the 27th because of the death of Allegra. But Byron's testimony, dated April 21, appears with that of the others in the official records at Florence.

104 From the original letter in The University of Texas Library.

105 W. M. Rossetti, "Talks with Trelawny" (*Athenæum*, July 29, 1882, p. 145).

106 Medwin, *The Life of Shelley*, pp. 380–81.

107 Tribolati, *Saggi critici e biografici*, pp. 227ff.

108 *Vie*, pp. 1129–30.

109 *Ibid.*, p. 1136.

110 *Ibid.*, p. 1139.

111 As told to Poujoulat (quoted by Prothero, *L. and J.*, VI, 412).

CHAPTER 8

1 See p. 74.

2 Shelley to Claire Clairmont, undated (*Julian*, X, 367).

3 Shelley to Claire Clairmont, undated (*Julian*, X, 355).

4 Byron advanced Hunt £250 on Shelley's security, paid another £50 for furniture, provided him with an apartment in the Palazzo Lanfranchi, gave him £70 at Pisa, and paid the costs of his moves from Pisa to Genoa and from Genoa to Florence. In addition he gave up his share of profits in *The Liberal*, to which he made over the copyrights of *The Vision of Judgment*, his Pulci translation—"the best translation that ever was or will be"—and *Heaven and Earth*. But Hunt, while acknowledging some of these obligations, complained that Byron doled out money to him, as if his disgraces were being counted, through Lega Zambelli. As Hunt's views on money were notoriously unconventional, however, one can hardly blame Byron for adopting such a protective measure.

5 Shelley to Hunt, March 2, 1822 (*Julian*, X, 361).

6 From the manuscript of Williams's journal.

7 Unpublished portion of Williams's journal.

8 Mary Shelley to Maria Gisborne, June 2, 1822 (Jones, I, 169).

9 *Ibid.*, p. 170.

10 Shelley to Claire Clairmont, May 29, 1822 (*Julian*, X, 396).

11 From the original letter in the possession of Sir John Murray.

12 Unpublished portion of Williams's journal.

13 *Ibid.*

14 Shelley to Captain Roberts, May 13, 1822 (*Julian*, X, 388).

15 The phrase is Williams's.

16 Mary Shelley to Maria Gisborne, June 2, 1822 (Jones, I, 171).

17 Unpublished portion of Williams's journal.

18 From the original letter in the possession of Sir John Murray. It appears with slight editorial alterations in the *Julian* edition, X, 391.

19 Byron to Shelley, May 20, 1822 (*L. and J.*, VI, 66–67).

20 From the original letter in the possession of Sir John Murray. It appears in the *Julian* edition, X, 398, dated [? June, 1822]. As the letter itself is dated

"Sunday" and is postmarked "Sarzana Giu. 11," it should be dated June 9, which was the preceding Sunday.

21 *Julian: Mr.*

22 The italicized words were added as an afterthought at the end of the page. They are intended to follow *welcome* rather than *rocks*, as in the *Julian* edition.

23 From the original letter in The University of Texas Library. It appears in the *Julian* edition, X, 399.

24 White (II, 628–29) discusses the vague chronology of the movements of Trelawny and Roberts. The unpublished portion of Williams's journal sheds a little light on the subject. It is clear that they arrived on the 13th, that Roberts and Williams went fishing ten miles up the river to Santa Stephano on the 14th, and that Roberts and Trelawny dined again at Casa Magni on the 15th. Mary Shelley gives June 16 as the date of Trelawny's departure for Leghorn in the *Bolivar*, but she was writing on July 7, with faulty memory, and has misled biographers. Williams, writing at the time, gives June 18 as the date, which is confirmed by this sentence in a letter of June 18 from Shelley to Trelawny: "We saw you about eight miles in the offing this morning; but the abatement of the breeze leaves us little hope that you can have made Leghorn this evening" (*Julian*, X, 405). There is no reason for hypothesizing two visits by Trelawny, as does White.

25 Trelawny, *Recollections*, p. 104.

26 *The Journal of Edward Ellerker Williams*, p. 65.

27 Mary Shelley to Maria Gisborne, August 15, 1822 (Jones, I, 179).

28 Shelley to John Gisborne, June 18, 1822 (*Julian*, X, 403–04).

29 Shelley to Horace Smith, June 29, 1822 (*Julian*, X, 411).

30 Unpublished portion of Williams's journal. Mary (in a letter of June 2 to Mrs. Gisborne, Jones, I, 170) says that the boat was 24 feet long and 8 feet wide.

31 From the manuscript of Williams's journal. Williams wrote: "At 7 launched our boat—With all her ballast in she floats three inches lighter than before." Garnett changes *her* to *our* and incorrectly divides the two sentences at the end of the *with* phrase.

32 Shelley to Leigh Hunt, June 24, 1822 (*Julian*, X, 408).

33 Hunt, *Lord Byron and Some of His Contemporaries*, p. 489. Mrs. Angeli disputes the date. (See below, note 57.)

34 *The Journal of Edward Ellerker Williams*, pp. 67–68.

35 See pp. 174–75.

36 *The Journal of Edward Ellerker Williams*, p. 68.

37 Mary Shelley to Maria Gisborne, August 15, 1822 (Jones, I, 183).

38 Taaffe, *Autobiography*.

39 Unpublished portion of Williams's journal.

40 White, II, 632, fn. 43.

41 Trelawny, *Recollections*, p. 116.

42 *L. and J.*, VI, 413.

43 From the State Archives at Florence.

44 Trelawny, *Recollections*, p. 105.

45 The following note from Henry Dunn, found with the Byron-Dawkins correspondence and probably addressed to Lega Zambelli, refers to the courier, Strauss:

Friday Morng
7th June/22

Sir

Please inform My Lord that Doctor Peebles called on me this Morning—to say that the sooner the Servant who is unwell is sent to Leghorn the better

—as the Doctor wishes to see him once or twice a day—If My Lord will send him to me I will procure a Room for him—and am

Sir
Yours very truly
H. Dunn

A visitor's permit good for a month was issued to Strauss by the Governor of Pisa, and Strauss went to Leghorn for treatment by Dr. Peebles. In a letter dated from Leghorn on June 12, Lega Zambelli wrote to Collini at Florence that Strauss was to be found in Leghorn under strenuous medical treatment and that he had not ceased spitting blood. He enclosed a medical certificate, drawn by a lawyer and notarized, certifying the man's condition (from the original letter in The University of Texas Library).

46 From the original letter in The University of Texas Library.

47 From an unsigned draft in The University of Texas Library which breaks off at the point where the complimentary conclusion was doubtless intended to begin.

48 In a letter of June 8 to Moore (*L. and J.*, VI, 80), Byron says, "A few days ago, my earliest and dearest friend, Lord Clare, came over from Geneva on purpose to see me before he returned to England." He remained only a day. Moore, from whom the letter derives, evidently misread Geneva for Genova [Genoa].

49 In the omitted portions of Hay's letter of May 1 (see p. 147) a long passage is devoted to the numerous victims of Austrian measures of repression in northern Italian cities.

50 From the original letter in The University of Texas Library.

51 The *Observateur Autrichien*, an excerpt from which is among the Byron-Dawkins papers. It states that a sergeant jostled the horse of one of Byron's friends, that Byron struck the man with a whip, and that in fear of retaliation by his comrades Byron instigated an attack on the sergeant by a servant. The sergeant was carried dying to a hospital, and the assailant was arrested and is standing trial.

52 Trelawny to Byron, May 1, 1822 (from the original letter in the possession of Sir John Murray).

53 This quotation and the several that follow relating to Byron's boat are from the State Archives at Florence.

54 The original estimate was £100 and the final cost £1,000.

55 From the original letter in The University of Texas Library.

56 Hunt, *Lord Byron and Some of His Contemporaries*, p. 9.

57 Hunt, *Lord Byron and Some of His Contemporaries*, pp. 9–14. As the police court records of the affray are dated June 28, Mrs. Angeli points out that Hunt was mistaken in thinking that he left Genoa on June 28. It seems to me equally possible that the police court records were simply misdated.

58 Origo, p. 317.

59 Hunt (p. 12) says that the servant, on his way out of the country, called on Shelley, "who was shocked at his appearance, and gave him some money out of his very disgust; for he thought nobody would help such a fellow if he did not."

60 Torelli says that this affair, with Byron's request to anchor the *Bolivar* on the coast and embark and disembark passengers at will, caused the government to study the means of making him leave Tuscany without acting directly. The result was the banishment of the courier and the hint to the Gambas to leave at once in order to forestall formal sentence of exile. Hunt believed that the affair was a remote cause of Byron's leaving Italy because it "increased the

awkwardness of his position with the Tuscan Government, and gave a farther unsteadiness to his restless temper." The Gambas, he continues, were admitted to Tuscany only on sufferance and had already come under the unfavourable notice of the authorities in the dragoon affair. And now, another of Gamba's servants having created a second disturbance, the distrust of the authorities was complete, and Byron's continued residence in Tuscany "was made uneasy to him" (p. 12). Williams wrote to Jane that "although the present banishment of the Gambas from Tuscany is attributed to the first affair of the dragoon, the continued disturbances among his and their servants is, I am sure, the principal cause for its being carried into immediate effect" (Trelawny, *Recollections*, p. 111).

61 Assuming for the moment that the date of June 28 which appears in the police records is accurate and not an error such as any clerk might easily make, it still makes no difference in the point at issue. The report of the second disturbance could not have reached Florence in time to affect the action taken, and it is clear from the Buon Governo order that it did not do so.

62 Count Gamba replied that only his son was with him and that he had no household; those servants who were supposed by the authorities to be his were in fact his daughter's, who was not mentioned in the decree; therefore the servants were not subject to its provisions. Except for Maluccelli they were allowed to return to Pisa with Teresa.

63 From the State Archives at Pisa.

64 From the original letter in The University of Texas Library. It was probably sent by Byron to Dawkins.

65 But see Byron's letter of July 4 (p. 176) in which the number of days is given as four.

66 Torelli, *Arcana politicae anticarbonariae*.

67 *Ibid.*

68 From the original letter in The University of Texas Library. The end of the letter, containing probably nothing more than the complimentary conclusion and signature, has been cut away.

69 Count Alborghetti, mentioned by Count Guiccioli as a partisan of Byron's.

70 From the original letter in The University of Texas Library.

71 From the State Archives at Lucca.

72 *Ibid.*

73 From the secret files of the Buon Governo at Lucca (translated into English by Nelson Gay).

74 Trelawny, *Recollections*, p. 119.

75 Mayne, p. 386.

76 Mary Shelley to Maria Gisborne, August 15, 1822 (Jones, I, 182).

77 From the original letter in The University of Texas Library.

78 Torelli recorded the death of Shelley with characteristic confusion of names: "On the 8th of July there was a terrible storm at sea. Captain Scellyny would-be Atheist, with William, another Englishman, wished to leave Leghorn in a little Schuner of theirs which they used to take trips at Spezia, where they had their families in a little country house rented by them. The Schuner was lost, and a few days later the sea threw up a body at the mouth of the Serchio which even though the face had been reduced to a skeleton by fishes was recognized by various signs as that of one of the two Englishmen."

79 Trelawny, *Recollections*, p. 123.

80 Presumably for the sale of the *Bolivar*.

81 From the original letter in The University of Texas Library.

82 One of the effects upon him, says Miss Mayne (p. 388), was to cause him almost to cease letter-writing for a long interval. "There are no letters from Byron between July 12 and August 3—an unusually long silence for him," she says. "We may conclude that, like the rest, he could think of nothing else, do nothing else but think, and wildly search, conjecture, inquire." The statement is almost true, but not quite. Since the publication of Miss Mayne's biography six letters written by Byron during the period of supposed silence have been discovered: the two to Roberts above, the two to Dawkins above, and two to Hobhouse, dated July 25 and July 31 (Hobhouse proofs).

83 From a copy of the letter, dated July 13 and written in French, in the State Archives at Lucca.

84 In writing to Dawkins on July 23 about the legal formalities required in claiming the bodies of Shelley and Williams, Trelawny added: "Lord Byron is sorry he did not see you on your way through Pisa he desires his compts—It appears our accquantance with you, is fated to be a very troublesome one indeed what can be expected from an intercourse with a Satanic club!" (From the original letter in the possession of Mr. Carl H. Pforzheimer.) Dawkins, in reply, wrote: "I am very sensible of Lord Byron's kindness, and should have called upon him when I passed through Pisa, had he been anybody but Lord Byron" (Trelawny, *Recollections*, p. 125).

85 From the original letter in The University of Texas Library.

86 From the original letter in The University of Texas Library.

CHAPTER 9

1 Taaffe's orthography is unmistakable, but I conjecture that this is the same minister whose name is rendered *Bombelles* in Dawkins's letter to the Marquis Mansi (see p. 179).

2 John Taaffe, Jr., to Byron, July 20, 1822 (from the original letter in the possession of Mr. Carl H. Pforzheimer).

3 Captain Hay to Byron, September 2, 1822 (from the original letter in the possession of Sir John Murray).

4 Medwin, *The Life of Shelley*, pp. 393–94. In his *Conversations*, Medwin dishonestly left the impression that he was present at the cremation ceremonies and took in even so careful a biographer as Miss Mayne. In *The Life of Shelley* he corrects the impression.

5 Forman, *Letters of Edward John Trelawny*, pp. 3–4.

6 Byron to Trelawny, August 14, 1822 (from the original letter in the Berg Collection).

7 Byron to Moore, August 8, 1822 (*L. and J.*, VI, 99).

8 From the same letter (*ibid.*, p. 101): "I have written three more cantos of *Don Juan*, and am hovering on the brink of another (the ninth)."

9 In almost identical letters to Hanson and Murray, both written on August 10, Byron had asked each to inform Kinnaird that the remittance had not arrived (*L. and J.*, VI, 102–03).

10 Byron to Kinnaird, August 15, 1822 (from the original letter in the possession of Sir John Murray).

11 At the time of the cremation of Shelley's body.

12 Byron to Kinnaird, August 20, 1822 (from the original letter in the possession of Sir John Murray).

13 Byron to Kinnaird, August 24, 1822 (from the original letter in the possession of Sir John Murray).

14 Byron to Kinnaird, August 31, 1822 (from the original letter in the possession of Sir John Murray).

15 Byron to Kinnaird, September 1, 1822 (from the original letter in the possession of Sir John Murray).

16 In the journal which Mrs. Hunt began in Pisa on September 18, 1822, she wrote: "Monday [September] 23d . . . Mr. Hunt was much annoyed by Lord Byron behaving so meanly about the children disfiguring his house which his nobleship chose to be very severe upon. How much I wish I could esteem him more! It is so painful, to be under any obligation to a person you cannot esteem! Can anything be more absurd than a peer of the realm—and a *poet* making such a fuss about three or four children disfiguring the walls of a few rooms. The very children would blush for him, fye Lord B.—fye" (*Bulletin of the Keats-Shelley Memorial*, Part II, 72–73). In a letter of October 6, 1822, to Mary Shelley, Byron (writing about a disputed sofa) said: "I have a particular dislike to anything of Shelley's being within the same walls with Mrs. Hunt's children. They are dirtier and more mischievous than Yahoos. What they can't destroy with their filth they will with their fingers" (*L. and J.*, VI, 119).

17 *The Liberal* died with the fourth number: "the cuckoo note, 'I told you so,' sung by his friends, and the loud crowing of enemies, by no means allayed his ill-humour," observed Trelawny (*Recollections*, p. 155). Hunt thought that Byron's friends were opposed to it because of its principles, but the reasons were probably more personal. "Mr. Hobhouse rushed over the Alps, not knowing which was the more awful, the mountains, or the Magazine," Hunt wrote bitterly (*Lord Byron and Some of His Contemporaries*, p. 48). "Mr. Murray wondered, Mr. Gifford smiled (a lofty symptom!) and Mr. Moore . . . said that the Liberal had a 'taint' in it!"

18 Byron to Kinnaird, September 26, 1822 (from the original letter in the possession of Sir John Murray).

19 Byron to Kinnaird, September 10, 1822 (from the original letter in the possession of Sir John Murray).

20 Byron to Kinnaird, September 12, 1822 (from the original letter in the possession of Sir John Murray).

21 Byron sold her eventually to Lord Blessington for 400 guineas, which, however, had not been paid at the time of Byron's death. (See *L. and J.*, VI, 290, 374–75.) Prior to the sale he had her laid up in port and dismissed the crew. Writing to him at the time, Trelawny said: "This is all I have to say on taking leave of your little schooner very sincerely regretting that—that which we anticipated so much pleasure from has been the occasion of nothing but disappointment, regret & vexation to all parties" (from a letter dated November 21, 1822, in the possession of Sir John Murray).

22 Trelawny, *Recollections*, p. 148.

23 "Do not go to Van Diemen's land," wrote Kinnaird in reply (from a letter dated October 15, 1822, in the possession of Sir John Murray).

24 Trelawny, *Recollections*, pp. 148–49.

25 Broughton, *Recollections of a Long Life* (London, 1910), III, 3.

26 Byron to Kinnaird, September 21, 1822 (from the original letter in the possession of Sir John Murray). Kinnaird, indignant at the imputation, replied: "You warn me not to let myself be cajoled by Lady Byron's banking with me —I should hope that if all her family banked with me, I might stand free from such a warning being thought necessary or fit to be given to me—I have already written to you that Lady Byron does not bank with me—" (from a letter of October 15, 1822, in the possession of Sir John Murray).

27 Byron to Hobhouse, September 26, 1822 (*Lord Byron's Correspondence*, II, 232).

28 Trelawny, *Recollections*, p. 150.

29 *Ibid.*, pp. 151–52.

30 Two further entries conclude the notices of Byron in Torelli's diary: (1) "Lord Byron has finally decided to leave for Genoa. It is said that he is already bored with his favourite Guiccioli. However he expressed the intention of not remaining in Genoa but of wishing to go on to Athens to be adored by the Greeks, who at that time were winning great victories on land." (2) "Byron, with Countess Guiccioli, left Pisa the 27th of this month in the direction of Genoa, where he thought to stay a little while and then go on to Athens, but at this point the Greek revolution ended with their complete defeat, and the occupation of the Morea by the Turkish army caused him to change his plans. Count Gamba, father of the Guiccioli, taking refuge in Lucca after his exile from Pisa, had already preceded his daughter to Genoa."

CHAPTER 10

1 Trelawny, *Recollections*, pp. 160–61.

2 Trelawny to Claire Clairmont, October 22, 1825 (Forman, *Letters of Edward John Trelawny*, p. 96).

3 Massingham, p. 305.

4 McAleer, *Dearest Isa: Robert Browning's Letters to Isabella Blagden* (Austin, 1951), p. 278.

5 Medwin, *The Life of Shelley*, pp. 407–10.

6 In the possession of Sir John Murray.

7 In a letter of October 20, 1829, written from Florence, Trelawny told Mary of being sent for by Mrs. Medwin, in the absence of her husband, and of advising her about her financial affairs. "He told her plainly that Medwin had run through her fortune of £10,000 and that his story of having £800 per annum was a lie" (Grylls, *Mary W. Shelley*, p. 217, fn.).

8 From a letter dated from Liverpool, January 15, 1833, in the possession of Sir John Murray.

9 Grylls, *Mary W. Shelley*, p. 189.

10 Byron to Teresa Guiccioli, October 29, 1823 (*L. and J.*, VI, 276).

11 Ginnasi was a brother-in-law of Teresa's paternal aunt. Of him Count Guiccioli wrote to his lawyer, Taglioni: [He] is opposed to me as buyer of national properties, he is a rock which it would be as well to sweep out of the way." (From the Guiccioli-Taglioni correspondence in The University of Texas Library.)

12 Origo, p. 387.

13 *Ibid.*, p. 389.

14 From the Guiccioli-Taglioni correspondence in The University of Texas Library.

15 Origo, p. 390.

16 Taaffe, *Autobiography*.

17 Origo, p. 407.

18 Mayne, p. 431 fn.

19 Nicolson, p. 279.

20 *Ibid.*

21 She had written earlier (on November 18, 1822) from Leghorn to thank Byron for an introduction to Mr. Dunn, "who is become my great & intimate

friend as He seems to have a perfect adoration for you & gave you such a character as did my heart good to hear. . . . I liked Mr. Dunn for his warm manner of speaking of you and also not the less for the share of his favour & utility that it procured me" (from the original letter in the possession of Sir John Murray).

22 Lady Hardy to Byron, February 13, 1823 (from the original letter in the possession of Sir John Murray).

23 Lady Hardy to Byron, March 22, 1823 (from the original letter in the possession of Sir John Murray).

24 At one time a captain of dragoons in Piedmont (an affiliation for which the Marchesa Gabuccini Taaffe disinherited him) and later a major in the Louth Rifles,

APPENDICES

1 The statement was as follows:

Transportation from Leghorn – – – – – –	£59	8	9
Entered Stationer's Hall – – – – – –		2	0
Advertising – – – – – – – – – –	8	16	6
	68	7	3
Sales – – – – – – – – – –	15	13	3
Balance due John Murray – – – – – –	£52	14	0

2 A note (probably in the hand of John Murray) reads: "ans. with statement £52 14—Mar. 18—1823."

3 Marginal note by Murray (?): "have these but not marked."

4 Marginal note by Murray (?): "have sent."

5 *Adelais.* See p. 201.

INDEX

The page numbers in italics refer to the Notes

Adelais (Taaffe's), 201, 213, 222, *249* (n. 5)
Adonais (Shelley's), 24, 34, 69
Adventures of a Younger Son (Trelawny's), 56, 194
Agnolo, Michel, 51
Ahasuerus (a "dramatic legend" by Medwin), 195
Albaro, 191
Alborghetti, Count, *245* (n. 69)
Allegra (Byron's daughter by Claire Clairmont), 2–3, 37, 39, 41, 140, 141, 155, 157, 190, *242* (n. 103)
Alphonso and Isabel or *The Last Eighteen Hours of Cadiz* (Taaffe's), 200
America, 176, 190
Andreucci, Justice (in dragoon affray case), 152
Angeli, Mrs. Helen Rossetti, 2, *230* (n. 53), *243* (n. 33), *244* (n. 57)
Angeloni, Justice (in dragoon affray case), 152
Arabic Grammar (Taaffe's), 202
Ardee (County Louth), 16
Ardenza, 170
Argiropoli, Princess, 11
Ariel, the (proposed name for Shelley's boat), 158
Arno, the, 5, 30, 50, 51, 65

Bagnacavallo, convent at, 37, 140, 141
Barletti (jeweller in Pisa), 101
Baroni, Domenico (Tuscan soldier), 145
Battaglini, Count Vincenzo Gamberini, 145
Batuzzi, Giacomo (Gamba agent), 99, 145
Beauclerk, the Misses, 22
Beauclerk, Mrs. Emily, 73, 120, 129, 169, *226* (n. 8), *239* (n. 34, 40), *240* (n. 51)
Belgrade (Taaffe's), 200
Bell, Dr. John, 1
Benzoni, Countess, 200
Bernardini, Signora, 11
Bertolini, Prof. Antonio (sculptor), 73
Bini, Captain (Gov. Viviani's adjutant), 104, 105
Bini, Giuseppe (witness in dragoon affray), *236* (n. 6)
Bisordi, Giuseppe (witness in dragoon affray), 100, 112, 121, 122
Blagden, Isabella, 194
Blessington, Lady, 193
Blessington, Lord, *247* (n. 21)
Boat on the Serchio, The (poem by Shelley), 30
Boccaccio, 5, 28
Boissy, Marquis Hilaire de, 199
Boissy, Marquise de (*see* Guiccioli, Teresa)
Bojti, Professor, 9
Bolgheri, 86, *235* (n. 103)
Bolivar, the (Byron's boat), 75, 144, 146, 158, 161, 163, 169, 170, 171, 172, 177, 179, 181–82, 187, 190, *243* (n. 24), *244* (n. 53, 54, 60), *245* (n. 80), *247* (n. 21)
Bologna, 37, 39, 47, 49, 140, 143
Bombelles, Count de (Austrian minister), 179, 186, *246* (n. 1)
Bradford, Lord, 118, 120, 121, 128, 129, 151, 169, *239* (n. 27)
Browning, Robert, 194
Bruen, Mr. (American ship captain), 177
Brussels, 147

Buon Governo (of Tuscany), 137, 140, 143, 152, 159, 167, 170, 171, 177, *245* (n. 61)
Buon Governo (of Lucca), President of, 179–80
Burdett, Sir Francis, 80
Burghersh, Lady, 131, *240* (n. 55)
Burghersh, Lord, *238* (n. 25)
Byron, George Gordon, 6th Baron, 3, 21, 28, 34, 36, 66, 117, 118, 119, 122, 127, 128, 152, 179, 180, 181, 186, 198, 199, 200, 201, 213, 215, 216, 217, 219, *229* (n. 38, 39), *240* (n. 44, 51, 53, 66), *244* (n. 48, 51, 60)
And Taaffe, 22, 56–58, 62, 68–69, 107, 110–11, 115–17, 120–21, 123, 130, 133, 135–36, 148–49, 150, 185–86; and Shelley, 37, 38, 39–44, 61–64, 66, 155–56, 159–60; last days at Ravenna, 39–47; and Teresa Guiccioli, 38, 40, 104–105, 166, 176, 177, 178–79, 180, 190, 197; and Moore, 39, 45, 64, 187, *228* (n. 7); agrees to found liberal journal with Hunt, 42; finds moving costly, 42–43; and Murray, 45, 48, 50, 59, 68–69, 78, 85, 189–90; quarrel with Southey, 46, 82–85; and Lord Clare, 47, 168, *229* (n. 39); passes Claire Clairmont on the road, 47; arrival in Pisa, 48; irritation, 48; and Kinnaird, 48, 50, 80, 81–82, 85, 124–25, *247* (n. 26); placated by Kinnaird's letter, 48–49; concern over money, 49, 78–82, 188–90, *246* (n. 9); at the Palazzo Lanfranchi, 51; calls on Shelleys, 51; centre of Pisan circle, 52; excuses himself from calling on Grand Duke, 53; habits at Pisa; and his riding and pistol-shooting party, 54, 91–92, 109; and his weekly dinners, 54–55, 73; and the rumoured *auto da fé*, 60–65; exhibits best qualities, 63; and Trelawny, 71–72, 75–78, 181, 187, 190; and boats, 74–75; and the proposed summer colony, 74; poses as man of the world, 76; and Lady Noel's health, 79; eager to assume the name *Noel*, 80–81; and Medwin, 83–84, 195; and John Hay, 86–90, 109–110, 125, 130–33, 147; and Mary Duff, 87–89; and the dragoon affray, 92–95, 98–100, 102–106; draws up report of the dragoon affray, 108; testimony for Tita, 112; and E. J. Dawkins, 113–14, 119, 125–27, 130, 131–32, 133–39, 140, 141, 142–46, 148, 165–69, 171–72, 176–79, 183–84, *246* (n. 84); attaches considerable importance to dragoon affray, 123, *239* (n. 40); sensitiveness to public opinion, 123–124; asks Mary to send account of affray to Hunt, 123–24; and Mrs. Beauclerk, 129, *240* (n. 51); complains of treatment of imprisoned servants, 132; welcomes suggestions of hiring lawyer, 134; inquires about legal fees, 135; feelings on death of Allegra, 141–42; attempts to save Tita, 137–47; applies to Auditor, 142; and Auditor's refusal, 142; on Tita's exile, 144–46; testimony of, 150, *242* (n. 103); attitude toward Papi, 153; disappoints Shelley about Allegra, 155; and the *Don Juan*, 158–59; vindictiveness toward dragoon, 160; complains against Tuscan government, 165–66, 168; at Montenero, 164–76; denied free use of the *Bolivar* at Leghorn, 170–172, *244* (n. 60); and the squabble at Villa Dupuy, 173–74; appeals for extension of time for Gambas, 175; renews complaints of treatment of the Gambas, 176–78; returns to Pisa 163, 176; and Captain Roberts, 181–82; joins search for Shelley and Williams, 182; shock of Shelley's and Williams's deaths to, 183, *246* (n. 82); and the cremation ceremonies, 187; regrets commitment to Hunt, 189; leaving Pisa, 191; fails to pay Mary's travelling expenses, 192; last days of, 193; funeral procession of, 196; liaison with Claire Clairmont, *224* (n. 30); petitions to practise shooting in garden, *230* (n. 61); on Lord Guilford, *231* (n. 1); his taste in horses, *233* (n. 48); and two curious Royal ladies, *233* (n. 49); on Mehemet Effendi, *236* (n. 3); note on Dr. Crawford's deposition, *237* (n. 12);

and Hunt, *242* (n. 4); on the Hunts, *247* (n. 16); Torelli on, *248* (n. 30)
Literary works: *Cain*, 45, 48, 49–50; *Childe Harold*, 76; *Don Juan*, 45, 46, 48, 49, 76, 81, 83, 188, 189, 193, 196, *246* (n. 8); *Heaven and Earth*, 59, *242* (n. 4); *Lara*, 19; *Manfred*, 45, 58, 75; *Marino Faliero*, 48, 49, *229* (n. 47), *241* (n. 83); *Sardanapalus*, 48, 78, *228* (n. 3); *Stanzas Written on the Road between Florence and Pisa*, 47–48; *Two Foscari, The*, 48, 83, *228* (n. 3); *Vision of Judgment, The*, 45–46, 82, 85, *233* (n. 70), *242* (n. 4)
Byron, Lady, 80, 88, 189, 191, 201, *230* (n. 48), *247* (n. 26)
Byron, Mrs. (Lord Byron's mother), 81, 87

Cain (Byron's), 45, 48, 49–50
Carloni, Coadiutore (in the dragoon affray case), 111
Casa Aulla, 28
Casa Finocchietti, 44
Casa Frasi, 5
Casa Mostardi (Taaffe's house), 107
Casa Negrito, 191
Casa Parra, 44
Casa Saluzzo, 147, 189, 191
Cassio, 113, 169
Castinelli family, the, 54
Celosci, Agostino (Tuscan soldier), 145
Cenci, The (Shelley's), 6
Cephalonia, 197
Charles I (Shelley's), 59, 162
Chauncey, Captain (of the U.S. navy), 176
Chiesi, Captain (Masi's commander), 121, 139
Childe Harold, 18, 75
Childe Harold (Byron's), 76
Chile, 190
Cisanello, 54, 91
Clairmont, Claire, 2, 3, 5, 24, 27, 31, 38, 54, 55, 114, 158, *223* (n. 1), *224* (n. 30)
Visits Allegra, 3; friendship with the Masons, 4–6; source of friction in household, 6–7; said by Paolo to be Elena Adelaide's mother, 8; leaves the Shelleys, 8–9; visits in Pisa, 13; goes to Leghorn for sea-bathing, 36; visited by Shelley, 37; glimpses Byron for last time, 47; Trelawny's sympathy for, 75; on Trelawny and Byron, 76; full of wild schemes, 155; her feeling shared by Shelley, 156; receives news of Allegra's death, 157; at Villa Magni, 162
Clare, Lord, 47, 49, 167, 168, *229* (n. 39), *244* (n. 48)
Cockburn, Robert (husband of Mary Duff), 88–89, *235* (n. 112)
Colbourne, Mr. (*see* Cockburn, Robert)
Colebrooke, Mrs. Belinda, 17–18, 20, 202, *225* (n. 3)
Coleridge, Samuel Taylor, 12
Collini, Lorenzo (Byron's lawyer in the dragoon affray case), 134–35, 136, 138, 139, 140, 141, 143, 144, 145, 147, 148, 150, 151, 159, 164, 166, 167, 168, 169, 177, 186, 191, *235* (n. 2), *241* (n. 75)
Comment on Dante (Taaffe's), 14, 22, 31–33, 56–57, 58, 69–69, 148, 161, 164, 213–22, *232* (n. 34)
Como, Lake, 35, 200
Conversations with Lord Byron (Lady Blessington's), 193
Corsica, 181
Courier, the, 83–84, 148, 186, *234* (n. 94)
Courier Français, the, 124–25, *240* (n. 44)
Crawford, Dr. James, 102, 113, 114, 125, 126, *237* (n. 12)

d'Albany, Countess, 199
Danoot (banker at Brussels), 147
Dante, 5
Davies, Scrope B., 88, *235* (n. 109)
Dawkins, E. J. (English chargé d'affaires at Florence), 115, 123, 124, 125, 132, 143, 146, 176, 181, 183, 184, 186, *237* (n. 14)
Receives letter from Byron about dragoon affray, 113–14; receives Taaffe's account of affray, 117–18; engaged in two-way correspondence, 118; answers Byron's letter,

119; reassures Taaffe, 119; further on the dragoon affray, 126–27; warned against Mrs. Beauclerk, 129; has "a most contemptible opinion" of Taaffe, 131; suggests employing lawyer, 133–34; disclaims private correspondence with Taaffe, 134; on legal processes, 136; on Taaffe, 136–37; more on the dragoon affray case, 138–39; warns Taaffe about his deposition, 139; Byron suggests new line of appeal to, 141; considers application to Auditor a blunder, 142–43; urges Byron not to leave Tuscany, 143; informs Byron of the fate of Tita's beard, 145; writes pessimistically about dragoon affray case, 147–48; on Collini, 148; advice to Taaffe, 150; disagrees with Byron, 166–67; offers to help the Gambas, 178; effort on behalf of Gambas, 179; on Byron, *246* (n. 84)
Death of Hector, the (Sgricci's improvisation on), 12–13
Dei Conti, Contessa, 11
Desdemona, 169
Didot, 69
Divine Comedy, The (Taaffe's translation), 22, 68–69
Don Juan, the (Shelley's boat), 158, 161, 162, 163, 164, 181, *243* (n. 30)
Don Juan (Byron's), 45, 46, 48, 49, 76, 81, 83, 188, 189, 193, 196, *246* (n. 8)
Dragoon, affray with (*see also* Sergeant-Major Masi), 22, 91–106
Drury, Henry, 198
Duff, Mary, 87 and fn., 88–89, *235* (n. 112, 113)
Dunn, Henry (Leghorn merchant), 160, 163, *243–44* (n. 45), *248–49* (n. 21)
Dupuy, Francesco, 164

Edgeworth, Maria, 52
Edgeworth, Mr. (brother of Maria Edgeworth), 52, *234* (n. 95)
Edinburgh, 17
Edinburgh University, 17
Elegy on the Death of H.R.H. Prince Clement, Duke of Saxony (Taaffe's), 22, 25, 117, 203–206, *239* (n. 26)
Empoli, 2, 47
Epipsychidion (Shelley's), 13–14
Epirus, 30

Falconcini, G. (Auditor to the Governor of Leghorn), 170, 176
Fano, 200
Ferrara, 198
Figi, Ranieri (witness in the dragoon affray case), 102
Filetto, 198
Fitzgerald, General Andrew, 20
Fitzgerald, Catherine (*see* Catherine Fitzgerald Taaffe)
Fletcher, William (Byron's valet), 51, 132, 173–74, 193
Florence, 1, 2, 3, 9, 26, 34, 39, 40, 44, 49, 117, 127, 130, 131, 138, 140, 142, 143, 144, 145, 147, 148, 149, 151, 154, 157, 164, 165, 167, 169, 176, 177, 178, 184, 185, 199
Florentine Academy, the, 19
Foggi, Elise, 8
Foggi, Paolo, 7–9, *224* (n. 30), *228* (n. 20)
Forestieri, Gaetano (Byron's cook), 102, 103, 172, *236* (n. 11)
Fortis, Mr. and Mrs., 21, 200–201, *226* (n. 7)
Foscarini, Dr., 103, 104, 105, 108
Foscolo, Ugo, 68, 221
Fossombroni (Tuscan Minister for Foreign Affairs), 119, 126, 131, *238* (n. 25)
Frassi, Francesco (witness in dragoon affray), 121
Fusconi, Dr. Sebastiano, 145

Gabrielli, Pietro (hearsay witness in the dragoon affray case), 112
Gabuccini, Marchesa, 200–201
Gabuccini, Marchese, 200–201
Galignani, Antoine (publisher of *Galignani's Messenger*), 149
Gamba, Pietro, 136, 146, 169, 183
Exiled from Romagna, 38; duplicates order for Byron's wagons, 43; arrives in Pisa, 44; makes social calls, 51, 52; and Byron's riding party, 54, 91–92; as author, 56; returns from Maremma, 66; and the dragoon affray, 94–95, 96, 99, 101, 103, 104, 105; said to have

struck dragoon with whip, 110; procures Dr. Crawford's statement, 111; precedes Tita to Florence, 145; and consequences of the dragoon affray, 165; and the squabble at Villa Dupuy, 172–74; reasons for exile, 174–75, *244–45* (n. 60); given notice to leave Tuscany, 175; in Lucca, 179–81, 184; accompanies Byron to Greece, 193; after Pisa, 199; his visitor's permit, *228* (n. 21)
Gamba, Count Ruggero, 53, 99, 122, 166, 167, 169, 183, 191, 198, *248* (n. 30)
Exiled from Romagna, 38; his visitor's permit, 44–45, 165, *228* (n. 21); returns from Maremma, 66; reasons for exile, 174–75, *244–245* (n. 60); given notice to leave Tuscany, 175; in Lucca, 179–81, 184
Gamba, Vincenzo, 44, 198
Gamba family, the, 36, 37, 39, 42, 45, 49, 51, 52, 163, 164, 166, 168, 176, 177, 178, 191
Garnett, Richard, 14
Gay, Nelson, *234* (n. 104), *235* (n. 104), *236* (n. 1), *237* (n. 8), *240* (n. 61), *245* (n. 73)
Geneva, 2, 27, 38, 55, 186
Genoa, 19, 23, 73, 74, 82, 129, 141, 147, 158, 167, 168, 169, 176, 177, 184, 186, 189, 191, 193, 195, 196
Gifford, William (ed. *Quarterly Review*), 50, 57, *247* (n. 17)
Gil Blas, 168
Ginnasi, Annibale (distant connection of Teresa's), 197, *248* (n. 11)
Giovani, Chancellor, 143, *238* (n. 25)
Gisborne, John, 2, 66, 162, *223* (n. 4), *233* (n. 73)
Gisborne, Maria, 1, 7, 13, 25, 29, 36, 56, 70, 114, 139, 157, 159, *223* (n. 4), *224* (n. 30)
Gisborne, John and Maria, 1, 7–8, 34, 36, *227* (n. 22)
Giuntini, Matteo, 99, 101
Globe Inn (at Leghorn), 181
Godwin, Mary Wollstonecraft (first wife of William), 4, *223* (n. 4)
Godwin, Mrs. William (second wife of William), 2, 4
Godwin, William, 1, *223* (n. 4), *224* (n. 30)
Goethe, 78
Gordon family, the, 89
Goring, Lady, 194
Goring, Sir Harry Dent, 194
Grainger, William (friend of Taaffe's), 35, 221, *227* (n. 33)
Greece, 29, 190, 193
Guiccioli, Count A., 178, 180, 197–199, *245* (n. 69), *248* (n. 11)
Guiccioli, Countess Teresa, 84, 136, 166, 178, 179, 180, 181, 184, 191, 193, 200, 201, *245* (n. 62)
Separated from husband by Papal decree, 38–39; joins father and brother in Florence, 39; and the Palazzo Lanfranchi, 42; arrives in Pisa, 44; on Byron's dallying at Ravenna, 46; social calls of, 51, 52; defends Taaffe, 57; her *Vie de Lord Byron en Italie*, 75; rides out with M. Shelley, 91; and the dragoon affray, 93, 97–98, 99, 102, 103, 104–105, 108; her testimony conflicts with Maluccelli's, 122; examination of, 150, *241* (n. 101); and identity of dragoon's assailant, 153; with Byron at Montenero, 164, 172; returns to Pisa, 176; wanted by Taaffe to appeal to Grand Duchess, 177; and Byron's love, 190; after Pisa, 197–99; and Count Guiccioli, 198; her visitor's permit, *228* (n. 21); Shelley on, *229* (n. 38); mentioned by Torelli, *248* (n. 30)
Literary work: *Vie de Lord Byron en Italie*, 75, 153, 172, 173
Guilford, Lord, 60, 62, *231* (n. 1)

Halford, Sir Henry, 79
Hamilton, Anne, Baroness (wife of Medwin), 196, *248* (n. 7)
Hamlet, 45
Hanson, John (Byron's solicitor), 49, 80–81
Hardy, Lady, 199, *248–49* (n. 21)
Harrow, 197, 198
Hawke, Martin, 88, *235* (n. 108)
Hay, Captain John, 52, 132, 133, 134, 150, *244* (n. 49)
And the dragoon affray, 73, 94–98, 103, 105; sends Byron a side of wild boar, 86; earlier

acquaintance with Byron, 87–89; arrives in Pisa, 89–90; and Byron's riding party, 91–92; Taaffe solicitous about, 107; condition improved, 108, 110; hears distorted rumour, 109; confirms dragoon's statement, 110; in Florence, 125, 130–31; on Dawkins's estimate of Taaffe, 131; deposition, 139; begs for news, 147; reads of Shelley's death, 186
Heaven and Earth (Byron's), 59, *242* (n. 4)
Heidelberg, 196
Hellas (Shelley's), 31, 58
Hentsch (Geneva banker), 147
Hill, William Noel- (English minister at Genoa), 183
History of the Holy, Military, Sovereign Order of St. John of Jerusalem (Taaffe's), 202
Hobhouse, John Cam, 70, 82, 124, 191, 195, 196, 199, 221, *247* (n. 17)
Hogg, Thomas Jefferson, 11 and fn., 197
Holland, Lord, 134
Hoppner, R. B. (English consul at Venice), 49, 144, 167, 168
Hoppner, Mr. and Mrs. R. B., 44, *228* (n. 20)
Hoppner, Mrs. R. B., 8
Horsham, 9, 196
Hotel de l'Europe, 186
Hunt, James Henry Leigh, 4, 5, 12, 41, 42, 59, 82, 123, 155, 156, 163, 172–74, 176, 187, 189, 191, 196, *234* (n. 93), *237* (n. 13), *242* (n. 4), *244* (n. 57, 60), *247* (n. 16, 17)
Hunt, J. H. L., and Marianne, 191
Hunt, Marianne (Mrs. J. H. L.), 4, 5, 53, 163, 189, *247* (n. 16)
Hymn to Intellectual Beauty (Shelley's), 55

Imola, 47
Inez di Castro (Sgricci's improvisation on), 13
Iphigenia in Tauris (Sgricci's improvisation on), 13
Ipselanti (Greek general), 30
Irving, Washington, 49

Jacob, Sir (*see* Sir Ralph Milbanke)
Jeffrey, Francis (ed. *Edinburgh Review*), 57
Jervoise, George, 27
Jones, Professor Frederick L., *226* (n. 13)
Journal of Edward Ellerker Williams (Garnett's ed. of), 14
Journal of the Conversations of Lord Byron in 1821 and 1822 (Medwin's), 65, 70, 85, 196
Julian, beard of, 146

Keats, John, 33, 35, 69
Kingston, Lord 4
Kinnaird, Douglas James William, 46, 48, 50, 79, 80, 82, 115, 124, 133, 148, 188, 189, 190, 191, *229* (n. 32, 47)
And *The Vision of Judgment*, 78; and Byron's finances, 78–79, 81–82; refuses to convey Byron's challenge, 85; advises Byron about bet, 88; corrects misstatements in English press, 124; indignant at Byron's imputation, *247* (n. 26)

Landor, Walter Savage, 194
Landrini, Domenico (witness in the dragoon affray case), 112, 121, 122
Lanfranchi family, the, 51
Lapacci, Angelo (witness in the dragoon affray case), *236* (n. 6)
Lapini, Cancelliere (in the dragoon affray case), 140, 149, 150, 153, *241* (n. 101)
Lara (Byron's), 19
Last Man, The (Mary Shelley's), 197
Leghorn, 1, 3, 7, 20, 26, 29, 130, 141, 144, 146, 147, 152, 161, 163, 164, 169, 170, 171, 172, 175, 177, 178, 179, 181, 185, 188
Leigh, Augusta (the Hon. Mrs. George, Byron's half-sister), 198
Leoni, Michele, 148, 149, *241* (n. 95)
Lerici, 146, 156, 157, 163, 181
Liberal, The, 85, 156, 176, 189, *242* (n. 4), *247* (n. 17)
Lionel and Melchior (Shelley and Williams), 30

Lodore (Mary Shelley's), 197
Lucca, 13, 40, 60, 61, 63, 120, 141, 176, 178, 179, 180, 181, 183, 184
Lucca, Bagni di (*see* Baths of Lucca)
Lucca, Baths of, 3, 7
Lucca, Grand Duchess of, 60, 64, 65, 179, 180
Lucca, Grand Duchy of, 180
Lucifer (in Byron's *Cain*), 48, 50
Lung' Arno (street in Pisa), 2, 5, 42, 44, 71, 100, 113
Lushington, Dr. (Lady Byron's trustee), 189

McDonnell, Mrs. Catharine (sister of J. Taaffe, Jr.), 221
Magawly, Count, 34
Magico Prodigioso (Calderon's), 71
Magnetic Lady to Her Patient (Shelley's), 66
Malta, 202
Maluccelli, Antonio (Teresa's servant), 91, 102, 112, 122, 125, 132, 147, 152, 153, 159, 160, 174, *235* (n. 2), *239* (n. 36), *245* (n. 62)
Manfred (Byron's), 45, 58, 75
Mansi, Marquis (Minister of Foreign Affairs in Lucca), 179–81, 183
Manton, Joe (keeper of a London shooting-gallery), 54
Marino Faliero (Byron's), 48, 49, *229* (n. 47)
Marley (?), 49
Marlow, 2
Masi (Leghorn printer), *223* (n. 21)
Masi, Sergeant-Major Stephani, 92–98, 100–105, 107, 108–114, 117, 118, 121, 122, 123, 124, 125, 126, 132, 133, 134, 135, 138, 139, 152, 154, 160, 165, 166, 169, 171, 174, 180, *237* (n. 12), *239* (n. 40), *244* (n. 51)
Masi affray, the, 173, Chapter VI
"Mason, Mr.", 4
"Mason, Mrs.", 4, 6, 8, 9, 41, 65, 161, 164, *223* (n. 10)
"Mason, Mr. and Mrs.", 5
Mavrocordato, Prince, 11, 13, 22, 29, 31
Mayne, Ethel C., 181, *246* (n. 82)
Medwin, Thomas, 2, 12, 28, 33, 90, 124, *223* (n. 3)
Early career of, 9; arrival in Pisa, 9; illness of, 10; as author, 10, 56; lures the Williamses to Pisa, 26; leaves Pisa, 27; rejoins Pisan circle, 52; social calls of, 53; and Byron's riding party, 54; and the rumoured *auto da fé*, 60, 61, 65; his *Life of Shelley*, 65; on Mary and Dr. Nott, 70; bores Mary, 77; and Southey's *Courier* letter, 83–84; on Byron's bet with Hay, 87; departure from Pisa again, 91; Papi admits guilt to, 152; misses cremation ceremonies, 186, *246* (n. 4); after Pisa, 195–96; Trelawny on, *224* (n. 37); on Papi, *237* (n. 13)
Literary works: *Ahasuerus* (a "dramatic legend"), 195; *Journal of the Conversations of Lord Byron in 1821 and 1822*, 65, 70, 85, 196
Medwin, Mrs. (*see* Hamilton, Baroness Anne)
Mehemet Effendi (Taaffe's Turkish friend), 91, *236* (n. 3)
Mephistopheles (Goethe's), 65
Mexico, 190
Milan, 21, 38
Milbanke, Sir Ralph (Lady Byron's father), 49, *230* (n. 48)
Milton, John, 50
Missolonghi, 193, 197
Moloni (Pisan bookseller), 60
Monbel, M. de (*see* Bombelles, M. de)
Montenero, 143, 146, 152, 153, 164, 165, 170, 178
Moore, Thomas, 39, 42, 45, 46, 49, 50, 61, 64, 68, 187, 189, *228* (n. 7), *247* (n. 17)
More O'Ferrall, Mrs. Cesira, *237* (n. 21), *239* (n. 33)
Morea, the, 30, 31
Morning Chronicle, The, 124
Mountcashell, Earl, 4, *223* (n. 10)
Mountcashell, Lady (*see* "Mrs. Mason")
Murray, John, 45, 46, 48–49, 50, 51, 57, 59, 68, 69, 76, 78, 82, 85, 142, 189, 190, 195, 196, 198, 213–22, *230* (n. 51), *233* (n. 70), *247* (n. 17), *249* (n. 2, 3, 4)
Murray, Mrs. John (wife of the publisher), 222

Naples, 3, 8, 186, 201
Neapolitans, the, 144
Newstead Abbey, 198
Nissi, Justice (in dragoon affray case), 152
Noel, Lady, 66, 79–80, 82, 189
Noel estate, the, 188, 189
Nott, the Rev. Dr., 70, *232* (n. 36)
Nottingham, 196

Observateur Autrichien, the, *244* (n. 51)
Observer, the, 124
Ode to Liberty (Shelley's), 6
Odysseus (Greek leader), 193
Ollier, Charles (Shelley's publisher), 10, 14, 33, 161, *223* (n. 21)
Origo, Marchesa Iris, 75, 153, 172, 173, *235* (n. 1), *241* (n. 86)
Oswald and Edwin (Medwin's), 56

Pacchiani, Professor Francesco, 11–14, *224* (n. 40)
Padilla, A Tale of Palestine (Taaffe's), 14, 16, 18, 21, 56, *225* (n. 5)
Palazzo di Giustizia, 145, 146
Palazzo Gabuccini, 200
Palazzo Galetti, 9–10
Palazzo Guiccioli, 40
Palazzo Lanfranchi, 42, 48, 51, 52, 53, 55, 61, 71, 84, 99, 100, 104, 105, 106, 109, 112, 122, 165, 191, *230* (n. 53), *242* (n. 4)
Palazzo Mocenigo, 200
Papi, Vincenzo (Byron's coachman), 91, 104, 112, 121–22, 124, 125, 152–154, 172–74, *237* (n. 13), *244* (n. 59)
Parnassus, 193
Pazienza (Auditor to the Governor of Pisa), 137, 142–44, 174, 176, *238* (n. 25)
Peacock, Thomas Love, 6, 7, 40, 55
Pelleschi (Claire Clairmont's voice teacher), *223* (n. 1)
Peru, 190
Petrarch, 5
Piagge gate (*see* Porta alle Piagge)
Pigot, Dr. John, 198
Pisa, Baths of, 8, 24, 32, 36
Pisan circle, the, 2, 26, 77, 139, 149, 150, 191, 196
Peculiar composition of, 52; social activity of, 51–53, *230* (n. 57); weekly dinners of, 55; literary activities of, 56; and the rumoured *auto da fé*, 60; have Christmas dinner at Byron's, 65; completion of, 73; anxiety over Masi, 110; relieved by Masi's recovery, 123
Pisans, the, 11, 152
Police, the Pisan, 108, 110, 111, 113
Porta alle Piagge, 54, 90, 91, 92, 94, 99, 106, 150
Poschi, Marchese, 28
Posthumous Poems (Shelley's), 196
Poujoulat, Jean Joseph François, 154, *236* (n. 3)
Professors, the Pisan, 143, 145, 146, 191
Prometheus Unbound (Shelley's), 22
Promise, or a Year, a Month, and a Day, The (Williams's unproduced play), 28
Protestant cemetery (at Rome), 195
Puccini, A. (President of the Tuscan Buon Governo), 137, 140, 143, 144–45, 165, 170, 171, 172, 174, *238* (n. 25)
Pugnano, 6, 28, 30

Quarterly Review, The, 68

Raffaelli, Justice (in dragoon affray case), 152
Ravenna, 37–41, 44, 49, 51, 55, 78, 180, 190
Recollections of the Last Days of Shelley and Byron (Trelawny's), 56, 75, 194
Records of Shelley, Byron, and the Author (Trelawny's), 56, 75, 194
Regny, Madame Artemisia Castellini, 19–21, 32, 200, *225* (n. 4)
Regny, Ida (daughter of Madame Regny), 32
Regny, Natalie (daughter of Madame Regny), 19
Reveley, Henry (son of Mrs. Gisborne), 28–29, *223* (n. 4)
Reveley, Mrs. (*see* Maria Gisborne)
Revolt of Islam, The (Shelley's), 9
Rivarola, Cardinal, 198

Roberts, Captain Daniel, 73–75, 158, 161, 163, 169, 181, 182, *233* (n. 53), *243* (n. 24)
Rogers, Samuel, 47, 49–50
Rome, 3, 152, 183, 193, 198, 201
Rosini, Professor Giovanni, 34, 145, *227* (n. 31)
Rossetti, W. M., 152
Russia, 30

St. Aubyn, Sir John, 27
St. John of Jerusalem, Order of, 201–202
St. Matthew, Church of, 100
St. Anna, Convent of (at Pisa), 13, 41
San Marco (near Leghorn), 178
Santa Chiara Hospital, 108
Santa Croce Quarter, Commissioner of, 143
Samson Agonistes (Milton's), 50
Sardanapalus (Byron's), 48, 78, *228* (n. 3)
Satan (Milton's), 50
"Satanic school" of poetry, the, 83–84
Schubalof, Prince, 109
Scott, Sir Walter, 17, 124, 220, 221, *230* (n. 59)
Sedillo, Canon (in *Gil Blas*), 168
Sensitive Plant, The (Shelley's), 6
Serchio, the, 9, 30, 182, 187
Serpent is Shut Out from Paradise, The (Shelley's), 66
Servia, 30
Settimello, 199
Sgricci, Tommaso (*improvvisatore* at Pisa), 11–14
Shakespeare, 113
Shelley, Clara Everina (child of P. B. and M. W. Shelley), 3
Shelley, Elena Adelaide, 8 and fn.
Shelley, Harriet Westbrook, 2
Shelley, Mary W., 26, 60, 110, 130, 153, 159, 185, 186, 187, 199, *241–42* (n. 101), *248* (n. 7)
At Florence, 1–2; on Pisa and the Pisans, 4, 11; and Mrs. Mason, 6; and Claire Clairmont, 6–7; on Shelley's *To a Skylark*, 8; and Elena Adelaide, 8; on Medwin, 10–11; on Emilia Viviani, 14; and Taaffe, 25, 32–33, 57, 114; and Teresa Guiccioli, 44, 91; and Jane Williams, 53, 197; on Shelley's health, 54; on literary activities of the Pisan circle, 56; resumes study of Greek, 59; and Dr. Nott, 70; and Trelawny, 71, 73, 77, 192, 194; and the dragoon affray, 93, 97–99, 102–105; her testimony, 122, 150, *241* (n. 101); sends account of affray to Hunt, 123, and Medwin, 124; at Villa Magni, 157, 162; suffers miscarriage, 162–63; and the search for Shelley and Williams, 181–82; and Shelley's burial, 183; precedes Byron to Genoa, 191; life after Pisa, 196–197; taken as a child by Mrs. Reveley, *223* (n. 4); and Mrs. Thomas (n. 10)
Literary works: *Last Man, The*, *Lodore*, 197; *Valperga: or Castruccio, Prince of Lucca*, 36, *228* (n. 39)
Shelley, P. B., 21, 39, 63, 65, 111, 175, 181, 185, 186, 189–90, 194, 195, 196, 197, *241–42* (n. 101), *244* (n. 59)
At Florence, 1–2; on Tuscan weather, 2; on Pisa, 4, 41; reads Greek with Mrs. Mason, 5; health at Pisa, 7; and Paolo's blackmailing attempts, 7–8; and Claire Clairmont, 7, 9, 37, 40; swears to birth of Elena Adelaide Shelley, 8; and Medwin, 9–11; and Mavrocordato, 13, 31; and Sgricci, 13; and Emilia Viviani, 13, 40, 44; and Taaffe, 22–25, 32–36; on Mrs. Thomas's verses, 23; religious views of, 23; and E. D. Williams, 27–29, 68, 85; and Jane Williams, 27, 67, 71; and boats and sailing, 28–30, 65, 74–75, 85–86, 111; at the Baths of Pisa, 31; visits Byron at Ravenna, 36–41; and Allegra, 37, 40–41, 44; and Teresa Guiccioli, 40, *229* (n. 38); persuades Byron to found liberal journal, 42; arranges Byron's move to Pisa, 42–44; on *Don Juan*, 46; member of Byron's riding party, 54, 72–73; calls on Byron, 51, 52, 55; effect of Byron upon, 55; translates Spinoza, 59; and the rumoured *auto da fé*, 60–65, *231* (n. 3); wager with Byron, 66; and Dr. Nott, 70; and Trelawny, 73–74, 77; and the

proposed summer colony, 74; and the dragoon affray, 91–98, 103–105; and tension after the affray, 109–10; learns of arrest of servants, 112; blames Taaffe, 114–15; on Tita's arrival, 146–47; intimacy with Byron grows irksome to, 155–56; sympathy with Claire and Hunt, 155–56; breaks news of Allegra's death to Claire, 157; at Villa Magni, 157–63; and the *Don Juan*, 158, 161–63; unwilling to prosecute dragoon, 159–50; expects Hunt family, 160; informed his copy of Taaffe's *Comment* ready, 161; and Mary's miscarriage, 162; meets Hunt, 163; disappears into fog, 164; search for, 181; discovery of body of, 182; cremation of, 187; influence on Byron, 191–92; disintegration of Pisan circle without, 192; Vaccà's friendship with, *223* (n. 3); and the funds, *233* (n. 73); Torelli's account of death of, *245* (n. 78)

Literary works: *Adonais*, 24, 34, 69; *Cenci, The*, 6; *Charles I* (unfinished), 59, 162; *Epipsychidion*, 13–14; *Hellas*, 31, 58; *Hymn to Intellectual Beauty*, 55; *Magnetic Lady to Her Patient, The*, 66; *Ode to Liberty*, 6; *Posthumous Poems*, 196; *Prometheus Unbound*, 22; *Revolt of Islam, The*, 9; *Sensitive Plant, The*, 6; *Serpent is Shut Out from Paradise, The*, 66; *To a Skylark*, 8; *To Jane*, 67; *Vision of the Sea, A*, 6; *With a Guitar: To Jane*, 67

Shelley, P. B. and Mary W., leave England for Italy, 3; at the Tre Donzelle, 4; at the Masons', 5; take lodgings at Casa Frasi, 5; at the Baths of Pisa, 8, 30; return to Pisa, 9; change their opinion of Medwin, 10–11; change their opinion of Pacchiani, 12; hear Sgricci, 13; meet Emilia Viviani, 13; call on the Williamses, 26, 52; move to Casa Aulla, 28; hear news of Greek Revolution, 29; move into Tre Palazzi di Chiesa, 51; and the proposed summer colony, 155; invite Claire to visit, 156

Shelley, Percy Florence, 2–3, 7, 196–197

Shelley, Sir Timothy, 66, 196

Shelley, William, 3, 183

Sienna, 152

Sismondi, 51

Sketches in Hindoostan, 56

Smarmore Castle (ancestral home of Taaffe), 16, 17, 202

Smith, Horace, 36, 40, 55, 67, 162

Sompting, 194

Southey, Robert, 46, 82–85, *229* (n. 33)

Spa, 186

Spannocchi, Governor (of Leghorn), 170–71, 175–76

Spezia, 142, 143, 144, 147, 155, 161, 162, 171, 185

Stanzas Written on the Road between Florence and Pisa (Byron's), 47–48

Stonyhurst (Jesuit school), 16

Strauss, Giuseppe (Byron's courier), 54, 91, 94, 96, 97, 99, 110, 111, 121, 152, 166, 174, 175, 177, *235* (n. 1), *243–44* (n. 45), *244* (n. 60)

Taaffe, Catherine Fitzgerald (wife of John Taaffe, Jr.), 20–21, *226* (n. 6)

Taaffe, Eliza (half-sister of John, Jr.), 16

Taaffe, George (brother of John, Jr.), 18, 221, *225* (n. 2)

Taaffe, Isias (daughter of John, Jr.), 20–21, 201, *226* (n. 7)

Taaffe, John (father of John, Jr.), 16, 21, 200

Taaffe, Mrs. John (mother of John, Jr.), 16, 200, 221

Taaffe, John, Jr., 11, 28, 66, 125, 126, 147, 160, 198, *233* (n. 49, 50), *239* (n. 40)

Visits the Shelleys, 14, 22, 51; and the Pisan circle, 15, 26, 52–53; biography of, 16–21, 199–202; poetic aspirations of, 17, 18, 200–202; his love affair with Mrs. Colebrooke, 17–18, *225* (n. 3); sets out on travels, 18; and Mme. Regny, 19–21, 200; and Mme. de Staël, 19; as author, 19, 25, 56–57; marries Catherine Fitzgerald, 20–21; two children born to, 20–21; appearance and character of, 21; study and translation of Dante, 22; religion of, 23; and Shelley, 23–25, 35–36, 161, 185–86; and Mary Shelley, 25, 32–33, 77; and Byron, 51–52, 53, 56–57, 111, 120–21, 123, 124, 127–30, 133, 135, 149, 176–77, 185–86; and Byron's riding party, 54, 72–73, 92; horsemanship of, 57–58, 61; on Byron's horsemanship, 58; and the rumoured *auto da fé*, 61–65; and Mehemet Effendi, 91, *236* (n. 3); and the dragoon affray, 92–93, 95, 97–98, 103–105, *236* (n. 5); reports on dragoon's condition, 107; inaccuracy of report, 108; and his statement on the affray, 108, 110, 115–16, 133; thought to have acquitted himself badly, 114; nicknamed "False Taaffe," 115; strained relations with group, 116; principal in previous police incident, 116, *238* (n. 25); and E. J. Dawkins, 117–19, 127-29, 131, 134, 136-37, 139, 148, 150–52; and Trelawny, 120–21; calls on Capt. Chiesi, 121; precarious position of, 127–130; and Mrs. Beauclerk, 129, *240* (n. 51); testimony of, 150–51, 208–212, *238* (n. 22); intended trip to Egypt, 145, 151–52; and Teresa Guiccioli, 177, 198, 201; after break-up of Pisan circle, 199–202; marriage to Marchesa Gabuccini, 201; visits Ireland and England, 201; death of, 202; correspondence with Murray, 213–22; genealogy of, *224–25* (n. 1)

Literary works: *Adelais*, 201, 213, 222, *249* (n. 5); *Alphonso and Isabel or The Last Eighteen Hours of Cadiz*, 200; *Arabic Grammar* (incomplete), 202; *Belgrade*, 200; *Comment on Dante*, 14, 22, 31–33, 56–57, 58, 68–69, 148, 161, 164, 213–22, *232* (n. 34); *Divine Comedy, The* (Translation), 22, 68–69; *Elegy on the Death of H.R.H. Prince Clement, Duke of Saxony*, 22, 25, 117, 203–206, *239* (n. 26); *History of the Holy, Military, Sovereign Order of St. John of Jerusalem*, 202; *Padilla, A Tale of Palestine*, 14, 16, 18, 21, 56, *225* (n. 5); *To the Baronness of Stael*, 22, 206–207

Taaffe, John (son of John, Jr.), 20–21, 200–202, *249* (n. 24)

Taaffe, Julia (sister of John, Jr.), 221

Taaffe, Mary, 221

Taaffe, Marchesa Gabuccini (wife of John, Jr.), 201–202, *249* (n. 24)

Taaffe, Nicholas, 6th Viscount, 200

Taaffe, Robert (brother of John, Jr.), 221

Taglioni, Vincenzo (Count Guiccioli's lawyer), 198, *248* (n. 11)

Tangier, 58

Tersitza (Mrs. Trelawny), 193, 194

Thersites, 75

Thomas, Mrs., 22, *226* (n. 10)

Thompson's Hotel (near Leghorn), 178

Tighe, George William (*see* "Mr. Mason")

Times, The, 124

Tita (Giovanni Battista Falcieri), 40, 91, 124, 125, 132, 147, 159, 160, 165, 171, *241* (n. 75)

And the dragoon affray, 99–100, 102; arrest of, 111–12; reputation, 112; held on technical grounds, 137; a favourite with the Pisan circle, 139; and his beard, 138, 145–146; receives decree of exile, 140; request for delay granted, 141; exile of, 143–46; rumoured aboard the *Bolivar*, 146; rejoins Byron at Genoa, 147; judged innocent of wounding dragoon, 152; accompanies Byron to Greece, 193

To a Skylark (Shelley's), 8

To Jane (Shelley's), 67

To the Baronness of Stael (Taaffe's), 22, 206–207

Todd, Dr. John, 105, 108, 121, 125

Torelli, Luigi, 53, 109, 112, 121, 146, 152, 153, 172, 174, 175, 176, 178, *242* (n. 101), *244* (n. 60), *245* (n. 78)

Tre Donzelle, Albergo delle (inn at Pisa), 2, 4, 9

Tre Palazzi di Chiesa, 51, 55–56, 70, 122

Trelawny, Edward John, 26, 118, 130, 136, 146, 148, 172, 183, 190, 191, 199, *243* (n. 24), *246* (n. 84)
And the Williamses, 27, 110; as author, 56; causes difficulties between Byron and Taaffe, 66, 120–121; arrives in Pisa, 70–71; and Shelley, 71–72, 77; and Byron, 71–72, 75–77, 193; and Byron's riding party, 72–73, 91–92; and Mary Shelley, 75, 76, 192, 194; and boats and boat-building, 73–74, 77–78; and the proposed summer colony, 74, 155; and Claire Clairmont, 75; and the dragoon affray, 92–98, 103–106; goes about armed, 109; learns of arrest of servants, 112; disapproves of Taaffe's call on Capt. Chiesi, 121; meets Masi out walking, 123; Mrs. Beauclerk requests Byron to interfere with, 129; names Papi as dragoon's assailant 152; at Genoa, 158; arrives with the *Bolivar*, 161; wants a sailor aboard the *Don Juan*, 162; unable to accompany Shelley and Williams, 164; his impression of Villa Dupuy, 165; on the *Bolivar*, 169; searches for Shelley and Williams, 181–82; arranges cremation details, 186–87; after Pisa, 193–95; death of, 195; on Medwin, 196, *224* (n. 37), *248* (n. 7); illiteracy of, *233* (n. 62); on *The Liberal*, *247* (n. 17); on the *Bolivar*, *247* (n. 21)
Literary works: *Adventures of a Younger Son*, 56, 194; *Recollections of the Last Days of Shelley and Byron*, 56, 75, 194; *Records of Shelley, Byron, and the Author*, 56, 194
Tribolati, Felice, 152–53
Tuscany, 2, 19, 114, 142, 143, 152, 165, 167, 168, 174, 175, 176, 178
Tuscany, Grand Duchess of, 120
Tuscany, Ferdinand, Grand Duke of, 53, 60, 61, 62, 65, 154
Two Foscari, The (Byron's), 48, 83, *228* (n. 3)

Ugolino, 51
Ulverstone (school near Preston), 17
Usk, 194
Ussero (inn at Pisa), 70

Vaccà, Dr. André Berlinghieri, 1, 7, 28, 42, 54, 104, 108, 110, 166, 179, 200, *223* (n. 3)
Valperga: or Castruccio, Prince of Lucca (Mary Shelley's), 36, *228* (n. 39)
Van Diemen's Land, 190, *247* (n. 23)
Vannuzzi, Giovanni (one of Byron's grooms), 122
Vantaggioli, Silvestrio (Tuscan police officer), 146
Venice, 3, 38, 200
Verona, 38
Viareggio, 187, 188
Vichi, Giovanni (one of Byron's grooms), 122
Vie de Lord Byron en Italie (Guiccioli's), 153, 172, 173
Villa Dupuy, 165, 168, 172
Villa la Podera, 54
Villa Magni, 157, 160, 162, 164, 182, 186, 194, 195, 197, *243* (n. 24)
Vision of Judgment, A (Southey's), 46, 83–84, *229* (n. 33)
Vision of Judgment, The (Byron's), 45–46, 82, 85, *233* (n. 70), *242* (n. 4)
Vision of the Sea, A (Shelley's), 6
Viviani, Emilia, 13, 14, 31, 66
Viviani, Marchese Niccolò (Governor of Pisa), 13, 104, 137, 140, 143, 165, 175, 176, *230* (n. 61), *237* (n. 12)

Wallachia, 30
Webb, W. (banker at Leghorn), 147
Wentworth, Lord (Lady Byron's uncle), 81
Wentworth, Mr., 182
Wilkinson (pistol-maker), 54
Williams, Edward Ellerker, 31, 61, 91, 100, 105, 111, 120, 121, 123, 130, 153, 156, 161, 174, 175, 181, 185, 186, 190, *243* (n. 24, 31)
Early career, 26; his play, 28; inspects Palazzo Lanfranchi, 48; and the rumoured *auto da fé*, 60, 65, *231* (n. 3), *232* (n. 14); and Byron's bet with Shelley, 66; and Shelley, 27, 28, 58–59, 157; and boats and sailing, 28, 29, 30, 65, 73–74, 85–86; and Mary Shelley, 36; and Byron, 52, 66, 129; renewed writing

attempts of, 56, 67–68, 85; and Trelawny, 70; goes house-hunting with Shelley, 85; records excitement after dragoon affray, 104, 110; learns of arrest of two servants, 112; thinks Taaffe "highly blameable," 115; testifies for Maluccelli, 122; as interpreter, 150; examination of, 157; and the *Don Juan*, 158, 161–163; writes to Taaffe, 160; goes with Shelley to meet Hunt, 163; disappears into fog, 164; discovery of body of, 182; burial of, 183; cremation of, 187; on exile of the Gambas, *245* (n. 60); Torelli's account of death of, *245* (n. 78)

Literary work: *The Promise, or a Year, a Month, and a Day* (unproduced play), 28

Williams, E. E. and Jane, 31, 41, 65, 74, 155, *230* (n. 56)

Arrival in Pisa, 26; second child born to, 27; move into Tre Palazzi di Chiesa, 51; and the Shelleys, 52; call on Taaffe, 52; hear account of dragoon affray, 104; at Villa Magni, 157

Williams, Edwin Medwin (child of E. E. and Jane Williams), 28

Williams, Jane, 159, 185, 187, 196

And Shelley, 27, 66–67; and Mary Shelley, 53, 197; good nature and beauty of, 67; introduces Trelawny and Shelley, 71; searches for Williams and Shelley, 181; after Pisa, 197

With a Guitar: To Jane (Shelley's), 67

Wollstonecraft, Mary, *223* (n. 4)

Worthing, 194

Zambelli, Lega (Byron's steward), 42, 99, 112, 124, 140, 143, 145, 159, *230* (n. 61), *242* (n. 4), *243* (n. 45)